# Restoring and Reupholstering Furniture

# Restoring and Reupholstering Furniture

Kenneth Davis, Thom Henvey,
Lorrie Mack and
Geoffrey Hayley

Rodale Press

Parts of this book were originally published under the
title *Restoring Furniture*

This edition is published by Rodale Press 1982

2 4 6 8 10 9 7 5 3 1

Printed in Singapore
ISBN 0 87857 429 8

# Contents

**Part 1: Restoring Furniture**                 6
The Amateur Restorer                             8
The Restorer's Tool Kit                          20
Stripping and Finishing Wood                     28
Project 1: Pine Desk                             34
Project 2: Two Chairs                            40
Project 3: Gate-leg Table                        54
Project 4: Chest of Drawers                      60
Project 5: Glass-fronted Cabinet                 68

**Part 2: Reupholstering Furniture**            78
Upholstery Terms, Tools and Materials           80
Project 1: Chair with Drop-in Seat              84
Project 2: Non-sprung Stool                      92
Project 3: Sprung Dining Chair                   100
Project 4: Occasional Chair                      108
Project 5: Square Armchair                       112
Project 6: Buttoned Wing-chair                   132
Project 7: Chesterfield                          152
The Care, Repair and Recovering of
Upholstery                                       164
Glossary and Further Reading                     174
Index                                            175

# Part 1: Restoring Furniture

# The Amateur Restorer

Indispensable professional advice on how to date and assess your old furniture, and the properties and advantages of different woods

Few workshop satisfactions equal those of restoring the beauty of old furniture, so often buried under layers of varnish and paint, covered with dust and oil stains or split and broken. The skilled replacement of damaged legs or mouldings, the renewal of hinges or inlay and the final finishing and polishing produce a period piece which is a joy not only to the craftsman but also to his or her family.

Furniture, both old and new, is becoming increasingly expensive. Wood commands high prices, so furniture is costly to build. And much modern furniture is designed under the eye of the production manager rather than the craftsman so that in a short period of time the consumer is forced to refurnish his or her home, again with inferior furniture. On the other hand, solid and attractive pieces are readily available in dilapidated condition and while rare antiques are bought by dealers and restored for resale at inflated prices, nineteenth- and early twentieth-century pieces or traditional country furniture can still be purchased at reasonable and often minimal cost.

With a willingness to learn the basic techniques of restoration—often surprisingly simple and requiring only straightforward materials and know-how—the amateur can easily transform seemingly ugly and repainted items into fresh and sturdy pieces of furniture. Often fairly modern pieces are in period style and only need knowledgeable rebuilding to restore them to the fine copies they are. Later, with the confidence gained tackling uncomplicated pieces, the amateur can gradually progress to work with more challenging and valuable antiques.

The possibilities will be demonstrated through the craftsmanship of Kenneth Davis, one of Britain's leading antique furniture restorers. He has rejuvenated furniture of all ages and styles and has the craftsman's eye and sensitivity together with an understanding of the processes that can be used by the layman in the restoration of pieces not fragile enough to warrant expensive, specialist treatment. His work is unsigned, and can be found in stately homes and famous historical buildings, seemingly untouched for centuries, a testimony not only to his learned craftsmanship but also to

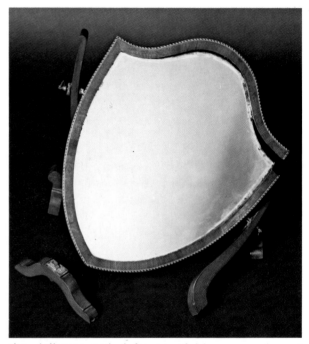

the delicacy and deftness of his approach and technique.

Furniture restoration is a relatively new craft. In the 1920s, after the upsurge and instability of World War I, collecting period furniture became fashionable and antique shops were crammed with the contents of country houses in Britain, Europe and America. Antique shops and auction rooms abounded with four-poster Victorian beds, Elizabethan oak chairs and seventeenth-century chests. But as the number of collectors increased, so did the demand for craftsmen who specialized in restoration. Many of these craftsmen, including Kenneth Davis, who have spent their lives rescuing antique furniture from decay, began their careers during this period.

Kenneth Davis displays all the skills of the furniture restorer. He is not only a master craftsman but he also has a keen knowledge of the history of styles and the use of wood throughout the centuries. In the various sections of this book he shares his special knowledge, suggesting how the amateur can furnish his or her home with durable, quality period furniture.

No special tools are needed for furniture restoration other than those of the ordinary carpenter. One or two new tools may be needed for repairing upholstery but they are inexpensive and, if you buy good quality, will last a lifetime.

The skills and methods examined here can be applied to almost all period furniture, whether it is a nineteenth-century chest of drawers or the more common Welsh oak dresser. A series of projects, photographed and described at each stage of the restoration, will show the techniques in their practical context. These projects have been chosen to demonstrate the full range of skills, from simple cleaning to total rebuilding.

A guide on how to buy old furniture is also

*Above left: With a few simple restoration techniques, a broken mahogany mirror can look as good as new (above). The joints were all strengthened and new mirror fittings were added. The whole piece was then revived and repolished to bring the wood back to its original brilliance*

included. This explains the faults to watch for, how to date pieces, recognize woods and veneers and how to tell if some restoration work—altering the style of the piece, for instance—has already been done. This will enable amateurs to make a quick evaluation of a piece of furniture seen in a second hand store or auction room. With this knowledge, you can furnish your home with taste and personality.

This book is intended for those who wish to learn the basics of restoration and those who are beginning to study furniture in more detail. The majority of repairs that confront the amateur restorer are simply a matter of following instructions. The furniture chosen for the projects was selected for its practicality in the modern home, as well as for attractiveness. It was also chosen to display the skills which apply to the restoration of a chest of drawers as well as to a writing bureau. The projects demonstrate how to remake joints, the best way to restore inlay, fittings and panels, the skills of mixing stains and polishes, the best ways to prepare decorative parts such as legs, cornices or brackets, and how to remove scratches and stains from old wood effectively. One project shows the way to restore a simple piece of cane furniture and an old woodworm-infested chair.

After completing one or two pieces, an amateur restorer will have gained the experience, natural deftness and confidence necessary to tackle more ambitious projects. The different projects are graded so that the pieces which require the more knowledgeable kind of workmanship come last. It is also to be hoped that as the beginner completes projects, the need for fuller knowledge about the history of furniture, wood and the styles of the cabinet-makers will become apparent. To track down elusive pieces, to date them to within a decade or so and then to repair and refinish them are all enjoyable and economic exercises.

### Finding furniture

Furniture restoration is becoming increasingly popular, and there is a corresponding growth in the number of dealers. These range from the renowned auction houses in the major cities to the local second-hand merchant.

Rare antique furniture is obviously too expensive for all except the professional buyers, specialists and private collectors. But there are a large number of auction rooms and old furniture shops where inexpensive originals and good quality reproduction pieces can be found. There are also many second-hand stores where the amateur collector can keep an eager eye open for the attractive bargains that occasionally crop up.

Auction rooms tend to provide a wide variety of old and new furniture at the cheapest prices since they are often essentially wholesalers. Through regular attendance at auctions you can learn how to handle pieces, and listen to dealers' evaluations

before attempting to bid. In this way you will gradually build up a fund of knowledge so that if you found it difficult at first to distinguish between mahogany and walnut, you will quickly learn not only to do that, but also how to differentiate rosewood inlay from tulipwood inlay. You will also learn the approximate prices of particular periods and styles and so will be able to pitch your bids without losing money.

This kind of knowledge will help a great deal when buying privately. Not only will you be able to date and evaluate a piece, but you will also be able to make an educated guess as to its mark-up price so that you can negotiate confidently.

Second-hand stores tend to be furniture graveyards and most of their furniture may be unsuitable. Nevertheless, they do have occasional bargains and so should not be totally ignored.

It should be stressed that it will be necessary to exercise caution, especially if you intend to invest relatively large sums of money. Some dealers do attempt to pass off reproductions as authentic pieces, and adjust the price accordingly. Establishing whether a piece is genuine can be a problem for some buyers. If a piece is well made, performs its function and is good value for money, it may not matter to you that it is a reproduction. But if you want to buy or unexpectedly find yourself in the position of being able to purchase genuine antiques there are ways to protect yourself. The safest thing is to have the piece checked by an expert. If you cannot afford this or if the price of the piece does not warrant such additional expense, the next best thing is to obtain a concisely written description of the article of furniture from the dealer so that you have a reasonable chance of returning the item for your money if it turns out to be other than the seller claimed.

### Dating furniture

Knowing what to look for when buying or dating old furniture is a skill that may take some time to acquire. Much wasted time, effort and cost can be avoided, however, by becoming acquainted with certain basic characteristics of good craftsmanship, knowing a few tips for testing authenticity and some general hints on evaluating its quality.

The term 'period' as used throughout the rest of the chapter applies to all quality-built, as opposed to mass-produced, furniture made prior to World War II. This will exclude furniture made with any kind of plastic, compressed particle board (such as chipboard or hardboard), plywoods or blockboards—sheet materials made from blocks of wood glued together and faced on both sides with

*Right: There are many places where furniture can be picked up second-hand. It pays to examine the furniture closely. Some shops specialize, as this one does in pine, and the furniture may have been renovated already*

a thick veneer. It will also exclude pieces made with mostly African timbers (such as Podo red or white Maranti) and Japanese timber. The furniture will not have pressed or lacquered metal hinges or fittings, rubber shod castor wheels, or wire nails or the more modern screws.

The timber most likely to be used would be a hardwood, such as English or Austrian oak, English or French walnut, sycamore, chestnut, birch, ash, mahogany, beech, teak, western red cedar, pine or rosewood. A good rule of thumb is that the main construction should be made of a hardwood, such as those outlined above, and the inside of drawers or bottoms of chests of any stable, common wood. In short, the parts of the piece of furniture in direct contact with room temperature will be made of hardwood.

Hardwood was used for quality furniture because of movement—expansion on cold days, contraction on hot days. This, together with the fact that wood is strongest along the grain and weakest across the grain, dictates the methods of construction of furniture if it is to be at all durable.

One of the most important things to look for is that the grain of any boards which are adjacent or at right angles runs in the same direction. If this is not so the resulting stress of contraction and expansion will eventually cause the wood to split. The larger surfaces of cabinets, wardrobes, chests, and clocks were usually made of several planks of solid wood to prevent excessive bowing. These planks were planed along their longest edges until they were flat and square. They were then placed together and rubbed against each other until they mated perfectly before being either glued along these edges or held together with tongue-and-groove joints. The grain ran vertically on the backs and sides of such pieces as a further measure against bowing.

However, there is usually some bowing in old furniture because of age and especially since the introduction of central heating in most homes. The outside surfaces on many old pieces will be slightly bowed and not as flat as when originally constructed. This is because the outside has been subjected to the varieties of room temperature while the inside, being unpolished, has dried out more over the course of time. The resulting shrinkage of the inside of the board will cause a slight contouring of the outside. This shrinkage is always in the width and never along the length of the grain.

This bowing will also occur if a hardwood veneer, such as walnut, was laid on a softwood such as pine, since the pine will have dried out more quickly and the veneer laid across its grain, resists shrinkage. This will particularly apply to Queen Anne furniture and to most early eighteenth-century pieces which immediately followed this period.

The behaviour of wood in old furniture will tell you a great deal about its quality and even its age. More details on this subject will be given in the section on woods and particularly in the section on the basic techniques used in restoration.

The finish is a good indication of the quality and value of a piece of furniture. The most likely finishes on old pieces of furniture are linseed oil for teak, beeswax and turpentine, lime bleach or fuming for oak and a shellac-based polish for mahogany, walnut and most other hardwoods.

The object of French or shellac-based polishing is to first make the surface as flat and smooth as possible and then to apply a coat of polish, rubbing it back to the wood to fill any crevices. Several coats used to be needed for a perfect finish, but with modern French polishes just one can often be sufficient. This process will bring out the depth

*Right: With experience, a knowledge of construction, and historical detail, the amateur restorer can easily assess and identify these seven chairs, all at various stages of repair.*
1. *An American rocker, Edwardian, in walnut*
2. *A round back Victorian bedroom chair in birch*
3. *A Victorian country bentwood chair in birch*
4. *A Regency bamboo chair*
5. *A bentwood chair, dated about 1860*
6. *A Victorian upholstered chair in walnut*
7. *A Windsor chair, 1780*

and iridescence of the grain, and the resultant lustrous sheen is known as the patina. This is the surface of the polish and years of repolishing will continue to enhance its depth.

By studying the patina carefully you should be able to estimate if the piece is genuinely old. A surface with a good patina should have an almost translucent, mellow tone and will usually be a little darker than the original colour of the wood. There are, as was mentioned, a number of liquids on the market today which, if used skilfully, can result in fairly convincing imitations of genuine French polishing, but the genuine French polished piece will have a mellow feeling while the modern substitute will usually be very shiny.

The veneer on a piece can also reveal a great deal. A veneer is a thin piece of wood which was cut by hand until the early nineteenth century. Veneers were traditionally used to enable decorative but unstable woods to be used in conjunction with stable but dull structural woods. And it was the use of veneering that subsequently made marquetry and inlay possible. Damage to veneers can easily be repaired. But if the whole surface is beginning to rise this can prove difficult to repair.

On the best furniture, mouldings and decorations are scribed or carved into the solid panels. They will not be pinned. If they are applied they will either be glued or jointed. Many inlays were added at a later date to period furniture to give it a look of authenticity and should be scrutinized.

On better quality furniture, fittings and hinges were made in brass or bronze; they were either handcut or cast and sometimes even soldered with silver. Their colour will have dulled and on very old pieces, unless the previous owners were obsessive, they will more than likely be scratched. If the piece is fairly inexpensive, you can ask for one of the fittings to be taken off so that you can see what the wood looks like underneath. The colour should look different and slightly newer, certainly not identical. There are likely to be rust marks where the metal has discoloured the wood.

These are most of the things you should look for to determine if a piece is old and of good

# The amateur restorer

*Left: Scratching with a coin on a hidden part of a heavily varnished piece will reveal the original wood*

*Below: Woodworm is a major problem, small holes can be easily filled but more seriously affected areas need to be completely replaced*

*Right: This fine mahogany hinged table has badly warped. Usually due to damp or too much heat, it is a major repair and should not be attempted*

## Finding faults

There are various obvious points to bear in mind when examining old furniture. Many faults, either due to botched restoration or because of the ravages of nature, come about through neglect or ignorance. Warping is a common fault, usually caused by exposure to unequal temperatures, such as when a table is placed against a radiator. This will bring about great strains in the wood, especially if the conditions are severe. Warping is perhaps most common in tables because the top is initially well polished, and frequently repolished, while the bottom is often left bare.

Examples of botched restoration are usually obvious, except where a dealer has done a superficial job to fool the inexpert. Watch out for oriental lacquer work, particularly red japanned work, which is usually black, heavily lacquered and resembles an egg-shell.

Stains, such as ink, wine marks and water crescents are other faults to watch for. These are not so serious and can usually be dealt with by rubbing down the spoiled area and then waxing. If the stain is more obstinate, use one of the other methods outlined later in this book.

Years of wear and tear on a piece of furniture can add a certain charm but some bruises may have defaced the wood. If they are not too deep they can be repaired although a slight scar may still be left. If there are deep gouges they may be beyond any kind of action.

Pests and diseases such as beetles or fungus are often ignored by people buying old furniture. Damage caused by the furniture beetle and woodworm is easy to recognize. Various products are on the market for dealing with these problems but if the damage has gone very far you may have to remove a foot, a bracket or a piece of moulding and replace it. This will involve many techniques discussed in the projects in this book.

## Wood

An understanding of wood, both old and new, is essential for the amateur restorer. It is simply not enough to know about styles and periods. It is

quality. Of course there are further points specifically related to the age and period of particular pieces, but this kind of detail will usually only apply if the piece is fairly rare.

There are also more esoteric differences on which to base your assessment of a piece, according to the tools used and the presence of any nails or screws. Before the eighteenth century, for example, wood was cut with straight saws. In the nineteenth century circular saws were introduced because they could cut faster, but they left distinct ridges around the cut which can be felt with the finger. Until the 1800s nails were handcut prior to being machine-pressed. Wooden screws were not tapered until the nineteenth century and the threads were handfiled into a shallow spiral. One test of authenticity in furniture in which nails have been used is staining in the wood caused by oxidation.

Many of these points will not apply to what has come to be known as country furniture, such as Welsh dressers and pieces from nineteenth-century American ranches. The wood used in antique furniture will usually be hard and heavy while country-made pieces will be heavier in construction but lighter, in woods with more porous grains. Much country furniture is extremely well made and has a charm and beauty within reach of the pockets of most collectors. The restoration of such pieces should be done with as much care as is given to a rarer antique.

imperative for the restorer to be able to identify the more common woods and to understand how they react so that he or she will be able to match old and new wood easily.

Every species of tree produces a different fine structure of cells making up its wood. This results in distinctive surface patterns, colours and lustres, plus qualities of texture, weight and hardness which can be readily recognized once you have had a little experience.

Woods are usually divided into softwoods and hardwoods. This division does not relate to hardness in any literal sense. Some softwoods are harder than hardwoods and *vice versa*. Balsa wood, for example, is a hardwood. The term softwood does not refer to lightness in weight or colour or imply weakness. It refers to woods from the family of coniferous (cone bearing) trees which are porous and moisture bearing. Pine is the best-known softwood. Generally, softwoods are strong and used in the unseen parts of quality furniture, drawers, for example.

Hardwoods derive from the broadleaved family of trees and include the oaks, teaks, birches and mahoganies. Hardwoods are used by cabinet-makers because of their hardness and good appearance, hence their survival and value in older antique pieces.

After trees are felled, timber is cut and seasoned. Seasoning is a controlled removal of moisture, and may be done naturally or in a kiln under controlled conditions. Generally, modern wood is not of the same quality as that used in the past. In the eighteenth century, one generation of craftsmen started the seasoning of timber for the succeeding generation to use. The timber was cut into long planks, stacked carefully under cover and allowed to dry out very slowly for up to 50 years, expanding and contracting to natural atmospheric conditions until it reached an ideal dryness for use. The internal stresses of kiln dried wood tend to result in warping and other defects because the moisture is extracted too quickly. One of the problems of restoration is finding a naturally seasoned wood if part of an old piece of furniture requires replacement, and knowing what to do should you have to match a modern mahogany with an older piece.

There is another problem in matching woods besides that of seasoning. The depth of colour of wood increases with age. A modern piece of oak is an off-white yellow while the oak used for Elizabethan furniture has mellowed to a deep rich brown. The amateur restorer may not encounter such extreme examples, but if he or she works with mahogany of most ages, the same problem will have to be overcome.

Each wood has its own peculiarities. In early walnut veneers there is always a depth of mellow faded colour which is difficult to copy or match. Queen Anne furniture, for example, made from walnut veneers, is difficult to restore because of colour matching.

*European Beech (hardwood)*
*Beech is a sturdy wood which is used extensively for all furniture, particularly for the solid parts in cabinet work and chairs. European beech is very enduring and stains and polishes well. One disadvantage is its tendency to shrink*

*Indian Rosewood (hardwood)*
*For more than two centuries Indian rosewood has been prized for fine cabinet work and inlay. Indian rosewood is plainer than other varieties of rosewood which usually come from Brazil. Rosewood veneers were popular in eighteenth-century England*

*European Oak (hardwood)*
*Traditionally the structural wood of legendary durability, European oak is used for all quality restoration work. It needs care when nailing and screwing, but stains, polishes and glues well. Oak is liable to corrode if in contact with metal*

*Sycamore (Maple in the U.S.) (hardwood)*
*This is a light-coloured wood with a very fine texture. It has an irregular grain and stains and polishes well. It is suitable for turned and cabinet work and is the traditional wood for the backs of violins*

*British Honduras Mahogany (hardwood)*
*From 1760 onwards this was the basic wood for quality furniture such as dining tables and cabinets. Today it is expensive but since it finishes so beautifully it is ideal for small dimensional work and it does not shrink or distort*

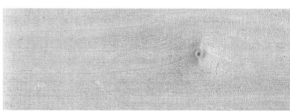

*European Birch (hardwood)*
*This is a very strong wood with an exceptional ability to hold tacks. In the nineteenth century it was used for wardrobes because it gave an interesting 'silky' finish. Today it is used for upholstery frames and interior work*

*Ceylon Ebony (hardwood)*
*This wood has a straight grain and its uniform black colour can, on rare occasions, be tinged with brown streaks. It is extremely brittle and difficult to glue but it polishes beautifully. Ceylon ebony is used wherever it can be shown to decorative advantage*

*European Ash (hardwood)*
*Ash is an outstandingly tough wood but its use for furniture making has always been limited. It is found in turned work, and is sometimes used for framing. It can act as a substitute for oak in some cases. Its best known use is in the making of cricket bats*

*American Whitewood (hardwood)*
*This wood was popular in the 1920s and*
*1930s but in England its use has been*
*restricted to interior joinery and the frames of*
*cabinets and cupboards. It is regarded as a*
*reliable foundation for veneering but is*
*unsuitable for any turned or bent work*

*Scots Pine or European Redwood (softwood)*
*This wood is extensively used in basic joinery*
*and frames and sometimes for veneers. It is*
*not very resistent to decay however, and is*
*regarded as a basic wood to be used where*
*it will not show*

*Teak (hardwood)*
*Teak is rarely found in old European*
*furniture although it is fashionable for*
*modern domestic furniture. However old*
*oriental furniture can be constructed with*
*solid teak. In restoration teak can be useful*
*as a show-wood but it tends to split*

*European Spruce (softwood)*
*This white, wild-grained wood is very tough*
*and easy to sand, glue and nail. It takes a*
*good finish and provides a base for veneering*
*but is not very resistent to decay. European*
*spruce tends to become lighter in colour*
*when exposed to the light*

*European Walnut (hardwood)*
*Walnut is an outstanding decorative wood,*
*sometimes with a wavy grain. The wood used*
*for furniture is taken from the base of the*
*tree near the roots. It is therefore very*
*expensive. It polishes and stains superbly and*
*is used in highly figured veneers*

*Bird's Eye Maple (hardwood)*
*This is a pale wood, sometimes called rock*
*maple, with an unusual 'bird's eye' figure.*
*It stains, polishes and glues well but is*
*difficult to nail. Bird's eye maple was very*
*popular for decorative veneering in the 1930s*

*European Cherry (hardwood)*
*Like other fruitwoods, cherry was used in*
*early provincial furniture, often as a decorative*
*veneer. It is inclined to warp and is therefore*
*used only in small sections but glues and*
*polishes well. It is widely used in America*
*for cabinet and furniture making*

*Ramin (hardwood)*
*Ramin will not be found in any antique*
*furniture since it was only introduced in the*
*1950s. Ramin provides an excellent substitute*
*for beech in carcass construction and*
*framing. It is used in long thin sections, such*
*as the rails of a chaise-longue*

The colour of oak, even over a relatively short period, mellows greatly. The older the piece, the more pronounced the change. You will immediately notice the depth of colour in old oak when it is cut to replace a panel, for example. Many of the problems of colour change can be overcome through various bleaching techniques and in the final staining or polishing of the repaired piece of furniture. These will be discussed in the section on polishing on page 30 and in the different projects.

Blending and harmonizing the colours of woods is a skill that can make a vast difference in a job of restoration. It is an area of restoration in which the greatest care is called for. In an old piece of furniture most of the colour is in the wood itself. This is why it is important to remove the polished surface without damaging the colour in the wood so that the wood can once again be polished to resemble its original patina. The beauty of age-coloured wood cannot be restored artifically with the help of modern dyes or bleaches, so any mistakes made in stripping are irrevocable. However, if you are careful, you can polish the carefully stripped surface to a good durable shine which will retain the depth of colour of the original patina.

Besides its use in major structural work, wood has also been used in ways which have become specialized crafts themselves. Such skills are generally beyond the scope of the amateur and are perhaps best left alone. A knowledge of the terms and techniques, however, is useful.

Marquetry is the use of different coloured woods to achieve a decorative effect. It is closely allied to inlay except that in the latter stones like lapis lazuli and agate, or ivory, mother-of-pearl and tortoiseshell are used instead of wood.

Both marquetry and inlay are done by cutting a shallow strip from the surface of a cabinet or table top. The groove is then filled with the coloured stones (inlay) or woods (marquetry). These can be arranged to achieve complex and beautiful patterns which are then polished. The greatest exponent of this kind of work was André Boulle, a Frenchman who lived from 1642 to 1732. The main materials he used were tortoiseshell, pewter and brass. His technique, called Boullework, has been copied through the centuries but it is a difficult craft and so pieces that need restoration should be avoided by the amateur.

Parquetry and intarsia are other forms of wood mosaic. In parquetry, woods of many different colours are inlaid to form geometrical patterns and then smoothed and polished. Intarsia is a similar technique but instead of geometrical shapes, the wood is inlaid to create pictures.

If you wish to try your hand at any of these techniques you could learn a great deal by reproducing a small piece from a furniture catalogue. In this way you will gain valuable experience before trying the technique on decorated and perhaps valuable pieces.

*Left: A chipped piece of veneer decorates this tea caddy from the mid-eighteenth century (Sheraton). The base wood is probably oak, with satinwood as the background. The major design is holly (the two central shapes), and the leaves and edging are in ebony and boxwood. By comparison, the detail on the right, from a late eighteenth-century Dutch serving table, is in perfect condition. Again the background is satinwood veneer with ebony and sycamore for the detail*

## Veneers

Veneering is a skill that can be tackled by any amateur restorer. A veneer is a thin layer of wood, originally cut by hand, but done by machine after the early part of the nineteenth century. Rare, expensive and decorative woods were cut into thin slices and then used to face common, cheaper wood.

Veneer can be successfully applied by hand without specialized equipment such as the heated presses used by professionals. It is advisable to begin by veneering flat surfaces before progressing to deal with curves.

Veneer may be hard to find in shops, and you will certainly have to spend some time looking for the better quality materials. The ideal way is to go to a specialist in veneers but they are usually only found in the larger cities and normally will only sell in large sheets. Some lumber yards stock the more common veneers but can order the exotic types at additional expense. Antique dealers who restore some of their own furniture may be willing to sell some, while an increasing number of art and handicraft shops sell small pieces for marquetry. A number of artificial veneers are on the market and although some of these are of good quality they can never look or feel as good as well-cut natural veneers. Modern veneers are thinner than the old veneers, so you may like to collect old broken pieces of furniture to cut up for materials.

Faults in veneer can range from simple blemishes which are easily corrected, to major repairs such as the replacement of marquetry. One of the most common faults is that of chipped corners and edges, especially near doors and drawers. Because of the continual friction, drawer runners often suffer from chipped veneer.

# The Restorer's Tool Kit

A good selection of tools is essential for any restoration job. This chapter outlines the basic equipment required for the work and the fundamental construction techniques used in the building of furniture

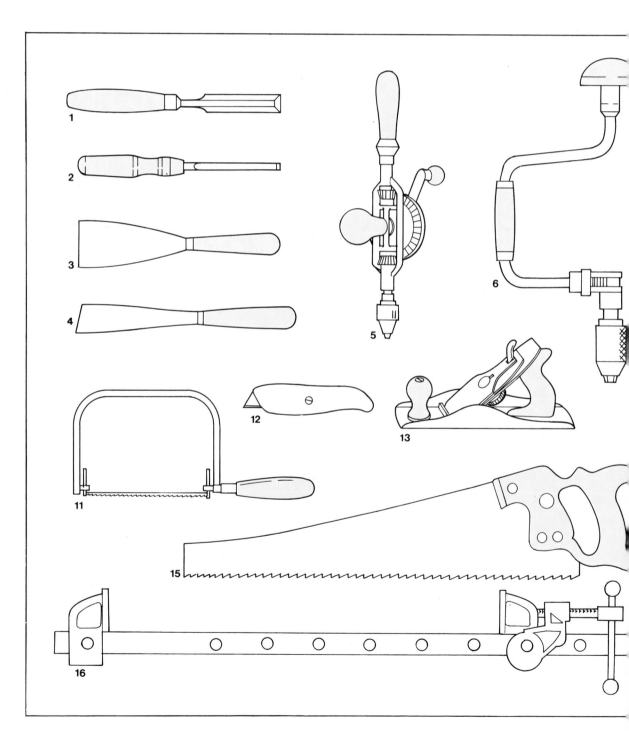

A skeleton tool kit, no bigger than that used for most ordinary do-it-yourself jobs, is all that is necessary for furniture restoration.

It is important that the tools are in good condition and that they are sharp, especially the chisels and planes. These can be sharpened by grinding them on a grindstone, if the edges are damaged, and then fining the edge with an oilstone. It is often necessary to cut off very thin sections of wood, so it is essential to keep your tools sharp.

If grinding the tools is unnecessary, then all that you need to do is to sharpen them on an oilstone. These are available in various grades and it is ideal to have both a coarse and a fine oil-stone. The coarser stone is used if the tool is in bad condition after cutting a hard or gritty material, while the fine stone will give that extra tone to a tool which is slightly dulled.

If you wish to have a still finer edge it will be necessary to hone the tools. This can be done on an old piece of leather with an abrasive paste coating in the manner of the old fashioned barber. Honing polishes steel and produces an edge as fine as a razor.

The most important tool to keep sharp is the steel scraper. Scrapers are made in various thicknesses. The very finest can be used for heavy lacquer work while the thicker scrapers can take off very fine shavings from wood, leaving a smooth surface ready for polishing.

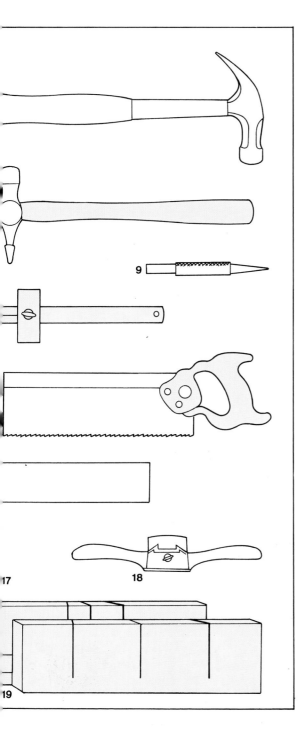

*Left: Some basic tools are essential to the amateur furniture restorer. A few are illustrated here and others will be shown throughout the special projects section.*
  *1. Bevel-edged chisel*
  *2. Mortise chisel*
  *3. Stripping knife or putty knife*
  *4. Filling knife or putty knife*
  *5. Wheel brace or hand drill*
  *6. Swing brace or brace*
  *7. Claw hammer*
  *8. Cross-pein hammer*
  *9. Nail punch or nail set*
*10. Gauge or marking gauge*
*11. Coping saw*
*12. Cutting knife or utility knife*
*13. Metal plane*
*14. Tenon saw or back saw*
*15. Panel saw or hand saw*
*16. Sash clamp or bar clamp*
*17. Try-square*
*18. Spokeshave*
*19. Mitre box*

*Below: A pine and curly maple tailoress's counter. This piece of Shaker furniture (1820–23) has a strong, stable construction with few embellishments. It is an example of the basic carcass construction of traditional furniture which is shown in diagrammatic form on the right*

## Basic Construction

The basis of any cabinet, sideboard, wardrobe, cupboard or bookcase is a carcass or box. This forms the main structure of the piece. A typical cabinet of almost any period will have the top and other major areas constructed from several large planks of wood, planed flat and then glued along their longest edges. If these boards are quite thick they are usually held together with tongue-and-groove joints.

The traditional method of construction is to make the back with one or more panels, the grain running vertically. The sides are constructed in one piece. These panels are then joined together by means of vertical strips of wood about three or four inches (80 mm to 100 mm) wide and three-quarter inch (18 mm) thick, grooved on both edges. The panels fit into these grooves making gluing unnecessary.

The constructed back panels are then fitted into grooves made in the wood on the sides, top and bottom of the piece. The sides themselves are normally constructed from one substantial solid end.

The front of most cabinets usually consists of rails running horizontally and vertically to form frames for the doors or drawers. The front is secured by mortise and tenon joints into the sides. In this kind of joint the end of one member

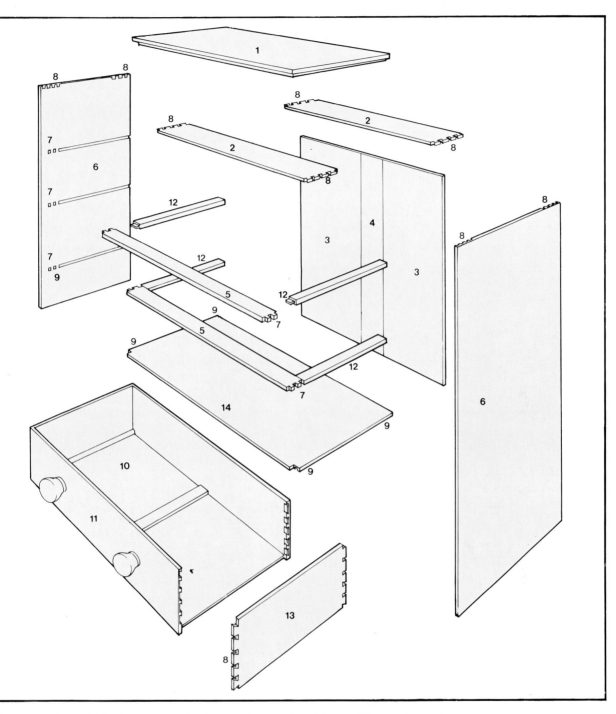

bears a slot which is rectangular in section and fits into a recess carved into the other member. The two are then held together with glue or dowels.

Drawers are usually made using dovetail joints, strong joints specifically used where the rail has to take weight. In constructing the drawers themselves, the bottom should slide in from the back into grooves cut into the sides and front. The entire drawer should then sit and run on hardwood runners. The base of the drawer may be made of two panels joined together by means of a strip of wood, much as the back of the carcass is.

When faced with the problems of carcass repairs you should not take apart more than is

*Above: The traditional carcass.*
1. *Top*
2. *Top carcass rail*
3. *Back panels*
4. *Vertical grooved strip*
5. *Rails, horizontal*
6. *Solid end*
7. *Mortise and tenon joints*
8. *Dovetail joints*
9. *Bottom shelf dovetail joints*
10. *Drawer bottom*
11. *Drawer front*
12. *Drawer runners*
13. *Drawer side*
14. *Bottom of carcass*

*Right: The traditional mortise and tenon joint, where the tenon is inserted into the mortise, glued and then clamped*

necessary. The repairs will usually fall into three main categories: the joints may have become loose or even broken, a whole section or panel may need to be replaced, or worn or shrunken parts may need to be replaced or repaired.

When dismantling, you may find it a good idea, particularly if you are inexperienced, to mark parts so that they are replaced in the correct positions. Do not strike the wood directly with a hammer or mallet. Instead, carefully knock the parts apart using a piece of scrap wood measuring at least two by one inches (50 by 25 mm), to ensure an even pressure and to prevent splitting. Apart from bruising the surface, the blow may crack a panel or break a joint.

Make sure before you do this that nothing else is holding the parts together. There might be a rail, back panel or moulding screwed or glued to both parts· which will prevent separation. There may even be nails from an earlier, unskilled restoration job. The separation of obstinate dovetail joints can sometimes be helped by damping and heating with a flat. iron; simply apply the fairly hot iron on a damp cloth placed over the cleaned area (this also removes veneer). Do not flood with water, especially on the joints, as this may cause the wood to swell.

When the parts are separated, clean up the area, removing old, dried glue with a chisel. Broken dowels can be removed with a brace and bit or an electric drill. To remake a joint, use a gauge to ensure accurate measurements and a tenon saw for easy working. Loose joints should be reglued using suitable clamping pieces.

When dealing with broken parts, it is best to dismantle locally around the area. The most common breaks in main panels are known as split ends. These usually occur when a moulding has been used in the construction. Because the moulding is glued tightly to the ends of the panel it resists shrinking tendencies. The panel, on the other hand, splits when it dries out. Another fault is a failed joint. This occurs, again because of shrinkage, when two panels, usually in the sides, are held at the ends by mouldings. The gaps caused by open or failed joints are usually straight and parallel, but may be curved to the grain.

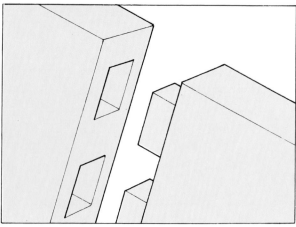

*Above: The stub tenon, where the tenon is cut shorter so that it is not seen on the outside. It more effectively conceals the construction where strength is not so essential, as for example, on drawer guides. The mortise should only be about two-thirds the width of the wood*

*Left: A through dovetail joint, the strongest and most common joint used on corners, particularly those on drawers*

usually includes worn edges (in friction with the runners), broken bottoms and loose joints. If the joints are loose it will be necessary to dismantle the drawer. Remove the bottom first, which may be held at the back by screws or nails and by small glue blocks along the underside edge of the drawer front. Chip the glue blocks away with a chisel. Tap out the sides from the front and back of the drawer using a piece of wood to prevent damage from the blows. Drawers are usually made with dovetail joints. Reglue the cleaned joints and reset, using a clamp if you feel it is necessary. Measure the diagonals for squareness. Replace the original glue blocks if these were present. When using the clamp do not place the metal directly on the wood. A piece of newspaper or plywood is the best separator to prevent scarring the wood.

If the edges of the drawer are worn it will be necessary to replace them. Cut a piece from the worn part making it as square as possible, and parallel to the top edge of the drawer. This can first be marked with a pencil and then cut with a chisel. Cut a replacement piece, a little larger than the damaged original, as you would when replacing a split end, and glue into position. When the glue has dried, plane the edge down level. A light coat of wax on all friction areas will help the drawer to run smoothly.

If the bottom of the drawer has split you may need to simply glue the split or repair it as a split end. In the first case you will have to do this while the drawer is dismantled. The underneath of the drawer bottom may have glue blocks which will need to be taken off and then replaced.

The most common faults found in doors are loose joints in the main framework, usually split mortises and split panels. You will have to dismantle to correct both of these faults, unless the panel split is a split-end type repair. If the joints are loose, dismantling will be easy. If not, make sure there are no nails holding anything and gently force the joints apart before cleaning off the old glue. Warps in the main framework can be cured by clamping it to another piece of wood and leaving it for a time. It is often just as easy to replace the piece, called a stile which is placed across the grain of the broken piece.

Clean out the split or joint using a saw or file. Prepare a strip of wood slightly thicker than the opening, and tapered in length if necessary. Plane it to a slight wedge shape so that it enters the opening easily in its length. Glue and tap it in with a small hammer and wait until dry.

When the glue has set, level the strip with a chisel, taking care to remove nothing from the adjoining surface. Sand to smooth.

Drawer runners often present a minor repair to the carcass. The chief fault is usually that of extensive wear where the lower edges of the drawers rub. The ends of the runners are normally scored into a trough by repeated use over the years. The runners may have to be repaired or replaced, depending on the extent of the damage. In either case, the runner will first of all have to be removed. They are usually held at the back with a screw and are stub-tenoned at the front, the outside edge being glued. A stub-tenon joint is essentially a smaller mortise and tenon joint. Simply undo the screw and prise the runner from the back. It is usually just as easy to replace the two outside runners as it is to carry out any repairs.

Some runners are not so complicated and are simply taken off and a replacement prepared and glued back on as Kenneth Davis shows in his repairs to the bottom part of the glass-fronted cupboard project on page 68.

The wear on the runners will usually be reflected in wear in the actual drawers. Damage to drawers

## The tool kit

Repairs to broken legs may mean that new pieces will need to be spliced on or that the whole fractured leg will have to be replaced. Small pieces that have broken off can simply be reglued and filled ready for polishing, if necessary. The fracture may be repairable by regluing and strengthening with screws. The screws should be countersunk, that is the screw head should not be flush with the surface. You can do this with a brace and bit or by simply gouging a hole with a chisel. The former is more professional. The countersunk holes can then be filled (bevelled) by gluing in 'pellets' or tiny dowels.

Turned legs can present a special problem. Breaks in turned legs can sometimes be repaired by dowelling the two pieces together and then gluing. If the breakage is near the base of the leg you may be able to drill upwards through the leg from the foot up into the main part. The two parts should first be glued together. Insert a new dowel in the bored hole with glue. This repair requires some experience. If the leg needs to be replaced you can probably buy a replacement, either ordered or ready-made, at a good joiners or cabinetmakers. If you are lucky and skilled enough to be the owner of a lathe you can make the new leg yourself.

Chairs are the most used and abused piece of furniture in the home and so old chairs are likely to have many faults. Most of these are in the legs and the techniques already mentioned apply. Corner brackets can reinforce the leg if they are placed in the corners at the top end, near the seat.

The most common fault in chairs is loose joints. This usually happens between the back legs and seat rails, and results from the strain of people leaning back and tilting the chair on its back legs. You may have to dismantle the chairs if all the joints are loose. When you have done this clean away the old glue and reset the joints. You will need clamps to make sure the joints fit tightly while the glue is drying. A tourniquet made from a clothes line is an alternative to a clamp.

Another common fault is a broken rail in the underframe. The rail should be removed, without dismantling if possible. Again, this is almost always due to loose joints which need to be clean and reglued.

When part of a chair, or any other piece of furniture, needs to be replaced, you can use the old part as a template to mark and cut out the new part. Kenneth Davis demonstrates this technique when replacing a section of the top for a gate-leg table on page 57.

*Right: An attractive cedar chest which is showing signs of wear and tear. One of the brass-bound corner pieces is missing—a specialist job to replace. It is also stained and scratched. The simple expedient of stripping and renewing the polish would turn it into a fine and valuable piece. A coat of wax will prevent more damage*

# Stripping and Finishing Wood

The restoration of wood to its original lustre and brilliance is one of the joys of restoration. Here the various techniques are discussed

*Above: When buying pieces of furniture which have been stripped in bulk, usually in tanks of caustic soda, watch for signs of damage. This small drawer from a pine washstand has suffered extensive cracking. Made from a single piece of wood, the surface has reacted to drastic treatment. Although still usable for storage, the bottom is now weakened and will certainly need to be repaired at some time in the future*

Besides a scraper, a paint brush or a grass brush will be of great value for stripping furniture of stains, polishes and paints. The paint brush should be regarded as expendable since once used it will be very difficult to clean to a standard suitable for painting. A grass brush made of coarse fibres is suitable for the application of bleaches and strippers which might destroy ordinary paint brushes.

Paint remover, methylated spirit or denatured alcohol, washing soda and vinegar are the main liquids needed for most stripping jobs. There are many abrasives available but you should be able to manage with coarse and fine steel wool, and some sheets of coarse and fine sandpaper. It is best to buy wet-and-dry sandpapers. By wetting the sheet before use you will avoid fractures which can scratch the surface of the furniture and may spoil the finish.

You can buy manufactured strippers from all do-it-yourself shops. These will have instructions regarding their use which should be followed implicitly. Washing soda should be used in solution of one part soda to ten parts water by weight.

There are two general procedures which you can use depending on whether the surface to be stripped is covered by a paint or a polish. To strip paint, apply the stripper and leave for a short period. When the surface begins to move, scrape in the direction of the grain. Several applications of stripper may be needed to reveal the bare wood. When all the paint has been removed, thoroughly rub down the piece of furniture with coarse steel wool and then scrub with soda diluted in hot water. Leave to dry and then wash again with diluted vinegar (approximately two teaspoons to 20 fluid ounces or half a litre of water). Leave to dry for 24 hours before sandpapering, working along the grain, as before. The surface should then be ready for staining and polishing.

To remove an old polish, cover the surface with methylated spirit or denatured alcohol and scrape when the surface begins to move. A second or third application may be necessary. Wipe dry with a cloth before rubbing with sandpaper along the grain. Remember to use a fine grade of sandpaper for this work.

Below: One sign that a piece has been
stripped in a soda tank is 'bleeding'. The base
of this piece is covered with a white
crystalline deposit of soda which can be
wiped away but will soon re-form. Cracking
and shrinkage are also common faults, since
the soda withdraws all natural oils from the
wood

More difficult cases of old polish can be treated
with caustic soda, but careful precautions are
essential as it can burn badly. Rubber gloves
should be worn, and the soda should be added to
the water, not the other way round. It is advisable
to do the job out of doors if possible. Caustic soda
should not be used on veneers as it will soften the
glue and pull the veneer away. After scraping,
wash the wood with a little diluted vinegar to
neutralize the caustic soda. The soda will, however, darken the wood considerably and this can
be counteracted later by washing the piece of
furniture with a peroxide bleach. Great care
should be taken here as this process can irreparably
damage the piece.

## Finishing

Once you have cleaned the surface the next step
is to stain it. Staining and finishing wood to give
it colour and enhance the grain is perhaps the
most enjoyable part of furniture restoration. After
repairing a piece of furniture you will want to show
it off to its best effect and to bring the dull but
sound wood back to life.

It is sometimes necessary, particularly in the
case of walnut or mahogany, to fill in the grain
prior to staining and finishing. This is done by
applying a wood filler paste, available in various
brands. The filler can be thinned with white spirit
or turpentine until it is the consistency and colour

29

of oatmeal. It should then be applied in a circular motion all over the surface of the piece with a piece of hessian, burlap or coarse rag. This should then be left for a few minutes and, when semi-dry, rubbed into the wood with a fresh piece of hessian or burlap. Do this by rubbing up and down the length of the grain. The grain pores of the wood should be uniformly filled and the surface free of all residues to avoid white-in-the-grain after staining (the white is left from the filler and, if present, the surface must be well sanded to remove it). Leave to dry for about 12 hours before lightly sanding with a fine paper. Most projects will not need filling, however, so you can normally proceed directly to staining or finishing as required.

There are three types of stains commonly in use and readily available: water stain, spirit stain and oil or wiping stain. Oil stain is the most popular of the three and is the easiest to use as it does not raise the grain when applied to the wood. Water raises the grain so that you should wet the surface, sand and then stain.

Before staining you can get the exact colour you want by testing the stain, which you may have either mixed yourself or bought, on scraps of matching wood. If the stain is too dark it can be diluted with white spirit or turpentine, while if it is too light more stain can be added.

Oil stains are powders which are mixed with turpentine, white spirits, naptha or similar oil products. They have great powers of penetration, but tend to build up over soft spots in the wood and for this reason they should be used sparingly. They should never be used on softwoods such as pine and spruce, or hardwoods such as beech or birch. The result could be patchy and uneven.

Oil stains are available ready-mixed under many brand names some of which are intermixable if you wish to achieve a special colour. However, by using white spirit or turpentine you can easily make them up yourself. They are fairly quick-drying and depth can be built up by repeated applications. To gain maximum adhesion leave the piece for about 18–24 hours between each coat.

Spirit stains are best for colouring in small patches but tend to be uneven over large areas. They consist of dyes and translucent pigments dissolved in denatured alcohol or methylated spirits. They can be added to French polish to impart more colour.

Water stains can be 'earth' colours, which are effective and cheap and reflect the browns of natural earth colours, but the most common are aniline dyes which give a brilliant effect and do not fade because of their deep penetration. The earth colours tend to fill the surface pores only, but they are suitable for certain types of old furniture. Water stains raise the grain a great deal but this can be corrected with sanding and the use of Vandyke brown dye crystals. The crystals should be diluted in water with a little ammonia, turpentine or white spirit to give a darkish oak stain.

After filling and staining you can coat the wood

by French polishing. It is necessary to begin by sanding with a fine paper before applying the polish with a brush or the pad described below.

The most popular polish, French polish, can be bought under a great number of brand names. There are many other types available such as pale, white and translucent polish. French polish is hard and dries quickly. If you wish to darken it you can add Bismarck brown, a powder which, despite its name, is red when dissolved in polish. Experiment with the quantities until you achieve the required colour.

After sanding, dip the pad into the polish, being careful not to make it too wet. The pad should be made from a wad of cotton wool rolled and then covered with a fine, porous rag, such as a clean handkerchief or piece of old sheet.

Rub the polish on to the wood, working first with the grain and then in circular movements. If the pad becomes sticky add a small drop of linseed oil to soften it. The more you rub the polish into the wood, the more lustrous the finish. When you feel that you have polished sufficiently finish off with the pad, using the polish without the oil.

Leave the piece to dry for about one hour before sanding with a fine paper lightly covered with linseed oil. Then wipe the wood dry with a rag and repeat the process. Finally, finish off with straight up and down movements along the grain.

Wax polishing is the best way to complete the finish. Traditionally, wax polishes were made from a mixture of turpentine, beeswax and carnauba wax. Modern waxes contain silicone compounds and are possibly superior as they protect against scratching or marking. This type of polishing is not particularly durable on raw wood so it is advisable first to apply a thin layer of polish or boiled linseed oil diluted with an equal amount of turpentine or white spirit and used sparingly. Softwoods are generally not suitable for oiling.

In many cases you do not need to do a complete finish and the piece of furniture may only need to be 'revived'. A simple method is to lightly sand the piece with a fine paper, then wash with a weak vinegar or detergent solution and then French or wax polish.

**Decorative Parts**

Besides repairs to the main parts of the furniture, you will also come across damage to the decorative features, which are often so vital to the quality and character of the piece. Decorative parts might include bracket feet, cocked beads, mouldings, banding and veneers as well as inlays, scrolls or carving.

Bracket feet can be repaired fairly easily. If the break is a new one the broken edges will be sharp, if old they will be dirty and chipped. A new break can simply be glued and refitted. The break line might be very obvious if you glue an old break, however, and you will probably have to

make a replacement. This can be done by making a template, drawn on a piece of thin white cardboard, from the other foot. Cut this shape out with a fret or coping saw, sandpaper the new foot and refit, ready for staining. All the legs can then be reinforced by blocks of wood screwed behind the bracket.

Cocked beads are found round the main panels of drawers and on the outside edges of the main framework of doors in some pieces of furniture. These are easy to repair. Merely reglue if you still have the broken piece or insert a new piece using the same type of wood. Glue and sand down flush with the old beading.

A fairly common problem is a broken or missing

*Above: The decorative parts are often missing from old furniture. Brass reproduction handles such as these can replace them. The selection shows a reproduction of an early plate handle (top), an eighteenth-century Sheraton handle (left of centre row), a swan neck and a Georgian lion head. The bottom handle is a Queen Anne type*

# Stripping and finishing wood

Applied moulding will often have missing sections. Cut the broken edges square to receive new pieces. You can buy lengths of moulding from a good timber merchant, and these can be cut as required and then fitted into place and sanded flush.

Damage to veneer can range from the smallest blemish to the major problem of repairing marquetry. When dealing with veneer faults remember that you can buy sheets of veneer from specialists. Broken veneer on corners and edges is a common fault. Deal with this by cutting the damaged veneer —always across the end grain—with a knife, at an angle of about 45°, so that the piece to be inserted will be diamond-shaped. Clean old glue away. Insert the new piece of veneer (cut a little longer than the original) using glue and a G or C clamp. Level the overhanging veneer when the glue has dried. The grain of the old veneer piece should be matched as closely as possible when buying your new veneer.

Veneer can 'bubble' when the old glue decays. This can be dealt with by cutting the veneer with a thin, sharp knife so that the cut is as fine as possible. Use a ruler to make it straight. Using the knife, spread the glue under the two edges of the cut. A palette knife would be the ideal tool. Clamp the glued piece, protecting it with a sheet of newspaper or cloth.

Large areas of veneer can be removed by covering it with wet rags and then placing a very hot, flat iron on top. Remove as much of the old glue as you can with a hot damp cloth, scraping if necessary. Replace or reglue the old piece when it has dried remembering to clamp it.

The repairing of inlays, scrolls and carvings can be carried out by the amateur if they are confined to regluing. If a new piece is required, you will probably need to have it replaced by a professional.

Carving is a specialist job. However, it is interesting to try and some people have a natural aptitude for it although they may lack the technical experience. If you wish to try it, you will need a set of carving tools. Try the simpler projects such as leaves, flower petals and motifs. Carvings should be glued back on to the piece of furniture.

In most restoration jobs there will be a part to be replaced which you may have to cut yourself. This covers a wide variety of jobs ranging from remaking a mortise and tenon joint to cutting bracket feet. The general procedure is to lay the part on a piece of cardboard and mark its shape in pencil. The copy should be slightly bigger than the original so that you can plane and sand it into a good fitting position. Cut out the pattern with a sharp knife. Place the cardboard on a new piece of wood and follow the outline. Cut with a pad or jig saw or with a fret or coping saw. Sand the cut piece and match constantly until you have a good fit.

Joints can be made by cutting with a tenon saw. You could use a template for a large dovetail joint. For a broken mortise and tenon you will need to

*Below: Fine carving is worth restoring and preserving. A small piece of matching wood should be glued on to this ornamental carving on a cabinet to replace a chip, and then carved to match. Staining and polishing will restore it completely*

moulding. It is called 'stuck' moulding if it is worked into the piece of wood at the edges. This is most commonly found on table tops. Applied mouldings are glued on to the surface.

Stuck moulding usually suffers from small indents or it may be broken at the corner, particularly on a table. The damaged corner should be cut off and a replacement made. The replacement should be cut wider and thicker than the original so that you can plane it to shape. The edge to be connected to the corner should be planed flat so that it can form a good glued joint. When the glue is set, plane down with a modern light plane so that it matches the rest of the moulding.

clean out the mortise. Measure the tenon with a gauge and cut a piece twice its length. This can then be recessed by gluing into a new mortise on the rail or piece on which the tenon was originally built. Clamp while waiting for the glue to dry.

Broken rails are fairly easy to replace, even when you have to make a tenon on both ends. When remaking a rail you may not need to make a template since you can simply mark out the shape onto another piece of wood. Cut with a jig saw or pad saw. An interesting variation to replacement is shown in the project on the chest of drawers. Parts of the bottom, suffering from dry rot, can be cut away to form new legs which, with some blocks to reinforce, are sturdy and attractive.

*Below: The central feature of this modern dining room is a huge Edwardian table which has been stripped to reveal the beautiful grain of the old pine, with chairs to match. A Victorian mahogany sideboard adds to the room's warmth*

# Restoration Project 1: Pine Desk

The complete renovation of this old pine desk involves waxing, repairing split ends, restoring the finish to the fittings, stripping painted wood, removing scratches and household stains, and colouring the pine

*Left: The untouched, unstripped desk.
Besides an ugly dark stain, it has chipped
wood, a split in the end, painted fittings, a
damaged handle, light scratches, and it needs
an entirely new finish*

This pine desk presents some of the commonest faults to be remedied in antique furniture. The desk is stained with a dark colour which gives it a heavy appearance. It would look its best if stripped to the pine and coated with a wax polish to protect the wood and recapture the beauty of the grain of the aged pine. This dark stain has also been coated on the door handle and other fittings. They will need to be cleaned and buffed back to their original state or replaced as in this project. The door handle is damaged and needs replacing.

Another fault is the chipped wood on the front of the drawer. Often small faults on drawers involve the replacement of veneer. They are easy to correct. When the veneered surface has developed a blister, it is almost certain that the glue used to fix the veneer has finally decayed. To repair this, cut through the blister with a very thin-bladed, sharp knife. A scalpel, which you can buy in an art shop or a department store, would be the ideal tool. Using the blade of the knife, spread some glue under the sides of the blister, covering as much area under the loose veneer as you can.

To press down the glued blister, warm a small hammer in hot water and press it on the outside edges of the blister, gradually working into the centre. Wipe off the excess glue and put a length of adhesive tape along the line of the original cut. This will prevent the edges from curling upwards while the glue is drying. After 24 hours remove the tape by dampening it, and clean the repair with fine sandpaper. Be very careful when doing this not to damage the veneer.

If a piece of veneer has to be replaced, follow the method which is demonstrated in the diagram on page 74.

Splits in the end panels of desks and other heavy pieces of old furniture are also common. In this case, there is no need to dismantle the carcass to remove the end itself. The method of dealing with this is shown in the diagram on page 36.

Splits in the actual panel are invariably tapered and follow the grain. This repair will be easier if you enlarge the width of the narrow end of the gap. The new insert is then shaped accordingly and glued into place. Then trim down the strip of wood. Splits along the joint of two panels are generally parallel and the insert requires little or no shaping. You will get a more professional finish if you match the grain of the insert to the original wood.

When the desk has been stripped, wax should be used as a finish. There are two kinds of wax used on old furniture, wax used exclusively as a finish and wax which is a 'dressing' on top of a stain. Beeswax is the best type to use for finishing.

Beeswax may be bought in block or flake form. It should be covered in turpentine and heated until the wax dissolves. Great care should be taken when doing this. A much easier method is simply to buy a proprietary brand of wax polish. For pine the wax should be uncoloured. The most important factor when waxing is not to apply second or third coats before the previous coat has completely dried. A waxed surface can be greatly improved by briskly rubbing it with a rag and then wiping with a duster.

After stripping the polish from a piece of furniture, you may find that there are a number of scratches, bruises, glass marks or ink stains underneath the paint. This may have been the reason for painting it. Scratches can usually be dealt with by sanding with a fine sandpaper dipped in linseed oil. For deeper scratches, simply fill with wax and then rub level with fine sandpaper. To remove bruises, lie a damp cloth over the bruise and place a hot domestic iron on top of it. Glass marks, like heat and water marks, can usually be eliminated by rubbing with linseed oil and turpentine mixed in equal quantities. The oil can be removed with vinegar.

Ink stains can often be removed by using an ordinary domestic chlorine bleach. Apply this only over the area requiring treatment. If bleach should fail you can use a proprietary brand of diluted nitric or oxalic acid. This will turn the stain white and this in turn can be removed with a proprietary brand of camphorated oil. You should not use any of these materials in the presence of children as they are poisonous and may be imbibed accidentally on the finger.

The major part of renovating this pine desk consists in stripping the old dark paint. Brush on a

To fill the split in the end of the desk, clean it out with a file or chisel and then prepare a piece of wood matching the length and widest part of the hole, but about quarter of an inch (six millimetres) deeper than the split. If the gap tapers slightly, it will be necessary to shape the insert correspondingly, using a surform smoothing plane. Chisel the wedge until it fits tightly enough so that you can hammer it gently into place, after glueing all edges, using a small cross-pein or pin hammer.

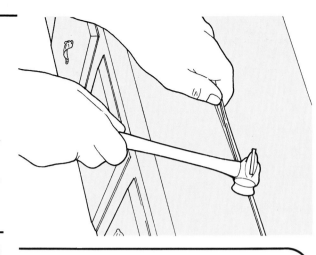

When the glue has dried, trim down the new insert, being careful not to damage the original surface of the desk. Use a bevelled wood chisel, paring thin slices at a time. Never try to take too much off at once as the chisel will rip along the grain of the inserted wood and you may have to start all over again. When you have pared flush, sand to get a really good finish. Check that the surfaces are level with the straight edge of a ruler or with the blade of a try-square.

It is sometimes necessary when restoring old furniture to remove the screws. You may need to clean paint from them, or they might prevent access to parts of the furniture you wish to repair. Using a screwdriver, take off all the handles and fittings. With some furniture, you may find that the screws are rusted and you cannot gain purchase when unscrewing. Carefully prise them out with pliers or pincers.

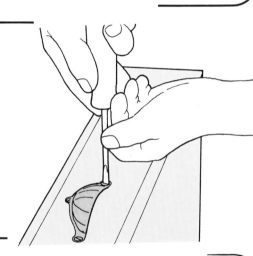

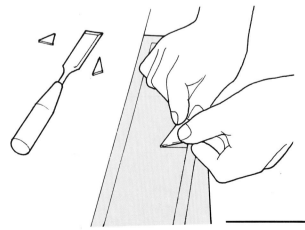

To repair chips to the wood on the drawer front, cut a new piece of matching wood, or, if the chip is shallow, use a piece of pine veneer. Glue the area to be repaired and insert the piece carefully. Wipe the area free of excess glue and allow to dry overnight. Sand the insert flush with the drawer front.

paint remover and then leave it for a short period until the surface begins to move or cockle. Then, using a scraper, remove the residues. You will need several applications of paint remover.

The important technique is to let the stripper do most of the work. You should not have to exert a great deal of force. If the surface of the paint does not cockle easily, recoat liberally with the remover. If you have to exert too much pressure when scraping, you are likely to damage the surface.

It is always a good idea when stripping to place the piece of furniture on some sheets of newspaper. A cloth would also be useful for wiping the residues of paint off the scraper when it

*Above: Kenneth Davis is using a steel scraper to remove the residues of paint after it has started to cockle and rise. Notice that he is working along the grain and is being careful not to allow the scraper to dig into the wood*

When all the paint is stripped from the desk, prepare the surface for staining by using a sheet of coarse sandpaper wrapped round a simple wooden block and sand the desk along the direction of the grain. Sand until the surface is perfectly clean and then wipe down the dust with a damp cloth. Leave to dry and then repeat the process with a fine sandpaper. Wipe down again. When dry the surface is ready for staining.

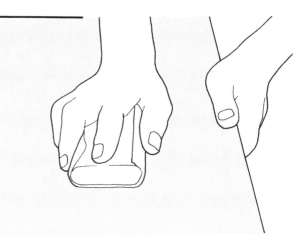

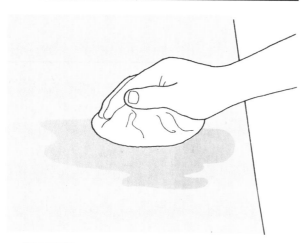

Staining is one of the most satisfying parts of restoration. You will need a home-made pad, described on page 30. For a pine desk use an uncoloured wax polish to heighten the natural colour of the wood. Using the pad, spread the wax in smooth, circular strokes. Leave for 24 hours after you have covered the whole desk. Then smooth the surface with fine steel wool before applying the final coat of wax.

Use fine wire wool and paint remover to clean all of the handles and fittings. To remove fine flecks of paint from inaccessible places you can finish the cleaning with methylated spirit or denatured alcohol. When clean, buff the fittings and handles to a shine.

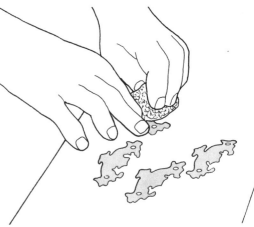

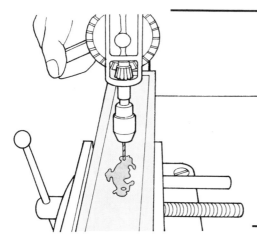

To replace the slightly damaged handle, buy a suitable replacement and mark its position before drilling the screw holes. It is probably best to remove the drawers and door so that you drill with the weight exerted downwards, ensuring a straighter hole and avoiding damage. Handles can then be screwed on.

begins to pile up. Do not dispose of the paper and cloth by burning. They will be highly inflammable.

When the paint is removed, the surface is thoroughly washed with soda dissolved in hot water, and coarse steel wool, although a scrubbing brush would do as well. After the surface has dried, it is again washed with methylated spirit or denatured alcohol and allowed to dry before being washed down with diluted vinegar. It should be left to dry for 24 hours before the surface is sanded to prepare for waxing.

Some proprietary brands of paint removers and strippers may carry specific instructions as to the best material you should use to clean them from the wood. In most cases this is methylated spirit or denatured alcohol but always check. It may not be suitable for mixing with the chemical in the remover.

The stripped surface when cleaned down may look attractive and give the piece of furniture a new lease of life. However, you may not be so lucky in every project you undertake. You may wish to lighten the colour of the wood still further or to darken it to hide various scratches and stains which you cannot remove to your satisfaction.

To lighten the pine use a peroxide No. 2 bleach with an equal volume of water. Bleaching will be necessary if you have to take the drastic and unpleasant step of removing the old paint or stain with a solution of caustic soda. This should only be used when all else has failed as it can cause

*Above: The waxed, natural pine now has a beauty which would look attractive in any home. The shiny fittings serve to enhance the colour of the wood and are not merely utilitarian. Many similar desks have been covered in layers of paint and may be unrecognizable as fine old pieces of pine furniture. Therefore amateur restorers should be on the lookout for such hidden treasure*

nasty burns and should be handled with care. If you are unused to these substances, take advice before you use them and make sure that you know how to treat burns should you have an accident.

To increase the colour, buy a dye or tint and mix it with the heated wax. There are many proprietary brands of coloured wax on the market and you may be lucky in finding the one you want without having to mix them. Remember when applying the mixture that each coat will darken the colour even more. This should be taken into consideration when selecting and mixing. Test each combination on an old piece of similar wood and allow it to dry before making your final decision.

Another method of deepening colour is to apply a single coat of stain before waxing. The best material to use in this case is French polish. If you do not bring it to too fine a shine, it will be an excellent base for waxing. It has the added advantage of toning and polishing new pieces of wood so that they are effectively disguised.

# Restoration Project 2: Two Chairs

This project presents two old chairs to be restored according to their different faults. Woodworm is treated in an old oak chair, legs are strengthened and the seat of a cane chair is renewed

*Left: The two chairs before restoration. The oak chair has a broken rail and loose joints but is in overall good condition. The cane chair needs recaning as well as a new rail*

Chairs take more strain and abuse than any other piece of furniture. The types of repair will depend on the individual chair as they are all constructed in so many different ways. The most common trouble is that the joints have broken or become loose. The rails, including those of the seat, can also become loose because they have had to take too much weight.

The first thing you should do with a chair you are about to tackle is to inspect it. Don't take the whole thing apart just because of one or two broken rails. Only take apart what is absolutely necessary. If it is possible to open the joint of the broken rail or leg, then deal with the repair locally.

A more serious form of damage is a rail which has been split in the middle. In this case it is often necessary to replace the old rail with a new one which you can easily make yourself.

The main problem with local repairs to rails and joints is how to get the joints back into place. The rail can be sprung back if the original joint is a tenon joint which is still intact. Another way of dealing with this is by making a loose tenon. The loose tenon is made and fitted into the leg so that it protrudes about two inches (five centimetres) after you have glued it into the original mortise in the legs (remembering to clean out the mortise first). Another mortise is cut in the rail but is cut open on the underside. Glue both the tenon and rail mortise. Slide the rail down onto the tenon. It should then be clamped.

Broken legs may be easy to make from a template but with the more complicated turned leg you may have to buy or have a replacement made, unless you have a lathe. If a square-sectioned leg is broken it is often possible to repair rather than replace it. It is usually better to splice on a new piece rather than just glue the two pieces together. Wood of the same kind must be used and the joint should be diagonal or tapered so as to give more gluing surface and consequently a stronger joint. You can gain even more strength if you screw the two pieces after they have been glued. Drill holes large enough to receive the whole screw head so that it can be hidden by a wooden plug glued into position. Smooth the plugs with sandpaper after the glue has set.

Apart from a broken rail, the faults and damage to this oak chair are minor. The legs of the chair are slightly loose, but can be repaired by inserting dowels in the joints. The split in the seat can be prevented from opening any further by placing a strip of canvas underneath it. The woodworm holes in the back rail need treatment by filling either with sawdust or commercial woodfiller.

Replacing the new rail is not so difficult because the legs are already loose at the joints. This means that a rail can be inserted by pulling the legs slightly apart. In many cases chairs either have to be taken apart completely or have a loose tenon constructed. Another way to deal with this problem is to cut a stub tenon, at an angle of about 30 degrees, in the upper corner of the top of the tenon. This enables the tenon to be fitted into the mortise without bruising the legs.

When the chair is repaired, the new rail should be match stained and the woodworm holes filled before wax polishing.

*Left: The oak chair is infested with woodworm and the holes can be seen on the back rail. Treatment is simple with products easily available to the amateur. The side rail is completely missing and will have to be replaced with a piece of matching wood. You may be able to find an old rail on a useless chair to match the one you are restoring.*

*The new rail roughly measures from the outside edge of one leg to the outside edge of the opposite leg. Cut along the grain with a tenon saw. When you are making this measurement ensure that splayed or broken legs do not distort the accuracy of the pencil mark. Although it is only a rough calculation, this kind of inaccuracy can make the cutting of the tenons more difficult.*

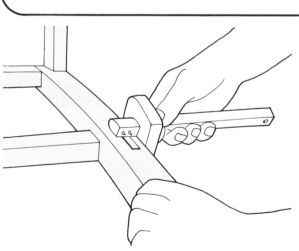

*Before marking the cutting outlines of the tenons on the new piece of wood, measure the old mortise in the chair leg with a mortise gauge. Set the two pins on the gauge to the width of the mortise. Then mark the outline for the tenon on the new rail, using the pins to scratch the wood. You can make the marking clearer if you pencil over the scratches. This will enable you to see the marking even if it becomes covered with sawdust.*

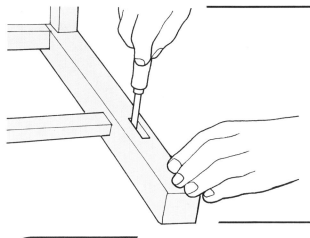

The old mortise holes in the legs can be cleaned out with a bradawl or small screwdriver. The important thing is to remove all the old glue from the corners and bottom edges of the joint. If the broken tenon of the old rail is still firmly glued into the mortise you will need a chisel to remove it. Shave off small pieces at a time with the thin chisel, making sure that you do not enlarge or cut into the rim edges of the mortise.

Now set about sawing the tenons using a tenon saw. Place the rail in a bench vice in a slightly slanted position as the picture shows. This can make the sawing position more comfortable. The tenon should be cut on the outside of the pencil marks to ensure that it fits tightly into the mortise. If it is too large you can always chisel it to size. You cannot add to it if it is too small.

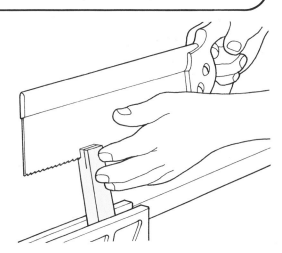

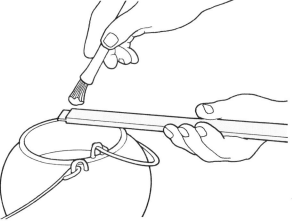

When the tenon is cut and sanded to size, cover it with glue smeared on with a paint brush. Apply a little glue to the mortise.

The glued rail is then inserted into the mortises by very gently prising the legs apart. Never pull the legs of any piece of furniture you are repairing too roughly.

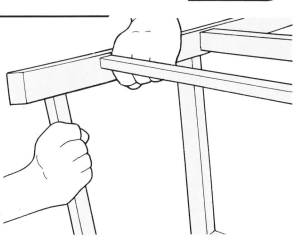

When the rail has been inserted and all excess glue wiped away with a piece of cloth, clamp the chair with a sash clamp. Place two pieces of wood under the feet of the clamp to protect the chair when it is wound tightly into place. The ends of the clamp should be placed directly opposite the repaired joints. If you do not want to buy or hire a sash clamp you can make a tourniquet of rope or cord. Bind the rope twice round the chair legs and tie a knot. Near a corner, insert a piece of dowel between the strands and twist it tight.

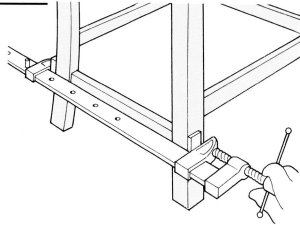

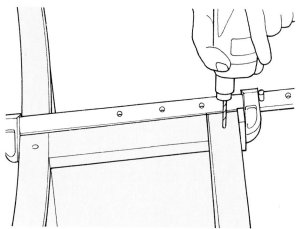

Bore holes into the sides of the legs so that dowel strengtheners can be used to reinforce the loose joints. Cut a piece of dowel about a quarter of an inch (six millimetres) shorter than the hole. Make a second cut along the length of the dowel and widen it with a file to form a V shape. This will allow excess glue to escape. The hole should be plugged with matching wood and glued into place after the dowel glue has dried. Sand.

The slight split in the chair can be repaired with a strip of canvas which acts as a reinforcement, preventing the split from opening further. For this type of hidden repair, plywood or even hardboard could be substituted for the traditional canvas. Linen is also used as a substitute. Cut the canvas into shape and glue. Apply glue to the underside of the seat. Then press the canvas firmly into place, squeezing out excess glue.

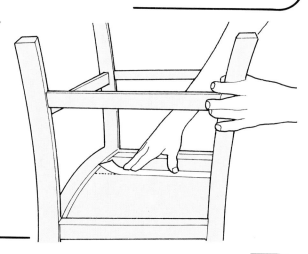

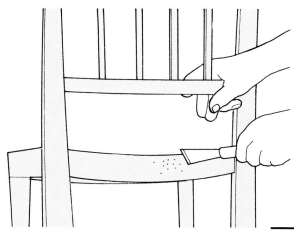

There are several ways to treat woodworm and, more particularly, woodworm holes. The first step is to spray the holes with an aerosol insecticide. This has to be done in the spring, in time for the mating of the insects. To fill the holes, mix some sawdust and glue and work it into the holes. Woodfiller, stained with a matching colour, is a good alternative. The finished chair on the right is now restored for many more years of use.

*Right: The cane chair before restoration. One of the rails needs replacing, staining and polishing, but the major part of the restoration involves complete recaning using a technique which seems difficult but is simplicity itself*

The restoration of a cane chair involves two processes: the woodwork to replace the missing rail and the canework.

The first step is to repair the missing rail and prepare the chair for caning. To prepare the chair all the old cane has to be removed and, if necessary, the chair must be repolished and restained. This should never be done after the caning is completed as it will cause discolouration to the canework. Also, the holes for the insertion of the cane lengths must be cleaned out so that the new pattern will not be distorted in appearance.

Caning requires few tools and many of these are already household items. Scissors are useful for cutting the cane. Any size is suitable as long as they are reasonably sharp. A small hammer would be ideal for tapping the pegs into the holes although you can probably get by without this. Tapping the pegs with a hammer instead of pushing hard with the hand will ensure that the pegs do not fall out and spoil the part of the weave you are working on. A small bodkin or even an upholstery needle will help if your fingers are not particularly nimble at weaving cane in small spaces. You will definitely need something to clear the holes when carrying out the preparatory work. This can be an improvised tool, such as a nail, a small screwdriver, a metal knitting needle or even a piece of metal coathanger with the point sawn off. The most important tool is a cutting knife. It will enable you to cut with great precision and in areas where other cutters cannot reach.

You will also need pegs for jamming the cane lengths into the holes temporarily while you are weaving. Any pointed sticks or dowels about two inches (five centimetres) long are suitable. Basketwood cane is ideal.

The cane used for chair seats and backs comes from a rattan creeper which grows to enormous lengths in south-east Asia. It is sold in handyman and artists' supply shops in two types and six sizes. Blue tie, the kind of cane normally used for antique furniture, is the best quality but it is expensive. Red tie is cheaper and is suitable for most projects.

Cane sizes range from the thinner number one to the thick number six. Numbers two and four are the sizes used for most chairs. The distance between the holes, measured from centre to centre, determines the size to use. The usual distance is half an inch (one centimetre), making it suitable for numbers two and four cane. If the holes are less than half an inch apart it is advisable to use numbers two and three because they are easier to weave in confined spaces. For very fine work, numbers one and two should be used.

There is another consideration to take into account when making your choice of cane sizes— cost and economy. One bundle of cane is more than enough material to cane a chair seat. If you buy two sizes of cane for one chair you will have at least half of each left over. For this reason you should choose to weave with only one size. However, what you gain in economy you will lose in quality and finish. A one-size cane weave does not look as attractive as a two- or three-size weave. And the material left over could be used for another project.

One of the simplest weaves for chairs is called the Seven Step Tradition. The seven steps in the weave are as follows:
1. First verticals
2. First horizontals
3. Second verticals
4. Woven horizontals
5. First diagonals
6. Second diagonals
7. Beading

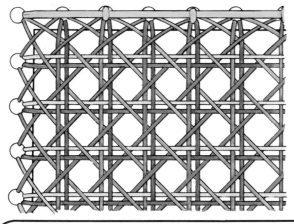

*Left: The Seven Step Tradition is here shown in diagrammatic form, the colours indicate the various steps*

1. First verticals
2. First horizontals
3. Second verticals
4. Woven horizontals
5. First diagonals
6. Second diagonals
7. Beading

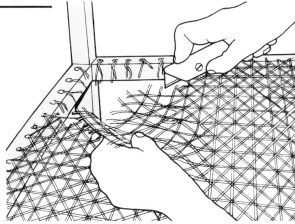

Prepare the chair by cutting away all of the old, ragged cane. Pull out any small nails or wooden pegs which may have been used to pin or jam the cane. You may find that it is easier to clear away the rest of the cane left in the holes by cutting at the tied strands under the rails of the seat and pulling them free. Do not mark the chair with the knife.

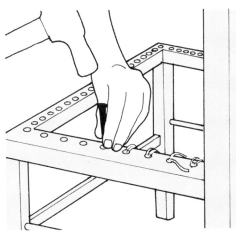

Clean out each hole individually with a blunt piece of wire, a long nail or a punch. It is important that the holes are cleared completely to prevent the new cane from sticking. When they are cleaned, locate the centre front and centre back holes. Lightly mark them with a pencil.

To replace the broken rail, measure a length of dowel to the required diameter with at least one and a half inches (four centimetres) extra for the tenons. After it is cut, sanded and fitted, glue the new rail into the mortises by slightly spreading the legs apart. Apply a sash clamp and wipe away excess glue. Now sand the new rail and stain it to match the rest of the chair. The whole chair should then be lightly 'cut' with fine steel wool, wax polished and french polished to revive the finish and bring out the inlays.

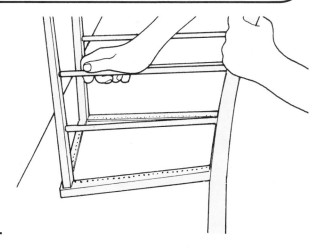

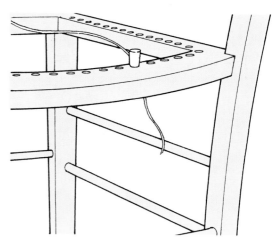

*Peg one end of cane into the centre back hole, leaving at least three inches (seven centimetres) through the bottom. String the cane, shiny side up, to the centre front hole. Working to either right or left, string the cane across to the next back hole. Continue across the frame to the last back hole. (Step 1) Then, repeating the same procedure, start again from the middle, stringing towards the other side of the chair. Do not use the corner holes for either verticals or horizontals.*

*Above: The chair after the first verticals have been inserted. The two strands at each side are strung between holes at the front and the sides. This means that the strands are kept parallel*

The lighter cane is usually used for steps one to four, changing to the heavier size for steps five and six. Beading is normally done with sizes two and six cane. If you have any doubts about which sizes to use, take the old cane which has been cut from the chair to the shop for reference. It is a good idea to make a drawing of the old weave before you cut it away. Make this a detailed drawing marking the direction of each strand, the number of holes and the number of canes in each hole. Do each step in different colours. If the chair is old it is probable that there will be no beading surrounding the weave. Beading is a relatively modern addition to the art of weaving.

Some professionals like to wet the cane before starting work. If you are a beginner, it might be a good idea to do so. Cane is very brittle and unless you are used to handling it, it is liable to split and crack.

It is inadvisable to soak the cane as this may cause discolouration. It is better, and just as effective, to wet the cane as you work. You can do this by passing it through a bowl of water just before you weave it. If the cane dries out too quickly while you are weaving you should wet

your fingers and pass them on the underside of the material, not the shiny side.

You should be careful not to step or kneel on the cane as you work as this will cause it to split lengthways. Even a tiny split is liable to creep up the whole length of the strand. Throw away all split pieces, they will make the work look unsightly. Keep checking the work as you go so as to avoid having to unravel the weave.

The cane should also be dampened for tying in the ends. Tying in is done when you have finished one length of strand and are starting a new length. The new end is passed twice around a short strand spanning the small space between two holes on the underside of the seat frame. It is then tightened by pulling gently. If you tie in the ends as you work you will not need many pegs for jamming the cane in the holes and you will not have as much finishing to do at the end of the weaving.

The alternative is not to worry about tying in the ends until you have finished and there are quite a lot of pegs holding various lengths of cane. The cane should be tied before you remove the pegs. To make this easier you can dampen the cane. Using scissors, cut each length of cane to a point. Thread the end twice around a loop spanning two holes, in the same way as described for tying in during weaving. Then take the end back under itself, pull tight and cut off the excess. If there are three or four ends coming out of the same hole you can use not only the loops immediately on each side but the next ones along as well.

In the past, nails, basket cane or wooden pegs were used to jam the strands permanently in the holes. These were never removed. But they tend to give an unsightly finish. The addition of the beading step has made them unnecessary. Beading gives not only a very professional and polished finish but also strength and durability so that the cane does not slip and sag when subjected to weight over a period of time. For this reason it is preferable to use a grade six cane for the beading. If the holes are larger than an eighth of an inch (three millimetres) then grade six will be necessary to cover them.

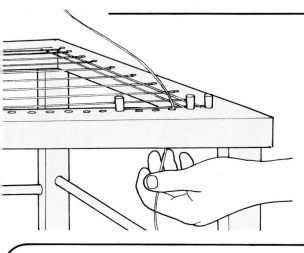

Next, string the horizontals from side to side, starting at the front and working straight through to the back without interruption. (Step 2) The horizontal canes should lie on top of the vertical strands. This will provide the basic frame for the diagonals.

Insert pegs as you string the horizontals. This will ensure that the strands are taut, but not overstretched. Jam the pegs into the last four or five holes you have used moving them as you work the strands from side to side, so that they 'travel' with the caning. Do not remove pegs which are holding loose ends.

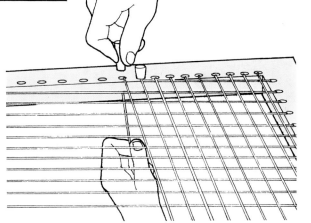

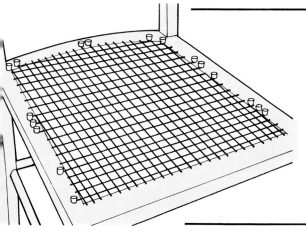

When all the horizontals are in place, the tension of the strands should be fairly tight and even but not at stretching point. The shiny side of both horizontals and verticals should be uppermost.

To place the second verticals, (Step 3) follow almost the same procedure as for the first, beginning at the middle and working out to either side. The second verticals are laid on top of the previous two steps but they should not lie directly on top of the first verticals, but parallel to them with a slight space between. Lay the strands to the right of the first verticals.

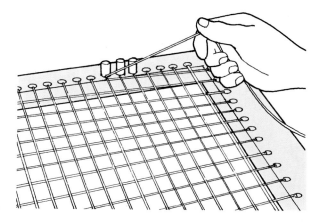

The second set of horizontals are woven **under** and then **over** the vertical pieces (Step 4). As for the first horizontals, peg one end of the cane with the shiny side up. Thread the cane under the first verticals and pull up through the two vertical strands, then over the second verticals. Repeat with each pair of verticals. Work from side to side towards the back of the seat. Occasionally run the cane through your fingers to check that it is not twisting. Do not worry if the weave looks a little untidy as the diagonals will square it up.

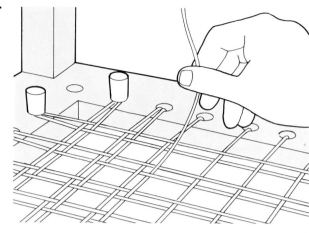

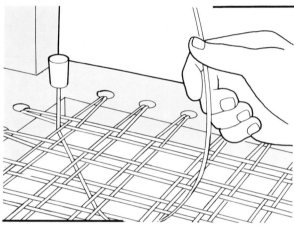

Start weaving the diagonals at the back left hand corner of the seat (Step 5). Peg the hole and insert the cane, shiny side up, **over** the first pair of horizontals and then **under** the first pair of verticals. Moving towards the lower right hand corner, continue weaving **over** the horizontals and **under** the verticals.

Try to keep the cane straight as you weave the diagonals. You should pull it tight every six inches (15 centimetres) or so. As you pull the cane through, the whole weave will tighten and begin to look like the finished product, but be careful that the cane does not break when in flattens into the intersection. When weaving diagonals you should proceed with patience and care, concentrating as you go. Remember that the only way to correct errors is to unweave all that you have already done.

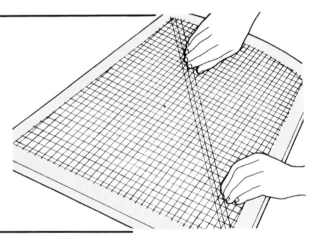

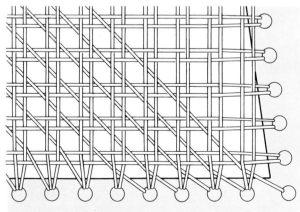

If the seat is not perfectly square, the diagonals, when pulled tight, will not hit the opposite corner exactly, since the strands will be at an angle of 45°. Peg the cane into the nearest available hole, missing one if necessary or using the same hole twice. Always use corner holes twice. Bring the cane up through the next hole in the front of the seat to your left, and then weave back to the hole on the left of where you started.

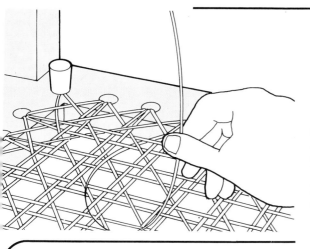

For the second diagonals (Step 6), you should start in the opposite corner and weave at right angles to the first diagonals. You should use the same corner holes twice. This time the strands pass **under** the horizontals and **over** the verticals.

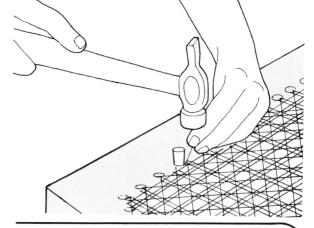

To prepare for the beading (Step 7) and achieve a neater finish, gently hammer a peg into every alternate hole (but not the corner holes). Any loose ends in holes that will not be pegged should be poked up into the adjacent one first and held in place while the peg is driven in.

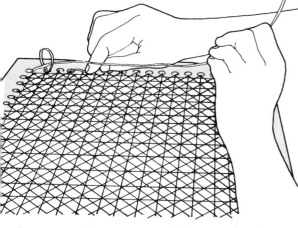

Securing the beading is the final step of the weave. It is usually done with two sizes of cane, numbers two and six. Start by pegging the thinner cane into the back corner hole, leaving about two inches (five centimetres) protruding from the top. Bend this short end down into the next unpegged hole and bring the long end up through the same hole to secure the short end. Then insert the heavier cane length into the corner hole and position it along the holes at the sides of the chair. The thinner cane is then looped over the thick and taken down the same hole.

Once you have successfully completed one caning project using the Seven Step Tradition weave, you will feel confident to try it again not only on chairs but also for screens, panelled doors, bed heads and even square light shades. Remember that you can cane chairs that have never been caned before. This often completely rejuvenates old dining room and sitting room chairs, especially if you also restain and polish them.

To cane a chair which has never been caned before you will have to drill the holes for weaving. They should be drilled all round the frame from top to bottom and should be at exactly the same spacing. To achieve this, measure the overall dimensions of the sides and the back and front. The centre front hole must line up with the centre back hole. If the seat is square this is not so important because you weave the verticals as you would weave the horizontals described in the instructions for the diagram at the bottom of page 50.

The size of the holes you drill will depend on the sizes of the cane you intend using. If you plan to use only grade six for a very strong seat, the holes can be quarter of an inch (six millimetres) in diameter. If you plan to use a variety of cane sizes, the holes should not be larger than an eighth of an inch (three millimetres). They should also be spaced at half inch (one centimetre) intervals.

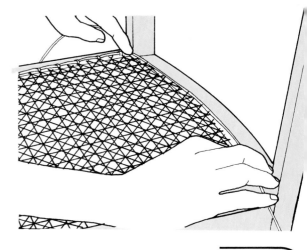

*The beading for the curved back of a seat is done with dampened cane. It must be curved by gently bending it round at one inch (two centimetre) intervals until it is the required shape. The thicker cane should be about four inches (10 centimetres) longer than the measurement from corner to corner. This is to give sufficiently long ends to start and finish the beading technique as described previously.*

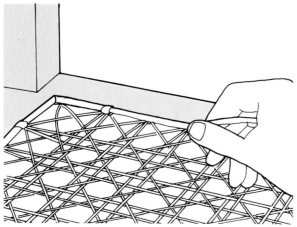

*Continue with the beading but just before the corner, bend the thicker cane gently into a mitre and do the same with the next piece of thick cane intended for the front beading. Place them both in the hole and hammer in a peg on the inside of the hole so that the front piece can fold over the peg, thus holding it. Continue using the same piece of thin cane you used for the first side of beading. Continue in this way around the chair until you reach the other back corner hole.*

*Use a sharp-cutting knife to trim and tidy up the ends on the underside of the seat rails.*

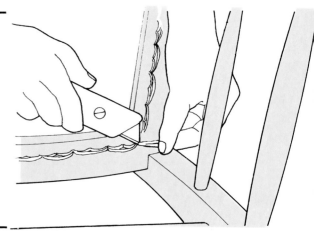

*Right: The finished chair after it has been revived, polished and recaned. The dark sheen of the newly polished wood complements the attractive light-coloured cane to great effect*

# Restoration Project 3: Gate-leg Table

A gate-leg table is given a new lease of life. Its loose framework is strengthened, the damaged gate sections are restored and a broken leaf is repaired

*Left: The gate-leg table before restoration, with the gate broken away from the main frame. Two rails are missing, one from the rail and the other from the gate. The swivel dowels are also smashed. The main task lies in replacing the missing section of the leaf which is broken at the joint*

Gate-leg tables are one of the most attractive and pleasing pieces of furniture. Despite its broken top, loose framework and damaged gate sections this one is no exception. The tightening of the whole structure is a routine part of restoration work but the repair to the broken leaf is a major job. The leaves of such tables are frequently broken. But such fractures are usually small and often only involve damage to the moulding. The two sections can either be rub jointed, as described in this project, or centre pinned with dowels. Four dowels should be used and they can be placed by scratch-gauging the centre thickness of the table edge. Then the two sections are placed face to face and the dowel positions marked with a square. Place the gauge along these positions and mark the centre of the dowel holes. Drill out the holes and glue the dowels into place. Then assemble and clamp. Remember to place two pieces of wood under the feet of the sash clamp so as not to damage the piece of furniture.

You can find the positions of the dowel holes using a slightly less orthodox approach. Hammer some pins along the face of one of the sections, after first cutting off the heads of the pins. Now press the old and new sections together. The impression made by the pins will give you the positions of the dowels. The pins should be removed before you drill.

If the fracture is quite small, the repair is still carried out in the same way. Rub jointing will probably not be needed and you will only have to use one or two dowels.

The rule joint (a series of three hinges which attach the leaves to the table top) on this table is in good working order but on some gate-leg tables it can be unreliable, usually because of swelling of the timber due to dampness. The leaf and the top are usually rule-jointed and held apart by a metal hinge. Swelling will cause the joint to bend so that the leaf does not lower correctly, although it is satisfactory in the raised position.

The best way to deal with this problem is to unscrew the hinges and allow the separated parts of the joint to dry out in a warm room. Remove the polish and varnish with a piece of sandpaper to speed up the drying process.

*The leaves of gate-leg tables are attached in a variety of ways, the most common on older tables is the rule joint, a series of three hinges countersunk on the opposite side to the joint. Each of these is held by four screws, which should be removed. The fixed part of the top is usually screwed to the cradle by up to six screws, recessed and inserted diagonally. These must be unscrewed.*

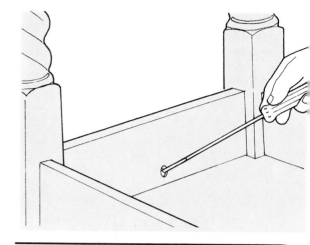

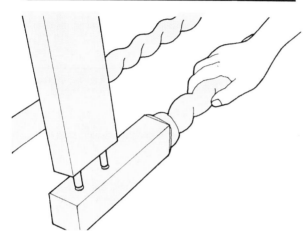

*After unscrewing all sections of the table, reglue joints which have become loose. The gates are attached to the main frame by strong dowels which allow them to swivel. When these are broken, the old dowels should be removed by drilling with an electric drill or brace and bit. New dowels are then fitted after being measured and glued into place.*

*Now fit the gates into the framework of the table, making sure the assembly is square by using a try square.*

If you have to replace any of the hinges, it is important that the hinge is embedded directly beneath the top of the moulded part of the joint. If this is not done correctly the leaf will become stuck when it is lowered and raised. Buy a hinge similar in type and size to the one you are replacing and screw it into place with the leaf in the lowered position. Smear wax or candle grease on the hinges to prevent stiffness and give a smoother action.

The gate sections of this kind of table also present problems. Swivelled on dowels, the gate folds snugly into the main frame by means of two housings, one in the leg of the gate, the other in the lower rail of the frame. The housing at the foot of the gate leg goes to a depth of half its thickness and a violent knock or a heavy weight placed on top of it, during removals for example, can cause a break.

You can repair this by cutting a piece of wood of the same dimensions as the part of the foot which formed the housing. Glue and dowel this into the top of the foot and then into the lower part of the leg.

The stop strip on the underneath of the leaves is often broken or knocked out of place because

*Left: Removing broken pieces of dowel. Dowelling is used in most gate-leg tables to enable the gates to swivel from the main frame*

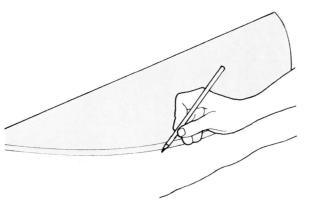

To repair the broken section of the damaged leaf, you will need a template. The first template is made by placing a sheet of strong paper on top of the complete, undamaged leaf and tracing its edge. This way of doing it prevents the paper from puckering if the leaf is accidentally pushed with the hand. But for the inexperienced, it is probably best to insert the paper underneath the leaf as shown in the diagram. Use a heavy pencil to get a firm clear line.

When the template is marked and cut, it is transferred to the broken section of leaf. A straight edge is used to mark the new section needed. It is again important to make sure that the template and the straight edge do not slide as you are marking. Press down on the straight edge and make sure there are no creases in the paper large enough to give you a distorted measurement, which could result in wasting a piece of valuable wood.

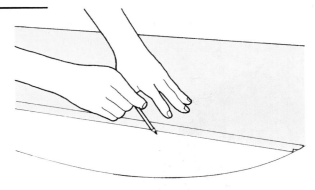

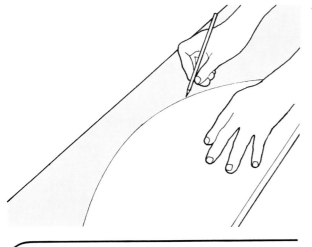

The completed template is then laid on a piece of matching wood. The section of the leaf needed is then carefully marked out for cutting. A jig saw, preferably electric, should be used to cut the wood. The new section is then sanded to give a smooth finish.

The new section of leaf is jointed to the old section by rub jointing. First place the old section tightly in a vice. The edges of both pieces to be joined are then glued. The new section is rubbed backwards and forwards along the edge of the old, not more than two inches (five centimetres) at a time. Both sections are kept level using the thumbs on one side and the forefingers on the other. The object is to create a vacuum between the two sections. When this occurs the joint sticks and great force will be needed to break it.

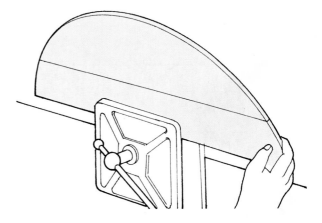

When the glue has dried, the new section is moulded with a spokeshave. The new wood is gradually rounded to match the shape of the edge of the old part of the leaf. The shaving should begin where the old and new sections are jointed. On this table the moulding has a vertical edge on the top and so the centre of the circumference of the rounded part of the moulding is lower than at first appears. This kind of moulding can also be done using a special tool called a moulding plane.

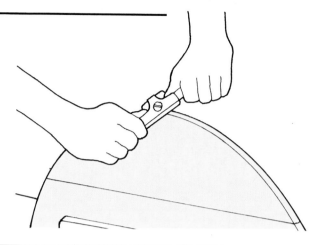

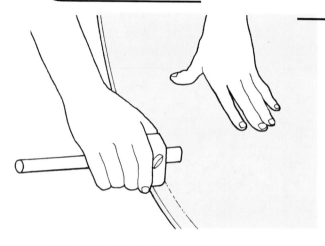

The vertical dip in the top of the moulding is marked out using a gauge. The depth of the dip is first gauged from the old section of the leaf.

The dip is then cut with a chisel. A sharp bevel-edged chisel should be used and held parallel to the side of the table. When this is completed, sand the new section to a smooth finish.

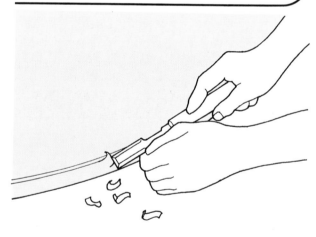

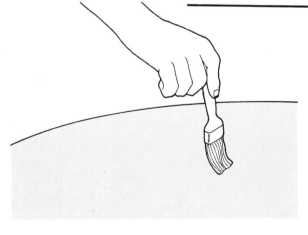

The new section of the leaf is stained to match the rest of the table and polished. After this has been done, revive the whole of the table, starting at the top, before wax polishing as a final finish.

the nails have rusted. It is best to glue these back into place. When you remove the broken pieces, an impression of the strip will be left so that there should be no difficulty in refitting a new piece of wood. Copy the dimensions of the old strip. To achieve an attractive finish you can taper the strips to about 45° so that the square edge does not knock anybody's knee when they are sitting at the table. Do not forget to water stain the new strips.

Finally if the top is warped you can clamp it to another flat surface after removing it from the frame. To avoid damage and to gain extra leverage, place a long batten under the soles of the clamps which should be placed at each corner of the top.

*Above: The gleaming table with all the restoration work completed. Besides the making of the template and the cutting of the moulding of the new section of leaf, most of the damage is easily corrected*

# Restoration Project 4: Chest of Drawers

A very worn and badly damaged, though still attractive, chest of drawers can be completely rejuvenated with the repair of drawer runners, replacement of fittings and knobs, and the reconstruction of the chest's back

*Left: The badly-damaged chest of drawers— one drawer is broken, the back is missing and most of the bottom has been gutted by dry rot. But the spare drawer means that a creative restoration can be carried out. This involves making a template so that specially shaped pieces can be cut for the bottom of the front*

This chest of drawers is in bad shape. The back is missing, the bottom is badly damaged by dry rot, one of the drawers is broken, and a knob is missing. In fact, the piece would probably be irredeemable except that there is a spare drawer which came with the chest. This drawer will provide the material for the necessary restoration work. By cutting the sides of the chest to form the two halves of bracket feet, you can then complete these feet and design a template from the front wood of the spare drawer.

The back of the chest is missing. Its replacement will not simply involve measuring and glueing the necessary amount of wood to make a square-shaped back, it will instead incorporate a shaped end which completes the bracket feet at the back of the chest.

Half of the four bracket feet are shaped from the overlap of the sides of the chest. These protrude beneath the bottom drawer by about five inches (twelve centimetres). These protruding sides are cut, after marking, in a trapezoid shape with sides jutting inwards by about 20 degrees. The slanted bracket feet are made up from the designed front and the new back.

Chips and dents in veneer, as on the front of the chest, usually present little problem. Their treatment depends upon the grain of the veneer. Curled, swirled grains should be matched if possible. The jagged edges should be cut back with a knife or chisel to give a straighter edge so that it will be easier to measure and insert the new piece. The waste should be carefully removed, taking care not to damage the new edge.

Broken knobs can be bought from a shop or, if this is not possible, you can have them specially turned. On most chests of drawers, knobs are fixed by boring through the drawer front and then glueing the knob into place. If a broken knob is tightly glued, take care when you remove it not to damage the adjoining surface, especially if veneered. The shoulder of the knob should be gently chipped away with a chisel. It should then be possible to tap out the dowelled part of the knob from the inside of the drawer.

Sometimes the rusted screws of metal knobs and handles enlarge the screw holes. When the knobs and handles are replaced the holes should be filled with wood plugs so that the new screws will grip. It may be advisable to drill new holes close to the old filled holes. Check that your fittings will cover the repair before drilling.

Most faults on chests are in the drawers. The drawer is a moving part and wear is inevitable, particularly as chests are often filled beyond their capacity. The damage usually includes broken and split bottoms, worn runner rails, loose joints, worn sides, split knobs and, on some drawers, damaged cocked beads.

There is really only one way of dealing with loose joints—take them apart and re-glue. Any screws or nails should be removed from the bottom. The sides should be separated from the front and back by knocking them outwards with a hammer and a flat piece of wood, if the joints are very loose, or by hitting them with a mallet. This is an extra precaution because a piece of wood inserted between the mallet and the drawer helps to avoid bruises or splits which may warrant a new side.

All the old glue should be thoroughly removed from the joints. If you use a chisel to do this, be careful not to gash the wood. If the joint is obstinate, it may be necessary to soften the glue with a little hot water. Too much water could cause swelling. The dovetails should be perfectly dry before re-glueing after which the joint should be re-assembled in the same manner as it was taken apart, with a mallet or hammer and wood. Wipe away the surplus glue with a rag. If the joints are actually worn from use you can mix fine sawdust to the glue to give added substance.

Sides are sometimes worn along the top edges. Most of the wear will be at the back of the drawer because drawers are sometimes left half open. The most effective way of dealing with worn sides, particularly if the wear goes down into the groove which holds the bottom in place, is to level off the edge and fit a new piece right along the length of the edge. Glueing a new piece should not present problems if the repair does not sink into the groove. If the wear is in the groove, make a small rebate with a rebate plane. In both cases, glue to the side edges only, not the bottom.

After removing all broken sections of the chest bottom, measure to replace it from the inside edge of the front rails to the edge of the back, and then along the length of the back, from the outside edges on both sides. When cut and sanded, glue blocks along the sides of the piece and then glue and fit them into position under the runners of the bottom drawer.

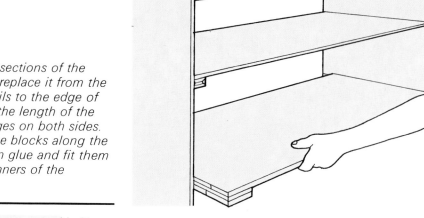

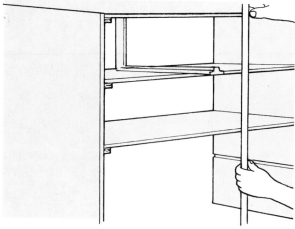

The length of the boards for the new back is measured from under the top of the chest to the lower edge of the glued blocks holding the bottom in place. The piece is then measured for width. The two end boards should extend, after the first cutting, right to the bottom of the chest. Cut them to form plain bracket-type feet. All the boards should be glued along their edges and then screwed to the carcass. To match the feet at the back, cut the sides of the chest to form plain bracket feet.

Check the end boards of the back to make sure they fit well, particularly the bracket feet. The uncut board, extending to the bottom of the chest, should be placed in position and a line drawn across at the lower edge of the new bottom. To determine the angle of the bracket feet, draw another line from the bottom of the board to meet the first line at an angle of about 20°. The side feet should be measured in a similar way.

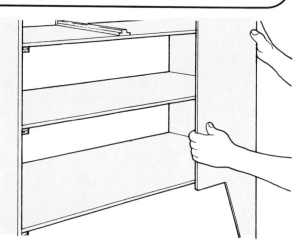

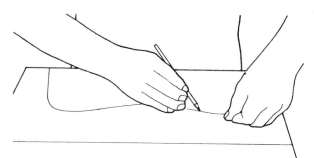

If you decide to use a spare drawer to form a moulded front for the exposed bottom of the cabinet, a template has to be designed first. Here it is designed freestyle, but if faced with a similar problem you can get ideas for your template from furniture catalogues and books. Draw your design on a piece of cardboard and cut out with a sharp knife. A template should also be designed for the sides to give a shape to the bracket feet.

Drawer bottoms are invariably made of two pieces of wood jointed in the middle. It is a common fault for this joint to break and sag under continuous weight. Both edges of the joint should be very lightly planed and then glued together again. To make the repaired joint straight, it will be necessary to place the two pieces of wood, after glueing, on a flat surface and weigh them down while the glue is drying. Place the weights at the ends, especially if the pieces of wood are bowed upwards. Remember that excess glue will spill from the bottom of the wood so that the flat surface on which you work should be protected by newspaper. A strip of canvas can be glued along the repaired joint if the drawer takes heavy items. Strips of canvas can also be used to cover small split ends.

Cocked beads are pieces of moulding glued along the edges of the sides, front and back of a drawer to protect the veneer. For this reason, they are frequently damaged. In some cases the whole length of beading has been damaged. In most cases, however, the damage is confined to small pieces that have broken off. Along the bottom and sides of the drawer the dovetails are made so as to allow a rebate to be inserted for the beads. The beading round the front of the top of the drawer is usually mitred. You can make these cocked beads up yourself by cutting a strip from an old piece of matching wood. Cut the beads to the width of the rebate which is already cut in the drawer.

Sometimes the front of a drawer is made from a solid piece of wood surrounded by a moulding which overlaps and stands proud of the carcass of the drawer. Often the corners of this moulding are damaged. Repairs entail glueing a section of similar wood into place, using a mitred joint if necessary. Instructions on how to use a mitre box are on page 70.

One of the first things you should check on drawers is whether the stops need repairing. Drawer stops are small pieces of wood, about one inch square (two centimetres), glued onto the rail just underneath the front of the drawer. Sometimes they consist only of dowels glued into the rail to protrude on top by about half an inch (one centimetre).

By removing the drawer the position of the stops should be obvious. If the piece of furniture is old and the drawers have been opened many times, the stops may have scraped, and therefore damaged, the back of the underneath of the drawer. If the sides and bottom of the drawer are repaired, the stops will not cause this problem. But it is wise to take the added precaution of placing the new stops in a slightly different position. The front of the stop should be placed against the inside edge of the front of the drawer. This can be gauged to the thickness of the front and then marked on the rail. The new stop should then be fixed with glue and pinned. The pins should be punched just below the surface to prevent the heads catching the drawer bottom. The grain of the stops should run from back to front. End grain wears better.

The usual damage to drawer rails (those attached to the carcass) is when they slightly curve in the centre, causing trouble to two drawers at once. The most effective remedy is to replace the rail completely. These rails are usually cut from a piece of pine and they act as a guide for the drawers to run on. Measure up for the new rail by noting the mark left by the old one. If you wish to correct this problem without cutting a new rail the following remedy can be tried. Chisel a dovetail about six inches (15 centimetres) wide into the rail, into which is glued a wedge of wood of comparable length. While the glue is drying, use a temporary wedge to prop up the sagging rail. This should be slightly overlength, by about quarter of an inch (six millimetres). When the glued repair has dried, remove this prop. This should cure the curvature if the rail is not too much out of alignment. The effectiveness of the repair depends on the degree of sag and the width of the dovetail. If the sag is very pronounced, the dovetail should be as wide as possible. It is possible to experiment as the repair is being carried out. If the first dovetail does not correct the curvature, remove the wedge and start again, this time using a wedge two inches (five centimetres) wider. Continue until you achieve the right width. Remember to keep the repair clean of glue each time you try this.

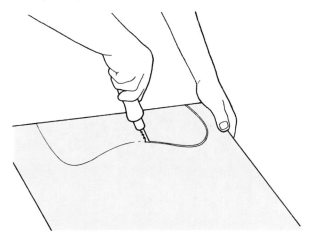

*When the template designs have been marked onto the front of the spare drawer and the sides of the cabinet, cut the shapes out using a pad saw. (An electric jig saw can do this much faster and, for the amateur, with greater accuracy.) Sand the pieces to smoothness.*

*Above: Hammering pins into the piece shaped from a template. If a spare drawer is not available with the chest of drawers you set out to restore, it may be possible to buy old, matching wood, or even to buy another old chest which is clearly beyond redemption and likely therefore to be cheap*

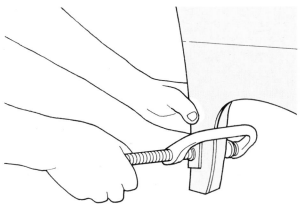

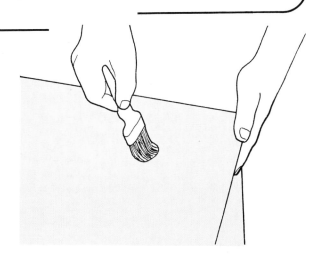

The designed front piece is then glued and pinned into place. Put wooden strengtheners behind the junction of the front and side parts of the bracket feet. Such strengtheners can be quite roughly shaped but should be small enough so that they are not visible when viewed from the front. Glue them to both sides of the bracket feet and clamp with a G clamp until the glue has dried. To make up the length of the designed front, cut a small rectangular piece of wood and glue it into place.

Stain the back of the cabinet and all new surfaces to match the colour of the chest, using a brush. A smaller artist's brush can be used for touching in the stains to any veneer which might show exposed wood. The undersides, bracket strengtheners, and edges of the designed pieces should also be coloured to match.

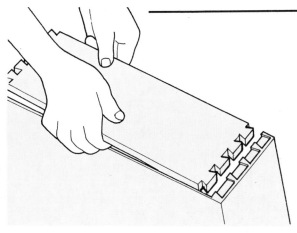

To mend the drawer, first take it apart by gently knocking the dovetails out with a wooden mallet. You should approach using the mallet with great care. Take your time and tap from the inside of the drawer. Clean the dovetails of all residue glue, then reglue and rejoin as much as possible by force of thumb.

Now tap the dovetails into place using a light hammer. This also forces out much of the excess glue which should be wiped off with a rag or it will dry in lumps and look very unsightly. The drawer should be gripped with a sash clamp while the glue is drying.

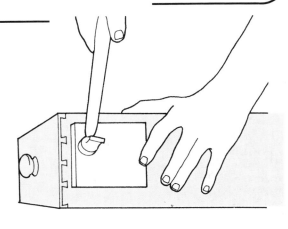

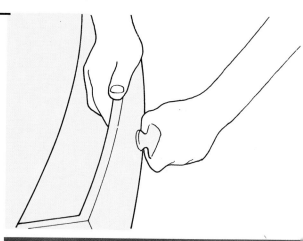

*A missing knob can be replaced either by making one yourself or by buying one to match. To make one you will need a lathe. The knobs for this kind of chest are held in place either by a small length of dowel or shaped wood glued in position, or by an open bolt with screw and washer.*

A prominent feature of many old chests of drawers are locks, and they are frequently damaged in some way. A common fault is for the screws to have come loose. The simplest remedy for this, if the thickness of the wood allows, is to use longer screws of the same diameter. Another easy remedy is to fill the holes with wood plugs thus giving new thread to the screws. If however the screw holes are very distorted, a more complicated repair will have to be carried out.

This is done by cutting small pieces of wood tapered to fit the old screw holes. Shape these with a chisel or knife and glue and tap them into position with a hammer. When the glue has dried, use a sharp chisel to trim the new plug flush with the level of the frame. This should then be sanded. New screw holes can be started with a bradawl or any pointed tool. Since old-type brass screws are fragile and can break when being driven into new wood, use a steel screw in all the holes to prepare the threads for the brass screws.

If you have to remove a lock, you should do so very carefully. Avoid damaging the screws or scratching the surface. The most common internal fault found with locks is a broken or loose spring. If you want to use the old locks again, you can get the spring repaired at a locksmith.

Splits around lock mortises can sometimes be repaired by re-glueing a piece which has still not completely broken off or by replacing it with a new piece. If a new mortise has to be cut into the new wood, it can be marked by smearing the bolt with dark oil and then opening the bolt until a mark is made on the rail. This mark should be the centre of the new mortise.

The designed front piece is cut from the spare drawer and as there is not enough wood, it does not meet in the middle. To cover this gap, square off the ends and cut a small rectangular piece of the same wood. Plane the rectangle to shape and surround it with a cocked bead. Then glue and pin into place. To do this it is necessary to apply glue blocks to the underside of the carcass and the back of the designed section.

For all the variety and number of repairs, a renovated chest of drawers not only looks good but is likely to last you for a long time

*Below: The finished restoration has brought about a complete transformation to the chest of drawers. What had seemed irreparable because of the extent of the damage, particularly to the bottom, has provided an attractive piece of bedroom furniture*

# Restoration Project 5: Glass-fronted Cabinet

The restoration of a glass-fronted cabinet can involve many different tasks. This cabinet will have its doors refitted, its top reblocked, and the plinth and cornice moulding restored

The work on the glass-fronted cabinet falls into two categories, that for the top of the cupboard and that for the bottom. On the top, the cornice moulding is badly broken and the moulding on the door has worked loose. The bottom needs more repairs, the most important of which is the work on the plinth. The drawer runners are worn away and the doors require refitting. There are missing sections of veneer on the main body of the carcass.

All the metal fittings on both top and bottom need to be cleaned and put back in place after stripping, staining and polishing the whole cupboard.

Before starting work, the two parts of the cupboard must be separated by unscrewing a sunken screw which is inserted through the base of the top into the top of the bottom.

Cornice moulding is usually fitted to the tops of cupboards and wardrobes by attaching it to blocks glued and nailed on to the top. There are usually about six of these blocks and the moulding is glued and pinned into them.

Besides replacing the moulding on this cabinet, it is necessary to reblock the top of the cupboard. When this is done, mitre the new moulding and fit it into position. Mitring, in this case cutting angles of 45° at both ends of a length of wood, is a simple task if a mitre box is used. It is imperative to make the mitres well so that they fit into each other tightly without gaps which will show both glue and pins.

Cornice and any other mouldings that are applied or worked on the tops and edges of pieces of furniture often become damaged. This is because they project from the main surface. When the damage is in the length of the moulding and not at one of the corners, a local repair will usually suffice. Two angled cuts are made and the damaged piece removed with a chisel. A new matching piece is cut to correspond with the angles already made. This is then glued into place and allowed to dry overnight before the piece is shaped with a plane and sandpaper and finished to the contours of the original moulding. Obviously this will only work for the amateur if the moulding is not too decorative and complicated in shape.

There are two basic types of moulding. Stuck moulding is worked into the solid carcass. The type of damage is confined to smashed corners, bruises and deep scratches. Applied moulding is so called because it is glued to the carcass. The most common damage occurs when it becomes loose or when it has gone completely missing. The door moulding on the glass-fronted cabinet is a good example of applied moulding. The shaped edge of the gate-leg table in one of the earlier projects is an example of stuck moulding.

With stuck moulding there is no difficulty involved in repairing it if the damage is small. Again, the damaged section should be removed by making two angled cuts and a new piece glued into place. If the moulding has to take weight, as does the moulding at the edge of a table top, the new section of wood should be dowelled into place as well as being glued. The new piece of wood should then be shaped using a plane or a spokeshave. (This method is described on page 58 in the project on the gate-leg table.)

For the purposes of repair, applied moulding can often be treated as stuck moulding. If the damage is small, the moulding should not be removed. Instead, a new section can be applied in the manner described for stuck moulding. There is usually no need to dowel applied moulding. In most cases, however, applied moulding is loose or has come away from the surface completely. If the moulding has lost some of its original shape, some form of clamping will be needed when you re-glue it back into place. One way of doing this is to bind the piece with string and use a stick or long nail to wind it tightly. An alternative is to turn the piece of furniture upside down or sideways and weigh the moulding down with a heavy object. In some cases conventional clamps can be used.

*Right: The untouched glass-fronted cabinet with a loose shelf is repaired by inserting two new supports along the marks of the old. There is also a broken cornice moulding, sections of oak veneer are missing and the plinth requires an additional piece. The whole cabinet is then stained and polished to look like new*

Take the cabinet apart by unscrewing the screw which is recessed into the part of the top which lies on the bottom section of the cupboard. On some cupboards there are up to three of these screws. Then remove the doors, keeping a tight grip to prevent the door from falling and being damaged further. This can easily happen if the screws are old and rusted.

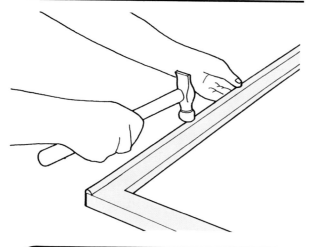

The moulding on doors on this type of cabinet are usually pinned in two or three places as well as being glued. On this cabinet the moulding has worked loose probably because the doors were slammed too often. Fresh glue is all that is needed to repair the damage. All the old glue is scraped away with a chisel.

Cornice moulding usually involves a more complicated type of repair. First measure the length of each piece of moulding required for the sides and the front. Each length is then mitred at the ends to make the corners. This is done simply by inserting the length of moulding into a mitre box and sawing along the 45° opening or groove.

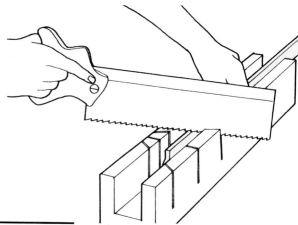

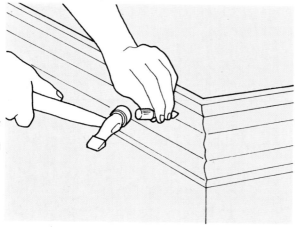

The cornice is then glued into place and the mitres pinned. Using a nail punch, sink the pins so that they do not show. The wax which is used in the staining process later in the project is sufficient to fill these holes.

*Below: Mending the shelf which had broken loose. The shelf rests on supports as well as being fitted into scalloped uprights. The insert on the left shows the top of the cupboard after the shelf has been repaired.*

To repair the damage to the plinth, first cut away a bevelled section beyond the area which has to be dealt with. The important point is to cut the piece as accurately as possible to make fitting a replacement easier, and to give it a more professional finish. You may find that the section you wish to remove is held with pins and glue. Pull the pins with pincers and lever away the glued piece, taking care not to do further damage to any other part of the plinth.

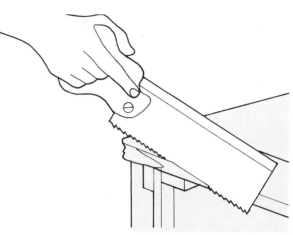

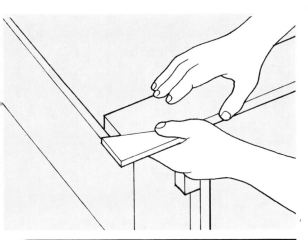

Bevel a new piece of matching wood and shape it to fit into the plinth. This should then be inserted into place, after the area has been sanded and cleaned, using glue and pins. The piece of wood used should be slightly larger than needed so that it overlaps the edges by a small amount.

When the glue has dried, pare the new section of the plinth with a chisel and then plane it to make it level with the rest of the plinth and veneers. Lightly sand the piece with a fine paper and wipe it with a wet cloth in preparation for staining. A wet cloth is used to remove wood dust.

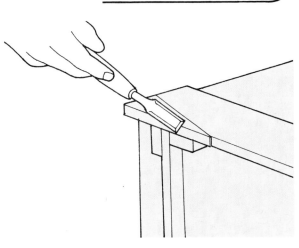

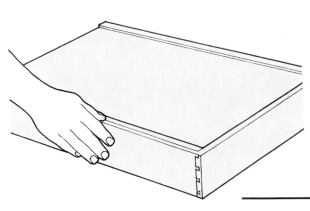

The drawer runners are badly worn and need to be replaced. First measure these up against the length of the side of the drawer. The old runners on the underside of the drawer are already flattened because they have worn down so much. The depth of the runner to be added can be gauged from the good runner. Glue the runners to the drawer.

When the glue has dried, prepare the runner by planing the edges. They should be planed so that the running edge is of a convex shape and will fit snugly into the runner troughs in the rail of the drawer. On the left the repaired drawer is being refitted into the cabinet. The runners need quite a lot of planing and waxing to ensure a frictionless action.

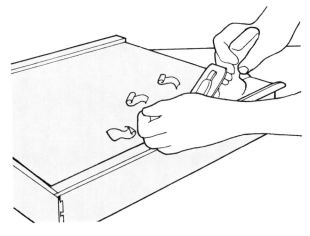

*To repair the broken sections of veneer on the main carcass, cut away the edges of the damaged pieces to give a straighter line. Then cut a new piece of veneer. Glue the area to be repaired and insert the piece of veneer carefully. Warm a hammer in hot water and use it to squeeze out any excess glue. Wipe the area clean and cover the repair with a piece of tape to prevent the outside edges curling upwards. Cut the overhang 24 hours later.*

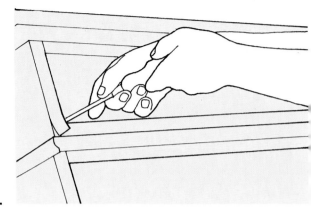

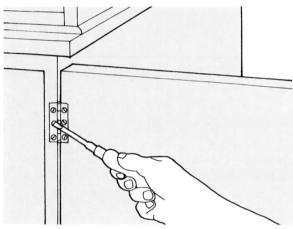

*The doors to the bottom part of the cupboard should be rehung after first repairing the hinge housing with wood filler, and then rescrewing the hinges into place on the door. The hinge housings on the carcass are repaired in a similar way before the doors are refitted.*

Remember before reapplying the moulding to clean off all the old glue. This can be scraped away with a chisel and lightly sanded. If the moulding splits or even splinters slightly when you are removing it, it should be replaced with a new piece. Unless you are particularly adept at glueing, the finish will not come up to a high standard.

The door moulding which needs to be repaired on this cupboard is of the simplest kind. It merely needs careful lifting and then reglueing in place and pinning with very slight pins. However by far the most complicated moulding found on doors is the barred or latticework type into which the glass is glazed. The moulding on this type of door is usually grooved to fit over the bars. For this reason, if there are any repairs needed on the bars these should be carried out first. Bars are joined together with different types of joint, depending on the type of cupboard or cabinet. If you have to carry out this type of repair, note which type of joint is used when you remove the bar and copy this if a new bar is required. By examining the moulding on the other bars you can work out how the new moulding should be fitted. You will not be able to make this kind of moulding so take a sample to a joiner's shop and replace it with identical moulding.

The other small repair needed to the top of the cabinet is the replacement of the bearer which supports the top shelf. This should be screwed back into position, or if it has cracked or dis-appeared, cut a new piece of similar wood using the other bearers for a template, and screw into position.

Having completed the restoration of the top of the cabinet, the necessary repairs to the bottom section should be carried out. These include adding a new section to the plinth, rerunning both drawers, refitting the doors, fixing the top and mending the upright support for the shelf.

A section of the plinth, which runs around three sides of the whole cabinet, is broken on the back corner and a new piece of wood must be inserted to replace it. This involves sawing just beyond the area of the break. The cut is bevelled or angled and the new piece is cut at the same angle so that the two pieces match and fit into each other. The other two sides of the V-shaped new piece overhang the edge of the plinth so that they can be planed and levelled with greater accuracy after the piece has been glued into place and allowed to dry overnight.

The drawer runners have badly worn and need to be replaced. The old runners are first planed down level with the front and back of the drawers. New runners of the required depth are then glued and fitted into place and planed into a convex shape so that they will run with greater smoothness in the troughs in the drawer rails.

The doors on the bottom of the cupboard should be removed so that they can be repaired for rehanging. The hinges are taken off so that the screw holes can be filled with wood plugs. The

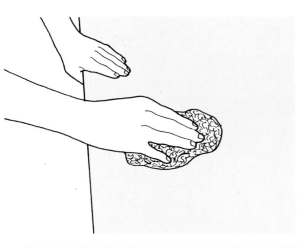

Care should always be taken when pre-preparing a piece of furniture for staining as it is easy to cause fractures and scratches which will spoil whatever stain and polish you apply. If you do not have any experience with steel wool, it is advisable to start with the finest grade. This should be slightly damp. After stripping the surface with steel wool, sand it to as smooth a finish as possible. Minor scratches should be dealt with at this stage.

Before staining, remove all handles, lock plates and fittings. Then apply the stain with a brush. When staining, take care to spread the liquid evenly so that bubbles do not form. Work methodically, starting at one edge and progressing to another. This will ensure that you do not miss any areas. Use a small brush for corners and places where access is difficult. It is also useful to have a soft rag handy to wipe off any surplus stain. Uneven applications give ugly finishes.

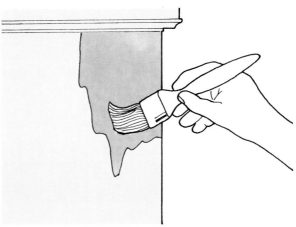

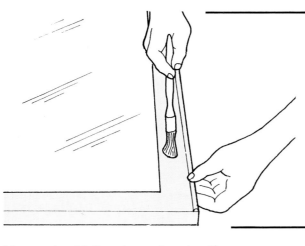

To stain doors, especially those with glass, you will need a small brush. A useful tip is to place strips of tape on the glass where it meets the wood. This will save you time and ensure a better finish as it enables you to concentrate on the job in hand without fear of painting over the glass.

hinges should then be replaced with new screws and the doors rehung.

Doors need refitting for a number of reasons. These can range from shrinkage in the timber, warping or swelling to loose hinges. Continual slamming or swinging back of the door can pull the screws and work the hinges loose. Besides the method described there are other ways of dealing with this problem. Longer screws of the same diameter can replace the old screws, if the thickness of the door will allow this. Wood plugs can also be used. Taper small pieces of wood to fit the old screw holes and then tap and glue them into place. The plugs should be oversized so that they can be trimmed flush with a chisel and new holes

started with a bradawl or similar sharp-ended tool.

Sticking doors are usually caused by swelling in the wood. The door should be removed and sanded where the edge is marked by continual rubbing. This allows moisture to escape, a procedure which can be considerably speeded up if the door is placed in a warm area of the house. Do not place it in front of a radiator or fire.

The reverse problem is often found—the door will not stay closed and springs open. This is usually due to the use of oversized screws in a previous repair. The best way to tackle this is to plug or fill the holes and use smaller screws which will go in flush. Another old repair which may be causing trouble is the replacement of the old

*After staining and polishing, clean all the fittings and rescrew them in place when any necessary repairs to the old screw holes have been carried out. In some cases you may find it necessary to replace damaged hardware fittings.*

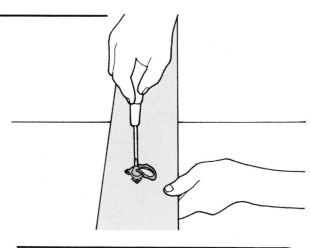

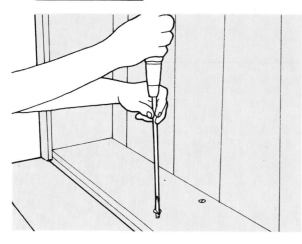

*When the restoration work is completed, place the top to the bottom of the cabinet and screw them together. In many old cabinets these screws sometimes rust and work themselves loose, making the insertion holes too large. Plastic woodfiller will remedy this problem. It is then preferable to drill new holes and fit new screws.*

hinges with new hinges which are too thin for the recessed housings. The recesses should be packed with old pieces of veneer or even cardboard so that the hinge is brought level with the side panels of the door.

Compared to refitting the doors, the task of stripping, staining, polishing and waxing the cupboard is a major one. But first remove all the metal parts which are in danger of being smeared with stain. These are usually already stained and need to be cleaned. Metal parts are easily cleaned by immersing them in methylated spirit or denatured alcohol and then scraping them clean with fine steel wool. There is a danger of scratching so that great care and delicacy is required if you do not wish to irreparably spoil the fitting.

For the task of stripping and staining, follow the procedure described in the pine desk project on pages 38/39. The polish is stripped from top to bottom and the whole surface is then sanded. The cupboard can then be stained to the colour required. All the colours are then levelled up and two coats of polish are applied, rubbing between coats. The piece is then finished with a coat of wax and all the metal parts are refitted.

This type of glass-fronted cabinet is fairly common and you should not have any difficulty in buying one. They are not only spacious but also very attractive whether finished with a light or dark colour or just waxed over the stripped wood in much the same way as the pine desk.

*Right: The restored cabinet in all its glory. It has been completely repolished and the cleaned handles and fittings greatly enhance the finish. Such cupboards can accommodate a great number of books and they are invaluable for any modern living room*

# Part 2:
# Reupholstering
# Furniture

# Upholstery Terms, Tools and Materials

**anchor** (twine or cord)
to drive a tack into the frame a short distance,
slip a looped length of twine round the tack, then
drive the tack home.

**back-tacking or blind tacking**
method of attaching outer covers which hides
the tacks used; also refers to the strip 13 mm
($\frac{1}{2}$ in) wide used in this process (available in
rolls). You can also use a strip of any stiff card
for the purpose.

**bias**
diagonal direction across fabric. Cutting cloth in
this way makes it slightly stretchy so it can more
easily be manipulated round curves.

**blanket stitch**
looped stitch used for edging or to join two
folded edges of fabric.

**blind (sink) stitch**
edge stitch made with twine on scrim-covered
hair or ginger fibre and forming a loop inside
the padding to consolidate it.

**bridle ties or quilting**
loops of twine which hold padding (hair or
fibre) in place.

**calico (muslin)**
plain unbleached cotton sometimes used as a
final cover for the padding before the covering
fabric is put on.

**cane or heavy wire**
bamboo cane 25 mm (1 in) thick or heavy wire
bent into a broad U shape and used to support
the front of an upholstered seat.

**chamfer (bevel)**
to file down a right-angled corner to make a flat,
angled surface.

**Courtelle or Cambric**
thin bonded polyester material, used as a final
padding underneath the covering fabric.

### Dacron
thick bonded polyester covered by a sheet of cheesecloth and used to wrap a central core of foam for cushions.

### double bayonet needle or double pointed needle
straight needle with a spear-shaped point at both ends, used for stitching rolls, anchoring stuffing and other jobs which are too heavy for a plain straight needle.

### drive home
to hammer a tack in as far as it will go, making a permanent anchor.

### facing
shaped, fabric-covered piece of plywood applied to the front of a scroll arm to give a neat appearance and conceal the tacks on the front of the arm.

### file
metal instrument with roughened surface used for shaping or smoothing wood.

### foam
dense plastic or rubber material, available in different qualities and used for seats, for back and arm padding and for cushions.

### gimp
narrow tape, available in a wide variety of colours, which is used to cover tacks and raw edges. Gimp is more expensive than ordinary braid because it is woven in such a way that it can go smoothly and flatly around curves and awkward corners.

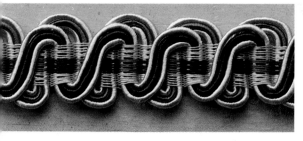

### gimp pin or gimp tack
thin tack with a tiny head used to attach gimp (q.v.) or braid. Usually available in a large range of colours.

### ginger fibre (coir fibre)
long, coarse fibres which come from the inside of the coconut husk; used as the first layer of stuffing over springs.

### grain
the lines of fibres in wood or fabric.

### hammer
see under magnetic hammer.

### hessian (burlap)
woven jute material used for separating different upholstery layers and especially for covering springs. Available in several different weights, although 340 g (12 oz) is the most commonly used.

### horsehair (curled hair)
usually, in fact, a mixture of hair from horses, cattle and pigs, twisted and heated to a high temperature to sterilize it and set the curl. It is the softest and springiest stuffing and, since it is very expensive, used most often for the top layer of padding only.

### lashing (cording) or spring tying
process by which springs are tied to each other and attached to the frame so they remain stable in use.

# Upholstery terms, tools and materials

**linter felt or kapok or silk floss**
soft, thick, coarse felted cotton, used as one of
the final layers of padding.

**magnetic hammer**
upholsterer's hammer with a two-pronged claw
and a magnetic head to pick up tacks. This is an
optional piece of equipment, and a non-
magnetized hammer will do just as well, as long
as it has a fairly small head so that the wood
surrounding each tack is not damaged.

**mallet**
wooden cabinet-maker's tool used to tap the
head of a chisel when removing tacks.

**panel pin or finishing nail or brad**
thin, headless tack used to fix a fabric-covered
piece of wood such as a facing (q.v.). It is
driven straight through the fabric, which is then
eased over it so it becomes invisible.

**piping cord or welting**
twisted cord, usually made of cotton. Covered
with a strip of fabric, it is used as a trim to give a
neat finish to final covers. (Wash and dry
piping cord before you use it, to shrink it.)

**rasp**
coarser version of a file (q.v.).

**regulator needle**
a flat-ended needle used to arrange, or
'regulate', the stuffing inside its cover. The flat
end is used to tuck fabric into narrow places and
for buttoning.

**ripping chisel**
flat-ended tool, similar to a screwdriver, used
with a mallet for removing tacks.

**rubberized hair**
horsehair (curled hair) bonded with latex
rubber and then compressed.

**running stitch**
simple in-and-out stitch used for tacking and for
anchoring layers of padding.

**scrim**
a loosely woven version of hessian, also made of
jute, used to cover the first layer of stuffing
before the edges are stitched.

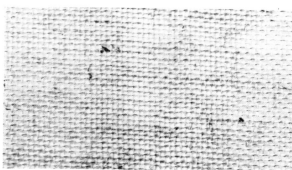

**selvedge**
side edge of fabric, woven very densely so that it
cannot unravel.

**skewers or upholsterer's pins**
straight pins with a looped end, used for
anchoring materials in place temporarily.

**sheet or skin wadding or cotton wadding**
compressed cotton fibres on a thin 'skin' of
cotton which holds them together. Used, skin
side up, to prevent padding — horsehair or
fibre — from working through the covering fabric.

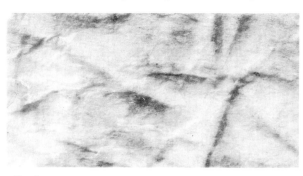

**slip knot**
simple and very common upholstery knot used
for fixing springs, for buttoning, and for starting
off a line of stitching.

**slip stitch**
nearly invisible stitch used most often to attach
the piped sections of covering fabric to each
other or to sew up the opening left in a cushion
cover for the pad to be inserted.

**slipping needle or curved needle**
small half-circle needle used for slip-stitching.

**slipping (buttoning) thread or nylon
stitching twine**
strong, fine twine or thread suitable for buttoning.

**springing needle**
large, curved needle used for attaching springs and sewing through stuffing. (Larger and stronger than a half-circle needle.)

**springs**
double-cone springs of different sizes and gauges (metal diameter) are used in the projects in this book. Their coils diminish in size towards their centre, or 'waist'.

**staples**
are a much easier and quicker way than tacks of fixing layers of material to the frame of a piece of furniture. Since, however, almost all frames are made of hard wood, a hand-operated staple gun will not exert enough pressure to drive the staples in, so you will have to invest in an electric or compressed air model if you want to avoid tacking. These are very expensive, but worthwhile for doing a lot of upholstery work.

**straight grain**
direction of fabric weave, either parallel to the selvedge or at right angles to it.

**straight needle**
slim, double-pointed stitching needle used mainly for buttoning.

**tack or tape roll**
highly compressed roll of foam which is tacked to the frame to replace back- and top-stitched edge rolls.

**tacks**
small-headed nails used to hold upholstery in place. They come in two main types: 'improved' which are fairly thick with a largish head, and 'fine', which are thinner with a smaller head. Within these types, tacks are available in various sizes. Remember that the tack chosen must provide a suitably strong anchor without splitting the wood.

**Tailor's tacks**
temporary stitches used in upholstery mainly to mark the positioning of buttoning on fabric.

**template**
piece of paper, card or thin wood used as a pattern for cutting out a section of fabric, or the front facings for scroll arms.

**temporary tack**
tack driven in only a short way so it can be removed and the material it is anchoring readjusted.

**top stitch**
edge stitch formed with twine (q.v.) on scrim-covered hair or fibre in order to make a firm roll, separate from the main padded area.

**trestles**
large, A-shaped wooden supports which can be used to raise a piece of furniture to a comfortable working height. They could be a useful investment if you were going to be doing a lot of upholstery; otherwise, a large sturdy table will do.

**twine**
strong, waxed fine twist made from flax and hemp or sometimes from various synthetic materials. All the twine used in this book is No. 2 upholsterer's twine.

**upholsterer's linen or cambric or dust cover**
closely woven black cloth used to make the cover for the base, or 'bottoming', of a piece of upholstered furniture.

**webbing**
strips of woven material usually 50 mm (2 in) wide, used to support the entire upholstered structure. We have used 'black and white' webbing (made from flax and cotton) throughout because it is the best quality, but jute can also be used.

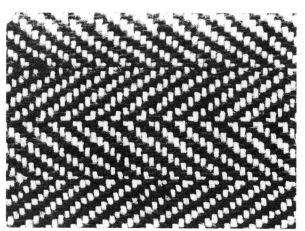

**webbing stretcher**
handled wooden tool used for stretching webbing over a frame. The one used in this book is called a 'bat' stretcher, and you can easily make one yourself by cutting a hole the width of your webbing in a rectangular block of wood and making a peg from a length of dowelling, attached to the wood with a cord. Shape one end of the wood into a handle for a comfortable grip. Alternatively, use a simple block of wood with a right-angled groove cut in it to pull webbing taut.

# Upholstery Project 1: Chair with Drop-in Seat

## Introduction

This type of chair (usually a dining chair) has a separate seat which consists of a simple wooden frame covered with padding which is supported by strips of webbing. The seat can be lifted out of the chair frame, repaired and then replaced; a few small dowels or screws may hold it in place, but once these are taken out, it should come free with a light tap from underneath with a hammer or mallet.

There are two important techniques, described for the first time in this project, which will be featured in almost every piece of upholstery you come across: attaching strips of webbing which support the whole structure; and making bridle ties which hold the horsehair or fibre padding in place.

Unless you are simply changing the outer covering, you will almost certainly need to strip the seat right down to its frame in order to reupholster it, since broken or sagging webbing is usually the main cause of any problem.

## Tools

mallet
ripping chisel
tape-measure
chalk or pencil
scissors or sharp knife
webbing stretcher
hammer
springing needle
regulator needle (or large bradawl)

## Materials

black and white (first-quality) webbing — see figure 3 for measurements and add 500 mm (20 in)
20 mm ($\frac{5}{8}$ in) improved tacks
280 or 340 g (10 or 12 oz) hessian — one piece slightly larger than the seat frame
13 mm ($\frac{1}{2}$ in) fine tacks
twine (upholsterer's twine is always sold by the reel)
horsehair — gauge approximately how much you need from the old stuffing
calico — approximately 1 m (1 yd)
10 mm ($\frac{3}{8}$ in) fine tacks
sheet (skin) wadding — enough to cover the top of your seat
60 g (2 oz) Courtelle — one piece slightly larger than your seat
covering fabric — enough to go over the top of the seat to the underside of the frame
black upholstery linen or hessian — 0.5 m ($\frac{1}{2}$ yd)

### Figures 1 & 2  Removing the old upholstery

As you remove the old upholstery, note how the different layers have been attached. Although it is extremely unlikely that you will be able to reuse any of the materials except the horsehair, you should keep them to estimate quantities.

Turn the seat upside-down and, with a mallet and ripping chisel, remove the tacks attaching the hessian which covers the underside of the seat frame, working carefully in the direction of the wood's grain and making sure that the edge of the chisel slides under the tacks. In the same way, remove the tacks holding the top, decorative covering fabric which should also be attached to the underside of the seat frame; keep this as a pattern from which to cut your new cover. If you find another cover just below it, untack it in the same way. Turn the seat over and remove these covers and the layer of sheet (skin) wadding just below them. You should now find a piece of calico, again tacked to the underside of the frame: remove the tacks in the same way as before and take it off. Under this layer is a horsehair pad fastened down with twine. Cut the twine and remove the pad. (You may be able to reuse this pad: if it is in good condition but very flat, tease the fibres until you have a thick, loose mass.)

Under the pad is a layer of hessian tacked on to the frame. Only when that has been removed will you be able to see how the webbing is attached. The cross-section (**1**) shows how the layers are constructed. Remove all the tacks holding the webbing in place (**2**). Once you are left with a bare frame, check its condition. If there are a great many tack holes, fill them in with plastic wood. It will help to strengthen the frame if you spread a layer of wood glue over its top surface and allow it to dry before you continue.

### Figures 3–8  Attaching the webbing

The whole structure of the seat must be supported by six strips of webbing, three running from side to side and three from back to front, and equally spaced. It is also important that they are all attached to the frame with the same degree of tension.

Measure the frame from front to back and from side to side to determine the central point on each rail (which you should mark with chalk or pencil) and the amount of webbing you will need, allowing for 25 mm (1 in) turnovers at each end of the webbing strips (**3**).

**Figure 1**

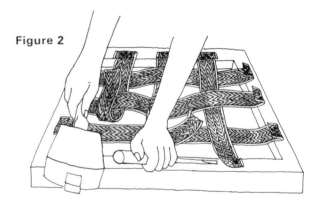

covering fabric    skin wadding    calico    frame

hessian    webbing    horsehair

Courtelle

cross-section

**Figure 2**

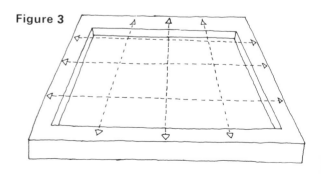

**Figure 3**

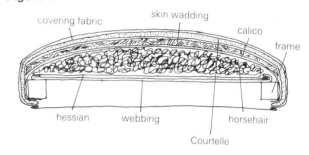

Turn over about 25 mm (1 in) of the end of the roll of webbing and, with the folded side up, attach this end to the centre of the back rail with five 20 mm (⅝ in) improved tacks through the two layers. These tacks should be arranged in a W-shape to prevent splitting the wood (**4**). Take a webbing stretcher and push a loop of the webbing through the hole in the stretcher from underneath, with the handle of the stretcher pointing towards the centre of the chair. Place the stretcher bar through the loop (**5**). Stretch the webbing over the front edge of the front rail at the centre, and pull the handle firmly towards you so that the webbing is tight over the frame without having undue stress put on it (**6**).

**Figure 4**

**Figure 5**

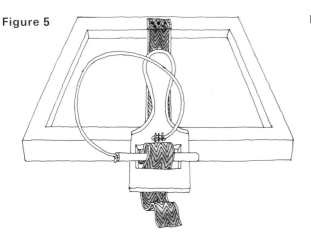

**Figure 6**

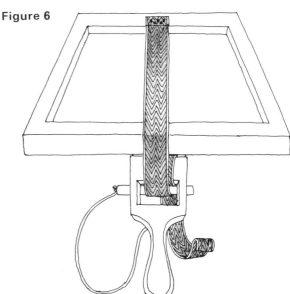

Tilt the frame up slightly from the work surface and hold the top edge of it firmly in one hand, bracing the front edge against the work surface with your knee (**7**). Using a hammer, drive three tacks into the webbing and frame. Cut the webbing so that it extends about 25 mm (1 in) past the edge of the frame, fold it back over the frame and hammer in two more tacks through the double thickness to make what would be a W-shape if all the tacks were visible (see figure 8). Attach two more pieces of webbing to the frame in the same way, on each side of and parallel to the first piece so that they are all equally spaced.

Take the loose end of the roll of webbing, pass it over the first piece of stretched webbing already in place, then under the middle one and over the next. Fold over 25 mm (1 in) and attach to the centre of one of the side rails as shown in figure 4. Stretch and tack it to the centre of the opposite rail. If the side rails are not parallel, fold the webbing so that the folded edge is parallel to the rail rather than at right angles to

**Figure 7**

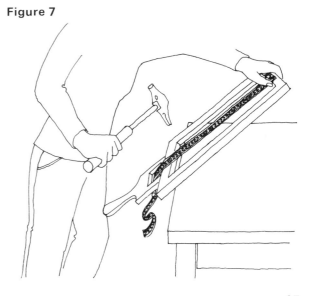

the webbing itself. Attach two more pieces of webbing at either side of and parallel to the first one, weaving them in the opposite way to it (**8**).

**Figure 8**

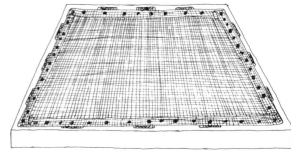

### Figures 9-11  Attaching the hessian

Take a piece of 280 or 340 g (10 or 12 oz) hessian 50 mm (2 in) larger all round than the frame. Lay it on the frame which has been placed on a work surface so that the back rail is farthest away from you. Turn up a 25 mm (1 in) hem on the hessian along the length of the back rail and place it so that it just covers the tacks on the webbing. Attach it to the centre of the rail with one 13 mm ($\frac{1}{2}$ in) fine tack. This 'temporary' tack may need to come out again, so do not hammer it flat. To square the hessian, pull it across the frame and again anchor it lightly with a tack directly opposite the first tack (**9**). Put one tack at the centre of each of the other rails in the same way. Pull the hessian taut from corner to corner and secure with another tack at each corner, also driven in lightly. In the same way, place additional tacks between those already in position. Only when you are satisfied that the hessian is positioned straight and taut should you drive all the tacks home. Trim the hessian to approximately 40 mm ($1\frac{1}{2}$ in) outside the tacks (**10**).

**Figure 9**

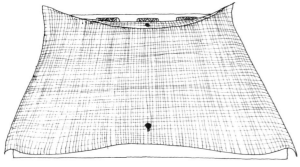

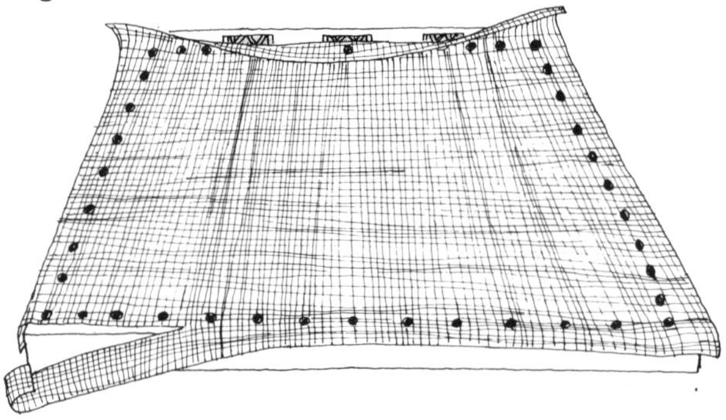

Now turn up a hem all round and tack it down, making sure that the tacks are evenly spaced and about 50 mm (2 in) apart. When you come to the corners, fold one hem over the other and secure with a single tack (**11**).

**Figure 10**

**Figure 11**

### Figures 12-14  Anchoring the horsehair with bridle ties

Thread a springing needle with enough twine to go one and a half times round the perimeter of the seat, and knot the end. Make a small stitch in the hessian 50 mm (2 in) diagonally in from the top left-hand corner. Pull the twine through, make a slip knot and pull it tight. Make another stitch in the top centre, with the needle pointing towards you so that it comes out slightly nearer the centre of the seat (**12**). Leave the loop of twine loose enough to insert, say, a couple of fingers.

At the top right-hand corner make another stitch in the same way (**13**). Make a fourth stitch by the centre of the side rail, and continue stitching round the seat to make loops — the bridle ties — until you reach the point where you started, bringing your stitch out above the first one.

Now make a small stitch in the middle of the seat, at right angles to the direction of the twine, and then make another right-angled stitch at the bottom right-hand corner. Fasten off the twine with a knot and cut (**14**).

Take up a handful of horsehair, tease it out slightly and gently insert it under and around the loops you have just made, as shown in the photograph, so that it makes a firm, even mass about 50 mm (2 in) thick and slightly higher in the middle to form a smooth domed shape. It is very important that there are no lumps or thin patches in evidence, so it is worth spending time making sure that the surface is as even as possible. Any very hard or matted pieces should be removed. Make sure that the horsehair is neatly tucked in around the edges and does not overhang the frame.

**Figure 12**

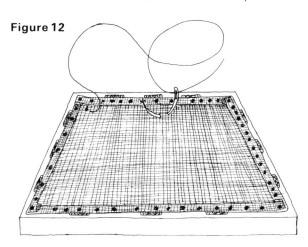

**Figure 13**

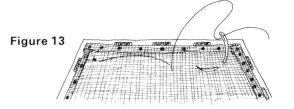

**Figure 14**

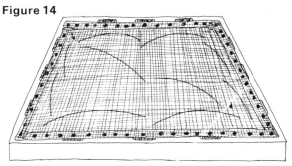

*Inserting horsehair around the bridle ties.*

## Figures 15–21 Attaching the calico

Cut a piece of calico large enough to go over the seat and a good 50 mm (2 in) or so beyond the undersides of the rails.

Turn the seat upside-down and centre it on the calico. Pull the calico up over the front rail and temporarily tack it with a 10 mm ($\frac{3}{8}$ in) fine tack in the centre (**15**). Stretch the calico very tightly

**Figure 15**

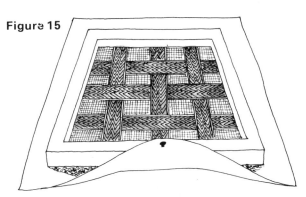

across the seat and secure it with another temporary tack on the opposite side. Attach the calico to the side rails in the same way.

To anchor the corners, begin by lifting each one slightly to free any horsehair (which must not go over the edge of the seat frame since this would prevent it being put back in the chair frame easily.) Pulling the calico tightly over the corner with one hand, ease and smooth it into position with the other (**16**). Keep it in position with one or two temporary tacks. When you have anchored all four corners, turn the seat the right way up and make sure they are rounded and firm and that no wood can be felt from the top of the seat. If necessary, remove the tacks, add more horsehair and retack. Now pull and smooth the calico as tightly as possible along each rail so that no excess hair will be forced down to the sides, and tack it lightly to the frame at 50 mm (2 in) intervals (**17**), leaving the temporary tacks in the corners. Check the padding along the edges as you go, adding more horsehair where necessary.

**Figure 16**

**Figure 17**

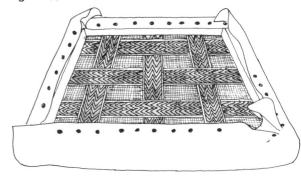

To finish the corners, remove the temporary tack from each one in turn, pull the calico tightly towards the centre of the seat and insert a 10 mm ($\frac{3}{8}$ in) tack firmly about 13 mm ($\frac{1}{2}$ in) in from the corner. Cut into the excess calico at each side of this tack to form a tongue shape (**18**). Pull one side of the calico down over this tongue and anchor it with two tacks about 25 mm (1 in) apart (**19**). Trim the calico to 13 mm ($\frac{1}{2}$ in) from the line of these tacks and to about 50 mm (2 in) along from the corner (**20**). In the same way, anchor the other side at right angles to the first and trim (**21**). Repeat with the other three corners.

Drive home the existing tacks along the rails and add more until they are positioned at about 25 mm (1 in) intervals. Finish trimming the calico to within 13 mm ($\frac{1}{2}$ in) of the tacks. You will now be able to see whether the horsehair is smoothly distributed across the seat. Any minor unevenness can be levelled by rearranging the hair with the point of a regulator needle.

**Figure 18**

**Figure 19**

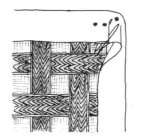

**Figure 20**

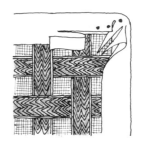

**Figure 21**

## Figures 22 & 23  Preparation for the final covering

Cut a piece of sheet (skin) wadding to exactly the same size as the top of the seat, making sure it does not go over the sides. This wadding prevents the prickly horsehair working through the covering fabric. Lay it over the calico (**22**); then cut a piece of 60 g (2 oz) Courtelle large enough to go over the seat to the underside of the frame. Turn the frame upside-down and place over the Courtelle centrally. With 10 mm ($\frac{3}{8}$ in) fine tacks, tightly anchor the Courtelle in place all round, stretching and pulling it at each corner to avoid bulk (**23**). Mark the front and back centres on the edge of the Courtelle with chalk or pencil.

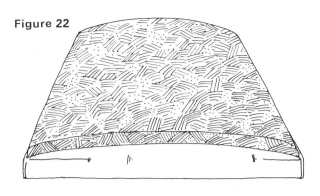

Figure 22

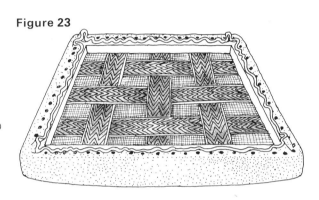

Figure 23

## Figure 24  The final covering

Cut a piece of covering fabric large enough to go over the seat to the underside of the frame, adding an extra 50 mm (2 in) all round. Make sure that any pattern is centred. Mark the middle of both front and back with a tiny nick. Place this in a centred position on the top of your seat and turn the whole thing over (**24**). Pull the covering fabric over the rails at the front and back, aligning the nicks with the chalk marks on the Courtelle. Insert a 10 mm ($\frac{3}{8}$ in) fine tack temporarily at both these points. Place a similar tack at the centre of each side rail. Attach the fabric to the rails in exactly the same way as you did with the calico (figures 16–21). At the corners, you may find it easier to trim away more fabric than you did with the calico to make two neat pleats at each corner.

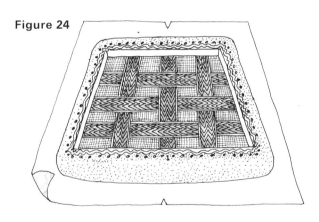

Figure 24

## Figure 25  Finishing off

Cut a piece of closely woven black upholstery linen (or hessian) 40 mm ($1\frac{1}{2}$ in) larger all round than the flat underside of the seat. Turn under a 6 mm ($\frac{1}{4}$ in) hem and, using 13 mm ($\frac{1}{2}$ in) fine tacks, fasten the linen down over the existing tacks, first putting one in lightly at the centre of each rail, then one in near each end. If you think the fabric is straight and taut, drive these tacks home. Put in more tacks, firmly this time, along the rails at approximately 25 mm (1 in) intervals, making simple square corners with turned edges (**25**).

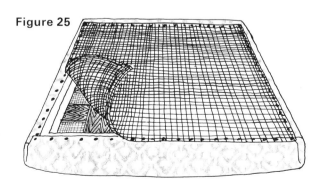

Figure 25

# Upholstery Project 2: Non-sprung Stool

## Introduction

The method used to upholster this stool is similar to that which might be used for a simple non-sprung chair. The most important new technique introduced here is that of making a reinforced roll of padding round the stool's edge.

The structure of the edge roll is used on most upholstered furniture; it protects the edge against wear, covers and softens the wooden frame, and provides a surround for the soft padding in the middle of the seat, where most of the sitter's weight will fall.

Apart from this important new feature, the basic structure of webbing, hessian, padding and several layers of covering is the same as that described for upholstery project 1.

## Tools

mallet
ripping chisel
scissors or sharp knife
webbing stretcher
hammer
file
felt-tipped pen
springing needle
double bayonet needle
regulator needle (or large bradawl)
four upholstery or kitchen skewers

## Materials

black and white (first-quality) webbing: see project 2, figure 3 for measurements and add 500 mm (20 in)

20 mm ($\frac{5}{8}$ in) improved tacks

280 or 340 g (10 or 12 oz) hessian — a piece slightly larger than the top of the stool

scrim — four pieces, one for each side of the frame, each 150 mm (6 in) wide and 100 mm (4 in) longer than the side to which it will be attached, for the edge roll

twine (upholsterer's twine is always sold by the reel)

ginger fibre — use the old stuffing to estimate quantities

10 mm ($\frac{3}{8}$ in) fine tacks

horsehair: gauge approximately how much you need from the old stuffing

sheet (skin) wadding: enough to cover the top of the stool

60 g (2 oz) Courtelle: see figure 32 for the amount needed

covering fabric — enough to go over the top of the stool to the underside of the frame

black upholstery linen or hessian: a piece slightly larger than the underside of your stool

## Removing the old upholstery

Using a mallet and a ripping chisel, and working always in the direction of the wood's grain, remove all the tacks holding the old upholstery in place. Detailed instructions for doing this are given in project 1, figure 1. As all upholsterers work in slightly different ways the layers may not be exactly as described, but it is always a good idea to examine carefully each layer of material and padding as you remove it, to see how the work was done originally and to help you estimate quantities. Keep the old top cover and use it as a pattern from which to cut your new covering fabric. If the horsehair is still in good condition you may be able to reuse it.

## Figures 1 & 2 Attaching the webbing and hessian

Keeping the frame level and preferably on a raised surface so that all parts of it are easily accessible, tack strips of webbing firmly to the four rails of the frame, using a webbing stretcher and suitable hammer, and spacing the strips approximately their own width apart (**1**). Instructions for this procedure are given in detail in project 1, figures 3–8. Place the hessian over the webbing, position it straight and taut, and attach it to the frame (**2**), as described in project 1, figures 9–11.

## Figure 3 Preparing the rails

With a large file, smooth away any sharp right angles at the top outside edges of the rails (**3**), to make a sloping surface at least 6 mm ($\frac{1}{4}$ in) wide all round the edge of the frame, into which tacks can be driven. This procedure is called chamfering or bevelling.

## Figures 4–28 Constructing a reinforced edge roll

Since a stool will receive the same amount of wear on all sides, it must be padded so that it looks and wears the same on all four edges, and the most effective way of doing this is to make the edge roll quite separately from the main padding, to go all the way round the stool. The roll is made with a strong material called scrim which is stuffed with fibre to form a sausage shape. This is then reinforced with one row each of two types of stitching: blind stitching and top stitching.

**Figure 1**

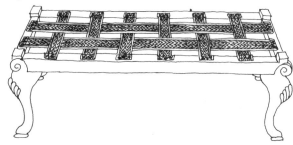

**Figure 2**

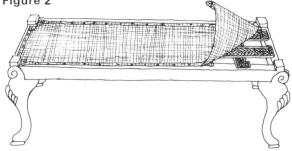

**Figure 3**

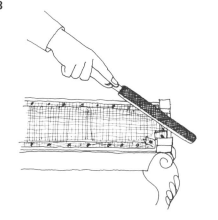

## Figures 4-10 Attaching the scrim to the hessian

With a felt-tipped pen, mark out a border on the hessian 75 mm (3 in) in from the edges along all four sides, as a guide for the edge roll (**4**).

Cut four pieces of scrim (one for each side of the frame) 150 mm (6 in) wide and each one about 100 mm (4 in) longer than the side to which it will be attached. Turn under a 13 mm ($\frac{1}{2}$ in) hem on the first piece of scrim, and place this fold along the border line you have drawn on the hessian, so that the raw edge of the scrim faces away from the centre of the stool. Anchor each end with a temporary tack.

Thread a 75 mm (3 in) springing needle with more than enough twine to go round the stool. Make a stitch in the scrim and hessian at one end of a rail, at the point where the two border lines meet (**5**). Pull the twine through almost to the end and fasten it with a slip knot. Make another stitch 13 mm ($\frac{1}{2}$ in) from the first one, and continue making neat 13 mm ($\frac{1}{2}$ in) running stitches along the length of the border line (**6**), being careful not to catch the webbing in the stitches.

Stop stitching when you reach the next border line (**7**), but do not finish off or cut the twine. Trim this end of the scrim to 25 mm (1 in) beyond the edge of the stool and remove the temporary tack. Lift up this loose end of the scrim and place the second piece along the second side exactly as you did with the first, having turned under a hem. Anchor this second strip with temporary tacks (**8**) and continue your running stitch at right angles to the first line of stitches without breaking the twine (**9**).

Continue in this way until all four pieces of scrim have been sewn round the four sides of the frame (**10**). Pull the twine through to the underside, knot it and cut it off. Remove all temporary tacks.

**Figure 4**

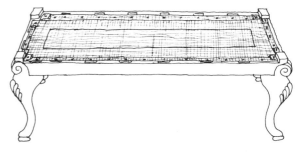

**Figure 5**      **Figure 6**

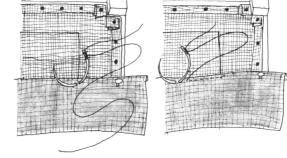

**Figure 7**

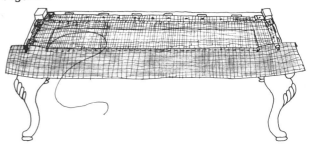

**Figure 8**      **Figure 9**

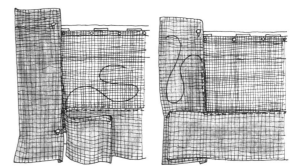

**Figure 10**

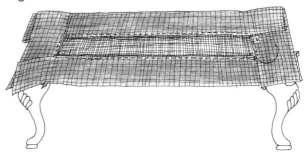

### Figures 11-17  Padding the scrim with fibre

The next stage is to make bridle ties which will keep the fibre in position in the edge roll. Thread the springing needle with a piece of twine long enough to go round the stool about one and a half times. Make a slip knot in one corner of the hessian at a point 40 mm (1½ in) outside the border marking, under the scrim you have just attached. Make loops about 150 mm (6 in) long, beginning each one just before the end of the previous one (similar to those in project 1, figures 12–14) and running them round the stool between the border line and the edge of the hessian (**11**). When you reach the starting point, finish off with a knot and cut the twine.

Tease out a handful of ginger fibre and, starting at one end of a rail, slip it under and around the first loop. Add another handful under this same loop (**12**), pull the scrim over the fibre to the edge of the rail and make sure it feels firm, looks nicely rounded and does not flatten under pressure. Continue in this way until all the scrim has been firmly padded.

Using 10 mm (⅜ in) fine tacks and starting in the centre of one long rail, pull the scrim over the fibre, turn under a 13 mm (½ in) hem and put a temporary tack through the scrim into the chamfered edge. Work outwards towards the ends of the rail, putting in temporary tacks at 50 mm (2 in) intervals (**13**). Do the same along the other three rails, leaving the corners open for the moment. If you are satisfied that the edge roll is even, rounded and firm, drive the tacks home. If there are any bare patches under the scrim take out the tacks at that place, add more fibre and then drive the tacks home. To make the surface even, insert the sharp end of a regulator needle (or a large bradawl) through the scrim and gently move it around in the fibre in order to smooth it out and distribute it evenly.

At each corner, pull back the two layers of scrim (**14**) and add a little extra fibre under that which is already there, for increased firmness. Now stretch the bottom layer of scrim over the top and sides of the fibre, fold the edge under and anchor it along the frame with permanent tacks (**15**); then fold the top layer of scrim diagonally under from the inner to the outer corner (**16**). Pull tight and tack down at the corner, and then turn down the remaining edge to neaten and tack it down (**17**). Use the regulator needle to smooth the filling.

Figure 11

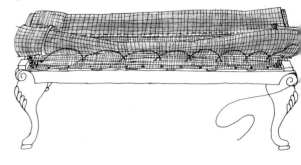

Figure 12

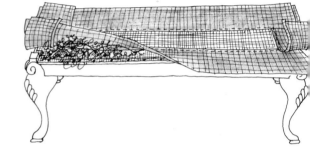

Figure 13

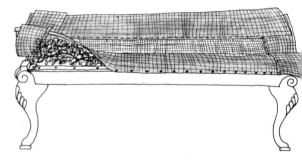

Figure 14

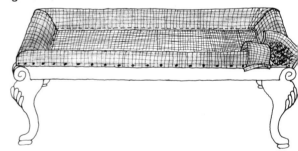

Figure 15          Figure 16          Figure 17

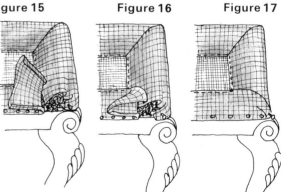

## Figures 18–24 Blind stitching

The purpose of blind stitches — sometimes called 'sink' stitches — is to bring the stuffing firmly towards the outside edges of the stool by catching it in loops of twine, as shown in the cross-section (**18**). Thread a 250 mm (10 in) double bayonet needle with enough twine to go one and a half times round the perimeter of the stool. Working from right to left, insert the needle into the outside of one corner, about 6 mm ($\frac{1}{4}$ in) above the rail and pointing it diagonally towards the centre of the stool (**19**). Pass it through the stuffing and scrim so that about 150 mm (6 in) protrudes at the other side, but do not pull it right through: the eye of the needle should now be inside the roll, about three-quarters of the way through the stuffing. Now manipulate the eye of the needle towards the right (inside the roll to catch the stuffing) and then push it back towards you so that it comes out 6 mm ($\frac{1}{4}$ in) to the right of the starting point (**20**). Fasten the end of the twine with a slip knot, but do not cut.

Insert the needle about 50 mm (2 in) to the left of the original point of entry, pushing it straight into the roll (**21**) until the eye of the needle is about three-quarters of the way through the stuffing. Bring the eye out again halfway between the two stitches (**22**), pull the twine taut, and make a knot by looping each end of the twine twice round the needle (**23** and **24**) so that the stitches do not loosen. Withdraw the needle completely and continue stitching round the stool, pushing the needle in at 50 mm (2 in) intervals, and returning it 25 mm (1 in) further back from the previous stitch. Use a regulator every two or three stitches to work the stuffing forwards as evenly as possible. When you get to the corners the needle should be pushed in so that it points diagonally towards the centre of the stool. When you have made the last stitch, knot the twine and cut it.

**Figure 18**

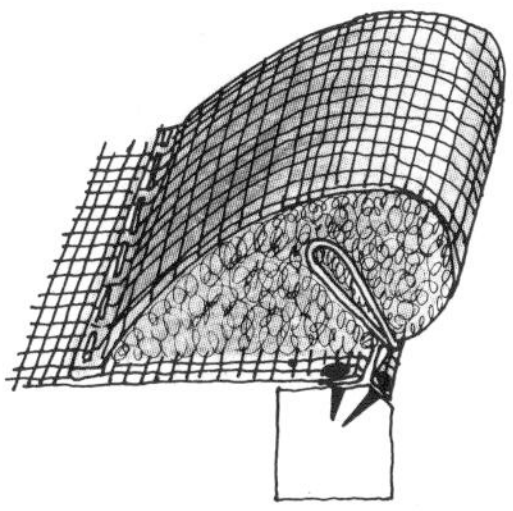

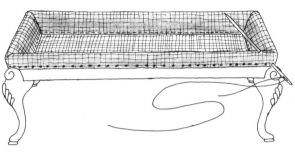

cross-section of blind stitch

**Figure 19**

**Figure 20**

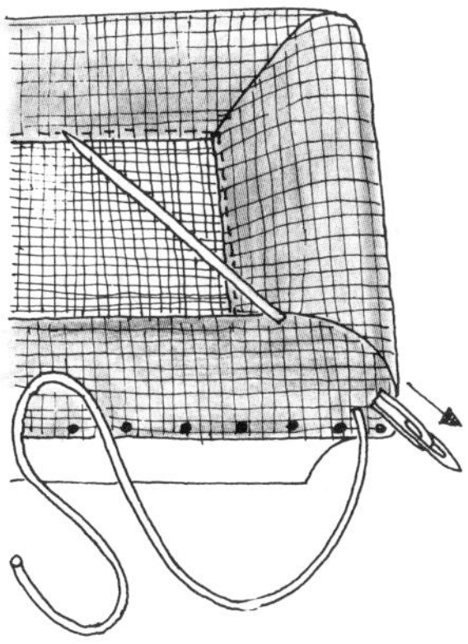

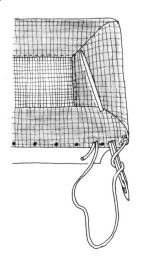

**Figure 21**

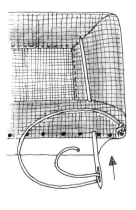

**Figure 22**

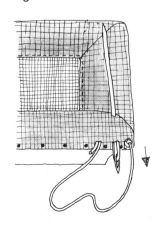

**Figure 23**

**Figure 24**

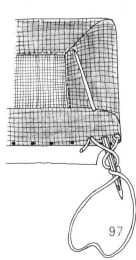

### Figures 25-28 Top stitching

These stitches are similar to blind stitches, except that the needle is pulled all the way through the stuffing so that it forms a line of stitches on both sides of the edge roll. When pulled tight, these stitches should form a firm roll about the thickness of a thumb along the top, as shown in the cross-section (**25**).

Thread the double bayonet needle with enough twine to go one and a half times round the stool. Working from right to left again, above the row of blind stitches, start by securing the end of the twine with a slip knot as in figure 20.

Now insert the needle exactly as if you were going to make a blind stitch (see figure 21), but this time pull the needle right through the edge roll to the other side. Now push the eye of the needle back through the roll at a point about 25 mm (1 in) to the right of where it went in until the needle is in the position shown (**26**). Loop the twine as before (**27**) and withdraw the needle to the outside edge, pulling the twine forward and in the direction that your stitches are running, to tighten the knot. Continue stitching in this way, making sure that the line of stitches and knots runs parallel to the edge of the roll (**28**).

You will need to use the regulator frequently to get a firm roll of even height and thickness. (Making both top and blind stitches is a fairly tricky and time-consuming job, but they are two of the most important techniques of upholstery.)

# Figures 29-36 Padding and covering

### Figures 29 & 30 Making bridle ties and anchoring the horsehair

Using a springing needle and twine, make a small stitch at one corner of the hessian now enclosed by the edge roll. Secure it with a slip knot and make bridle ties (see project 1, figures 12–14) in a zig-zag pattern (**29**). Tease out the horsehair in the same way as you did with the ginger fibre and tuck it under and around the bridle ties to fill the central part of the stool with a firm, even layer of horsehair. Make this more thickly padded in the middle (**30**), so that it is slightly domed in shape.

**Figure 25**

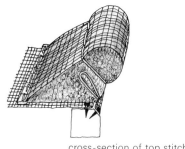

cross-section of top stitch

**Figure 26**

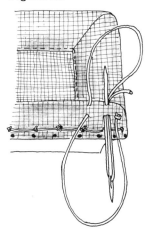

**Figure 27**

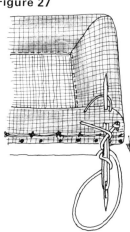

**Figure 28**

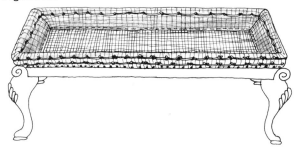

**Figure 29**

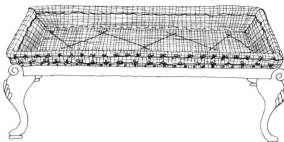

**Figure 30**

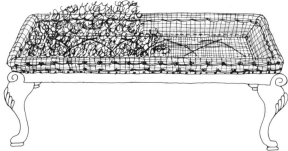

## Figures 31 & 32 Preparation for the final covering

Cut a piece of sheet (skin) wadding large enough to go over the top of the stool and slightly over the edge roll. Lay it over the horsehair (**31**) and anchor each corner with a skewer stuck in straight, at right angles to the top.

Cut a piece of 60 g (2 oz) Courtelle large enough to cover the stool and fasten underneath the side rails, and lay it over the top of the stool. With 10 mm (⅜ in) fine tacks, tack it down near the bottom of the side edge of each rail, removing the skewers as you come to each corner. When you are doing this, remember to stretch and smooth the Courtelle carefully, making sure no horsehair escapes from under the wadding. Trim at the bottom edge of the rails (**32**).

## Figures 33–36 The final covering and finishing off

Centring the pattern if necessary, cut a piece of covering fabric the same size as the Courtelle and lay it on the stool. Fasten it down with a temporary tack at the centre of each rail and another near both ends of each rail (**33**), making sure that the fabric is straight and smooth. Put in more temporary tacks all round at 25 mm (1 in) intervals, pulling the fabric taut and stopping about 75 mm (3 in) short of the corners. Once you have made any minor adjustments necessary and you are satisfied that the cover is smooth and straight, drive the tacks home.

At the corners, ease the fabric so it fits as neatly as possible round the legs, making a small pleat if necessary. Anchor the fabric with a closely spaced row of tacks (**34**). Trim the fabric as close to the tacks as possible all round (**35**).

Cover the tacks by gluing a strip of braid or gimp over them at the corners and along the bottom edge of the four side rails (**36**).

Turn the stool over and cover the bottom with a piece of black upholstery linen or hessian using the technique described in project 1, figure 25.

**Figure 31**

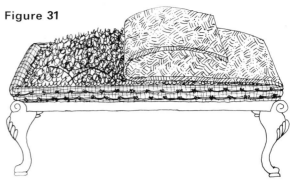

**Figure 32**

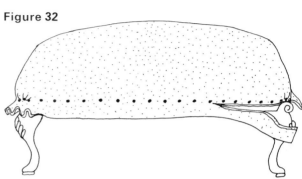

**Figure 33**

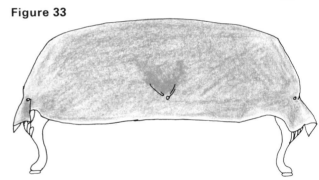

**Figure 34**          **Figure 35**

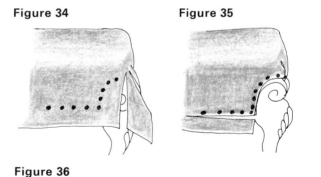

**Figure 36**

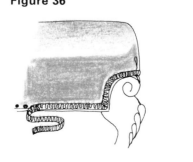

# Upholstery Project 3: Sprung Dining Chair

## Introduction

This project introduces the basic and important technique of springing. The way in which the springs are anchored (or lashed) to the frame and to each other will determine the degree of comfort and support provided by the chair as well as its appearance and durability.

The procedure involved is not difficult but it does require concentration, and you will need to practise before you are able to do it quickly and well. You should get used to working with springs on a fairly small project such as this before you attempt anything larger and more complex, even though the basic skills remain the same. It is worth taking time to work very slowly – even to redo certain steps if necessary – until you are totally satisfied with the result and feel familiar with the techniques. The chair shown here has five springs, but some have only three and others as many as nine; make sure that, however many springs you are working with, they are evenly spaced over the seat area.

The reinforced edge roll is another important feature of this project. Although the most complicated part of it, the stitching, remains the same as for the stool, the padding in this instance is applied in one stage evenly over the entire seat, then pulled to the edges; the edge roll is not made separately from the central area of padding. When you are working on a chair (as opposed to a stool), the two methods are interchangeable – use whichever you find easier.

As always, it is important to remove the old upholstery carefully. Working with a mallet and chisel and following the procedure outlined in project 1, remove all the layers until you are left with the bare frame. You will find it useful to keep the old padding so that you can refer to its structure as you work.

## Tools

mallet
ripping chisel
scissors
webbing stretcher
hammer
springing needle
double bayonet needle
regulator needle
tailor's chalk

## Materials

black and white (first-quality) webbing: see figure 1 for measurements and add 500 mm (20 in)

20 mm ($\frac{5}{8}$ in) improved tacks

five 100 mm (4 in) gauge 10 double-cone springs: you will probably be able to use the ones you have removed from the chair

twine (upholsterer's twine is always sold by the reel)

laid cord (also sold by the reel)

280 or 340 g (10 or 12 oz) hessian – one piece slightly larger than the seat frame

13 mm ($\frac{1}{2}$ in) fine tacks

horsehair – use the old stuffing to gauge approximately how much you need

scrim – one piece large enough to go over the padded seat and fasten to the outside faces of the seat frame

sheet (skin) wadding – one piece the same size as the top of the seat

covering fabric – enough to cover the padded seat and attach to the outside faces of the seat frame

braid or gimp – enough to go round the seat frame

# Upholstery Project 3

### Figure 1  Attaching the webbing

Following the instructions given for attaching webbing in project 1, figures 3–8, tack six pieces of webbing underneath the frame, making sure the central pieces in both rows are straight and at right angles to each other. If the frame is wider at the front than the back, the strips of webbing running from side to side should be parallel to the front and back rails and to each other, while the side strips of webbing running from front to back should be parallel to the side rails (**1**).

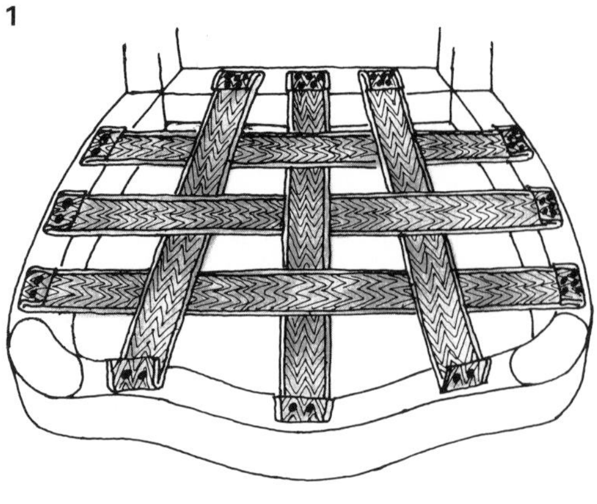

### Figures 2-5  Attaching the springs to the webbing

Stand the chair upright, and place five 100 mm (4 in) gauge 10 galvanized steel double-cone springs in position at the junctions of the webbing, so that the knots at the top of the springs are facing the centre of the chair (**2**).

You should attach each spring to the webbing with three equidistant stitches around the base of the spring. To do this, thread a springing needle with approximately 2 m (78 in) of twine. With the chair facing you, insert your needle into the webbing from underneath, at the base of the spring at the top left-hand corner. Catch the spring in a single stitch and push the needle back through to the underside of the webbing. Fasten the twine with a slip knot. Bring your needle up again, make a second stitch over the base of the spring and, when your needle is back on the underside of the webbing, knot the twine to the long stitch just formed. Make the third stitch (**3** and **4**) in the same way. Repeat this procedure for all the springs, working in the shape of a Z from the first spring to the last (**5**). Finish off with a double knot.

**Figure 1**

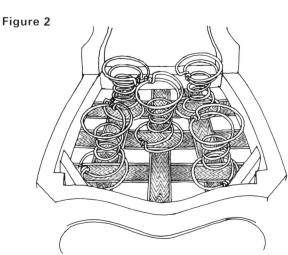

**Figure 2**

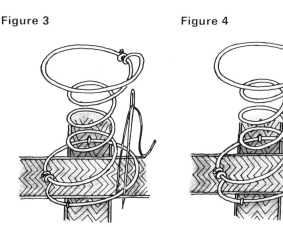

**Figure 3**          **Figure 4**

**Figure 5**

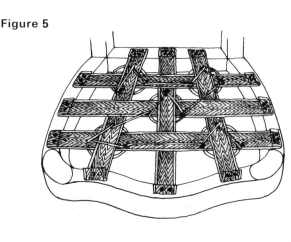

## Figures 6-12  Lashing the springs

The purpose of this process (also called cording) is to keep the springs upright and under tension, so that when the chair is sat on they are all depressed together.

**Figure 6**

**Figure 7**

**Figure 8**

Drive in three 15 mm ($\frac{5}{8}$ in) temporary tacks along each rail in line with the centre of each spring (see figure 11). Cut six pieces of laid cord long enough to go very generously across the frame, over the tops of the springs. Make a single knot at the end of one piece and slip it over one of the temporary tacks (**6**). Make another single knot (**7**), pull it tight and drive the tack home (**8**). Attach all six pieces of cord along two adjoining rails in this way (see figure 8).

**Figure 9**

**Figure 10**

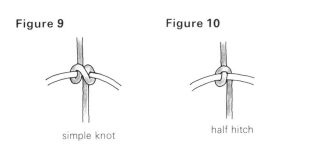

simple knot

half hitch

The springs must be lashed so that the top coil of the outer ones leans towards its nearest corner, making an overall domed shape (the central spring remains upright). Starting with one of the pieces of cord on the side rail, make a simple knot (**9**) round the nearest point of the top coil of the nearest spring, pulling the cord tightly so the spring leans a little towards the rail. Then make a half-hitch knot on the top coil opposite the first knot (**10**). Take the cord to the next spring in a straight line, and knot it with a half hitch. Compress the springs about 13 mm ($\frac{1}{2}$ in); this will loosen the two half hitches and you should now tighten the cord, taking up the slack so that the springs stay under a slight degree of tension. Then make another simple knot opposite the second half hitch. Anchor the cord to the appropriate temporary tack with two single knots, pulling it so that the top coil of the second spring leans toward the nearest rail at the same angle as the first spring (**11**). Trim the cord.

**Figure 11**

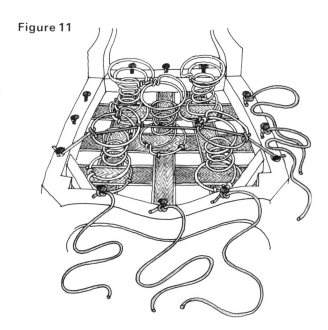

Lash the second row of two springs in the same way and parallel to the first, then lash the central spring using two simple knots. Compress it as much as the other four springs, but keep it upright. Now lash the central spring from front to back, looping the cord round the existing lashing where the two cords cross, before making your second knot.

Lash the outer springs from front to back, knotting as before and looping the cord round the existing lashing as you cross it.

When you have finished this lashing, all five springs should be compressed equally, the top coil of each outer spring leaning toward its corner and the central one remaining upright (**12**).

**Figure 12**

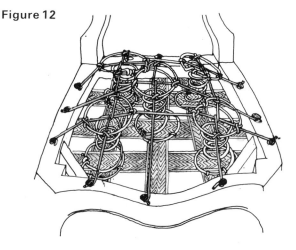

## Figures 13-17 Attaching the hessian to the frame

Cut a piece of 340 g (12 oz) hessian 100 mm (4 in) larger all round than the seat of the chair. Turn up a 13 mm ($\frac{1}{2}$ in) hem along one edge and anchor it to the back of the frame with a 13 mm ($\frac{1}{2}$ in) fine temporary tack at the centre of the rail. Pull the hessian taut over the springs and fasten it with a temporary tack at the centre of the front rail. Repeat from side rail to side rail (**13**).

At this stage, you will be able to see from the level and angles of the springs whether they have been properly lashed, and you should make any necessary adjustments to the lashing before you continue. When you are quite satisfied with the springs, drive the tacks home.

Make a diagonal cut into the hessian at the two back corners so that it can be folded round the two upright rails of the chair back. Tack round these corners (**14**), then tack along all four seat rails at 50 mm (2 in) intervals. Trim the three sides of the hessian which do not yet have a hem to 13 mm ($\frac{1}{2}$ in) beyond the frame (**15**), then turn up a hem and tack it to the frame, putting the tacks between those which are already in place (**16** and **17**).

**Figure 13**

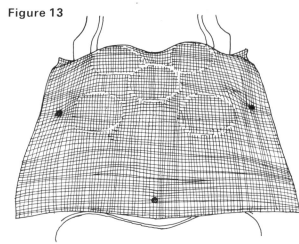

**Figure 14**

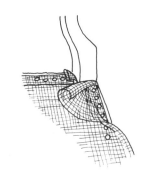

**Figure 15**

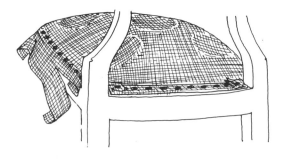

**Figure 16**

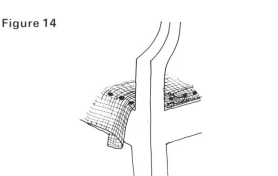

**Figure 17**

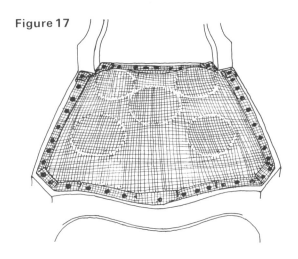

## Figure 18  Attaching the hessian to the springs

The springs must now be attached to the hessian in exactly the same pattern as they were to the webbing, that is, with stitches at three equidistant positions round the top coil.

Thread a piece of twine approximately 1·5 m (60 in) long through a springing needle. Starting at the back left-hand corner, insert the needle into the hessian and bring it out again, catching the front of the spring underneath. Tie this tightly with a slip knot. Take the twine to the back of the spring and catch and secure it in a half hitch. Bring the needle back to the front of the spring and catch the spring once more so that the twine forms an inverted V-shape on the hessian. Repeat this procedure with the right-hand back spring, then the central one and then the two front ones (**18**). Fasten the last stitch with a double knot and cut the twine.

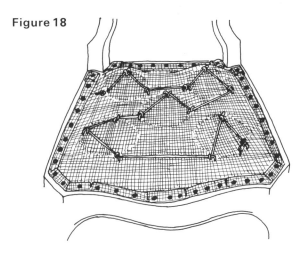

Figure 18

## Figure 19  The first set of bridle ties and first layer of horsehair

Thread the springing needle with a piece of twine long enough to go about one and a half times round the perimeter of the seat. Make bridle ties round and across the seat as described in project 1, figures 12–14.

Take a handful of horsehair and tuck it under the first loop of twine, working it under and around the loop and pressing it down firmly (**19**). Continue adding more hair and pressing it down until it feels firm and thick. Fill all the ties, blending the hair together so that the surface is smooth and even. Add more hair to the centre of the seat, blending it with the surrounding hair. Continue adding to it until the seat feels solid and you cannot detect the springs.

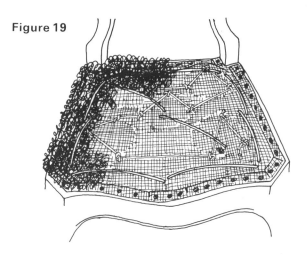

Figure 19

## Figure 20  Attaching the scrim to the frame

Measure the distance from one bottom edge of the frame, over the horsehair, to the bottom of the opposite edge at the widest point. Add 50 mm (2 in) all round and cut a piece of scrim this size. Lay it over the hair and tack it neatly with 15 mm ($\frac{5}{8}$ in) improved tacks temporarily to the centre of the outer faces of the four rails (**20**). Adjust if necessary, drive the tacks home and, working from the centre outwards, secure with more tacks spaced about 40 mm ($1\frac{1}{2}$ in) apart (see figure 21). Cut into the scrim at the back corners and fold it under to neaten.

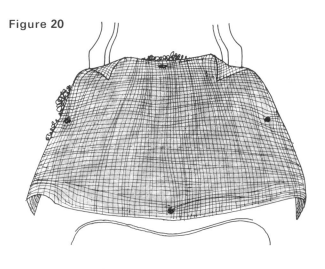

Figure 20

### Figure 21 Anchoring the padding

Thread a double bayonet needle with a piece of twine 1·5 m (60 in) long. Make a stitch in the scrim 75 mm (3 in) in from the left side of the frame at the back and secure with a slip knot. Push the needle down through the seat, avoiding the springs, to the bottom of the chair, so that the eye of the needle just clears the hessian. Then push it straight up so the other point of the needle comes out about 13 mm ($\frac{1}{2}$ in) away from the point of entry on the top of the seat. Knot, but do not cut, the twine. Repeat this stitch at the centre of each rail and at each corner, keeping 75 mm (3 in) in from the rails as shown. Knot and cut the twine (**21**). Turn up the excess scrim all round the edges of the seat, tack it down between the first row of tacks, and trim (see figure 22).

### Figures 22 & 23 Reinforcing the edges

To ensure that there is sufficient padding round the edges where it is most needed, and to cover the hard rail, the edges of the chair should be reinforced with blind stitches (**22**) and top stitches (**23**) in a manner very similar to that used for the stool in project 2, figures 18–28. Manipulate the hair towards the outer edges with a regulator needle, keeping the surface smooth and even.

### Figure 24 The second layer of padding

The edge roll you have just formed makes the chair seat somewhat saucer-shaped; the depression must be filled in so that the edge is not detectable as a separate entity.

On the scrim, make another set of bridle ties slightly tighter than the first set – make them loose enough to be able to put just your thumb under them. Insert a layer of horsehair about 25 mm (1 in) thick under and around these ties (**24**), making sure you do not go over the reinforced edge and that the surface is smooth, even and slightly domed.

### Figure 25 Attaching the skin wadding and the calico

Cut a piece of sheet (skin) wadding slightly larger all round than the top of the seat and lay it in position.

Now cut a piece of calico approximately 100 mm (4 in) larger all around than the top of the seat. Anchor this with three temporary tacks to the

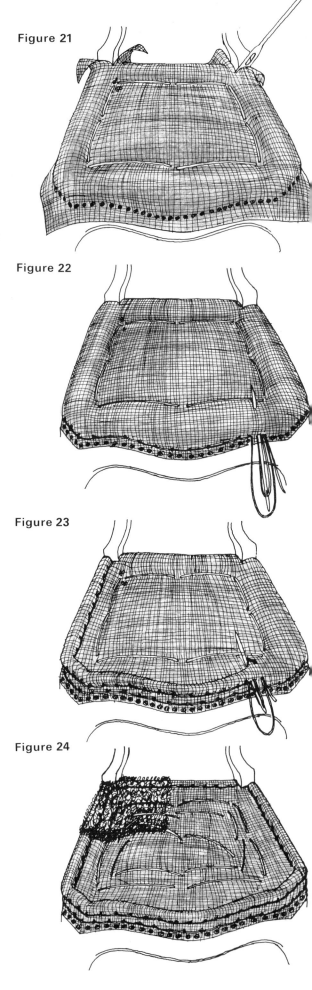

Figure 21

Figure 22

Figure 23

Figure 24

outer face of one rail at the centre, pull it taut across the chair and fasten it with three more temporary tacks to the centre of the opposite rail. Repeat across the other two rails. Neaten at both back corners by making a diagonal cut towards the centre of the seat (**25**), turning the calico under and tacking it neatly round the chair back. If necessary, use your regulator needle to neaten and tuck it in. This chair has very gently rounded corners at the front, over which the calico can be stretched and tacked in a straightforward way. See below for how to pleat round square or more sharply rounded corners. Drive home the temporary tacks in the centre of the rails and add more, spaced about 25 mm (1 in) apart.

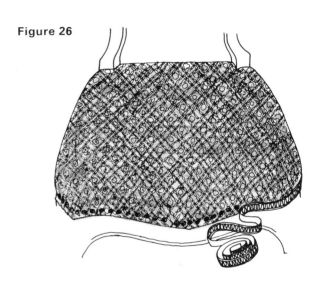

Figure 25

## Figure 26 Finishing off

Cut a piece of covering fabric 25 mm (1 in) larger all round than the measurement from the bottom face of one rail, over the seat and across to the bottom face of the opposite rail at the widest part, making sure that any pattern is centred. Measure and mark the centre of the front and back rails. Make a small nick at the centre front and back of the fabric and place it over the seat, aligning the nicks with the central points marked on the rails. Anchor the fabric with three temporary tacks at the centre back. Pull taut and proceed exactly as you did with the calico cover (see figure 25).

Conceal the tacks and raw edges with a length of suitable braid or gimp (trimming) glued on and turned under at the ends (**26**).

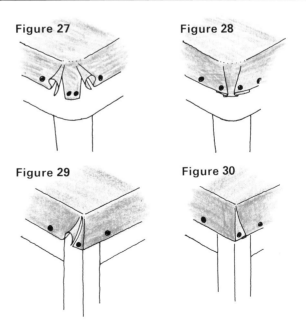

Figure 26

## Figures 27 & 28 Finishing rounded corners with a double pleat

Pull the fabric down over each corner and tack it there securely, making sure there is an equal amount of fabric on each side of the tacking point. Fold this fabric to form two pleats facing towards the corner. Cut away any excess material (**27**), pull both pleats taut and secure each one with a tack (**28**).

Figure 27

Figure 28

## Figures 29 & 30 Finishing square corners with a single pleat

Pull all the loose fabric at each corner round to one side and fix it there with a tack. Cut away any excess fabric (**29**), leaving enough to pull back to the other side of the corner, making a pleat over the first tack. Put in a second tack (**30**), then slip-stitch down the fold, concealing the stitches on the inside.

Figure 29

Figure 30

# Upholstery Project 4: Occasional Chair

## Introduction

This Edwardian occasional chair has a fully sprung seat which should be upholstered according to the instructions given for the sprung dining chair (project 3). There may be more springs in a chair of this type since the seat area is usually quite large, but this does not affect the techniques involved.

The new feature of this project is the simple, non-sprung padding on small areas of the arms and back, which provides some degree of comfort while leaving the carved and inlaid wood (called 'show' wood) as the main visual feature of the piece. In order to display this to its best advantage, you should choose a fabric in a plain colour or one with a small subdued pattern.

When you buy the braid or gimp for covering the tack heads, ask your retailer's advice, since there are some types specially designed to go smoothly and neatly round fairly sharp curves like these.

To remove the old padding, use a mallet and a ripping chisel in the usual way, taking great care not to damage the areas of exposed wood. If your chair is very old and has delicate carving like this one, you may find it more satisfactory to use the tip of a small screwdriver, bradawl or regulator needle to work the tacks loose. Be very gentle as you do this, since one hard knock against the frame might split the wood.

## Tools

mallet
ripping chisel
scissors
webbing stretcher
hammer
springing needle
double bayonet needle
regulator needle

## Materials

black and white (first-quality) webbing: see instructions for measurements and add 500 mm (20 in)

20 mm ($\frac{5}{8}$ in) improved tacks

100 mm (4 in) gauge 10 double-cone springs (the number will vary according to the size of your chair – you will probably be able to use the ones you have removed)

twine (upholsterer's twine is always sold by the reel)

laid cord (also sold by the reel)

280 or 340 g (10 or 12 oz) hessian – three pieces, one slightly larger than the seat frame, and two slightly larger than the back padding

13 mm ($\frac{1}{2}$ in) fine tacks

horsehair – use the old stuffing to gauge how much you need

sheet (skin) wadding – enough to cover the top of the seat, the arm pads and back pad

scrim – three pieces, one large enough to go over the padded seat and fasten to the outside faces of the seat frame, and two large enough to cover the areas of arm padding

covering fabric – enough to cover the padded seat and attach to the outside faces of the seat frame, to go over each arm pad and to cover the back pad (on the inside and the outside of the back)

braid or gimp – enough to go round the seat frame, the arm pads and the back pad, inside and out

ginger fibre for padding the arms – use the old stuffing to estimate quantities

Courtelle – four pieces, two large enough to cover the arm pads and two the same size as the back pad

linter felt – enough to cover the back pad

## Figures 1-8 Padding the arms

Cut a piece of scrim three times the width of the arm pad area and twice its length. Cut a piece of twine about 75 mm (3 in) longer than the arm pad area. Put in a temporary tack at one end of this area, knot the twine round it and drive it home. Repeat the process with another tack at the other end, making the twine loose enough to be able to pull it about 40 mm ($1\frac{1}{2}$ in) away from the arm at its centre (**1**).

Turn under a 13 mm ($\frac{1}{2}$ in) hem along one side of the scrim and tack it along one side of the area to be padded. Fold the scrim back and tuck handfuls of ginger fibre under and around the twine until you have a tightly packed layer of fibre about 65 mm ($2\frac{1}{2}$ in) thick along the length of the twine. Pull the scrim over this layer and temporarily tack it down in the middle of the other side, turning under another hem (**2**). If the fibre does not feel smooth and firm under the scrim, add some more and then put more temporary tacks along the arm to anchor the scrim (**3**), adding more fibre where necessary. If the fibre still feels lumpy, insert the point of a regulator needle into it and work it around until the surface is smooth.

Pull the scrim over the fibre at one end, turn under a hem and put in temporary tacks at each side of this end, trimming and folding the scrim neatly at the corners. Repeat at the other end.

Check your padding for symmetry, firmness and smoothness. If any adjustment is needed, remove some or all of the tacks and add, remove or rearrange the fibre as necessary. When you are satisfied with the look and feel of the padding, drive the tacks home. In order to make sure the pad keeps its shape, sew a row of top stitches round it as described in project 2, figures 24–26.

Press a thin layer of horsehair over the top of the hessian to fill in the bumps and hollows formed by the top stitches (**4**). Now cut a piece of sheet (skin) wadding the same size and shape as the top of your padding and lay it over the horsehair.

Cut a piece of Courtelle large enough to cover the padding and be attached to the arm rail below it (**5**). Anchor it with a temporary tack halfway along one side, then along the other side, then at each side of both ends and finally all along the sides. Adjust if necessary and drive the tacks home in the usual way.

**Figure 1**

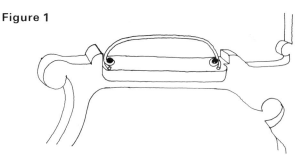

**Figure 2**

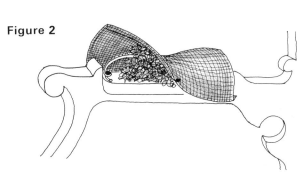

**Figure 3**

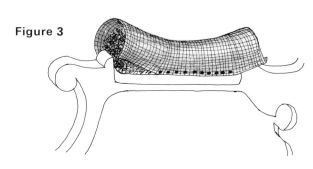

**Figure 4**

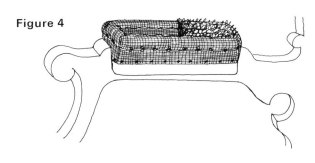

**Figure 5**

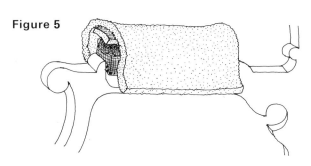

Cut a piece of covering fabric slightly larger than the Courtelle. Anchor it with temporary tacks to one side of the arm rail, pull it over the padding and put in more temporary tacks along the other side, as for the Courtelle.

At each end of the fabric, make a V-shaped cut from the middle to the outside edges of the arm rail where the padding begins, as shown (**6**). Fold the fabric neatly at the corners, trim it if necessary and tuck it down between the wood and the padding with the point of the regulator needle (**7**). Finish the corners according to the instructions for square corners in project 4 (figures 29 & 30). Check for neatness and drive all the temporary tacks home. Glue on a length of braid or gimp to hide them (**8**).

## Figures 9–11 Padding the back

Begin by laying the chair on its back so that you can work on a flat surface. Cut a piece of 340 g (12 oz) hessian slightly larger than the area to be padded. Tack it down along one side, beginning with one tack in the middle and spacing the tacks 50–75 mm (2–3 in) apart. Pull taut to the opposite side and anchor, then fill in this side with tacks. Repeat at top and bottom, and trim the hessian as closely as possible to the tacks.

Cut or tear a piece of linter felt the same size as the opening and lay it on top of the hessian; no anchoring is necessary (**9**). Cut a piece of skin wadding slightly larger than the area being padded and tack it down in the same way as you did the hessian. Trim close to the tacks (see figure 10). Cut, tack and trim a layer of Courtelle in the same way (**10**).

To attach the covering fabric, cut it slightly larger than the padded area, turn under a small hem and tack it down in the same way as all the layers of padding, but instead of tacking it permanently immediately, anchor it with temporary tacks so that you can adjust it if necessary. When you are satisfied with it, drive all the tacks home, then cover them with a glued-on length of braid or gimp (**11**).

Treat the outside back in the same way as the front, except that you do not need to add a layer of linter felt for softness.

**Figure 6**

**Figure 7**

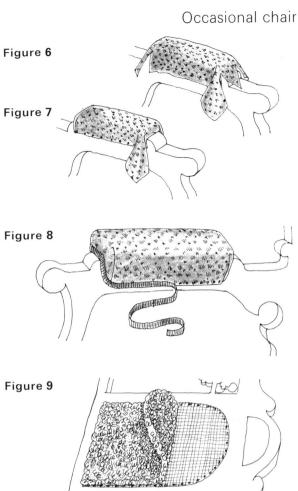

**Figure 8**

**Figure 9**

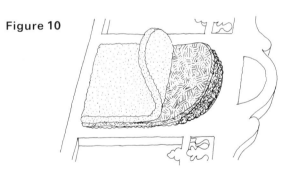

**Figure 10**

**Figure 11**

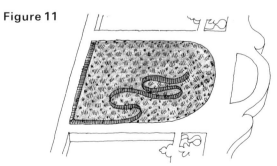

111

# Upholstery Project 5: Square Armchair

## Introduction

An upholstered armchair is much larger and more complicated than any of the upholstery described so far and you should have tackled at least one or two of these, including the sprung dining chair, before you proceed with this one. Allow yourself plenty of time and make sure you have a large, clear work area which can be left in disarray until the chair is finished.

Following the steps oulined in project 1, remove all the layers of old upholstery until you are left with the frame. As with the smaller projects, keep all the old layers so you can refer to their structure as you work, and use them to help you estimate the number of springs and the amount of padding and covering fabric you will need. Your chair may, of course, be larger or smaller than this one, so quantities and sizes may differ.

You will find a piece of cane (or occasionally metal) bent in a broad U shape supporting the structure of the seat at the front. If this is not broken, you can reuse it; otherwise you will have to make a new one from a piece of ordinary garden cane. To do this, measure the total length of the old cane and cut a new piece to this length. Bend it by carving a V-shaped nick halfway through the diameter at the appropriate points and pressing the two halves of each nick together to form a right angle.

You will notice that at each part of the chair (arms, seat and back) the final covering fabric is attached before you proceed to the next. This is because the rails to which you attach the cover become inaccessible when you put on the padding at the next stage. The arms are always done first.

Although it is fitted, the cover of this chair is constructed much like a loose cover, that is, in parts which are completed separately, then fixed in place.

## Tools

scissors
pencil
tape-measure
hammer
webbing stretcher
springing needle
pins
skewers
double bayonet needle
tailor's chalk
regulator needle
slipping needle

## Materials

black and white (first-quality) webbing: see project 1, figure 3 for measurements and add 500 mm (20 in)

20 mm ($\frac{5}{8}$) improved tacks, 13 mm ($\frac{1}{2}$) fine tacks

340 g (12 oz) hessian — enough to cover the arm frames, the seat over the springs (see figure 26) and the chair back (front and back)

linter felt — small pieces for front arm pads and filling in hollows, one large piece for covering the seat and front panel and one piece for covering the front panel

D7 polyether foam — two pieces the size of the tops of arms but 25 mm (1 in) longer

contact adhesive

twine (upholsterer's twine is always sold by the reel)

horsehair — use the old stuffing to gauge approximately how much you need

sheet (skin) wadding — enough to cover the inside and top arms, over the padding

60 g (2 oz) Courtelle — enough to cover the inside arms, the seat and front panel (see figure 46), and the back (front, back and top rail)

covering fabric — enough to go over all surfaces of the padded chair and attach to the frame, and to make the seat cushion

piping cord — enough to pipe the seams, as
shown in the diagram of the covered chair
overleaf

springs: we used twelve 225 mm (9 in) gauge 9
and five 130 mm (5 in) gauge 10 springs for
the seat, and six 150 mm (6 in) gauge 12
and three 125 mm (5 in) gauge 10 springs for
the back

galvanized staples

cane for the seat front — use the one you
removed with the old upholstery if you can
(see figure 25) or make a new one from a
length of garden cane (see introduction)

sticky tape

aid cord

ginger fibre for padding the back and round the
seat springs — use the old stuffing to estimate
quantities

25 mm (1 in) thick rubberized hair — a piece large
enough to go over the seat (see figure 37) and
a piece for the inside of the chair back (see
figure 59)

40 mm (1½ in) curtain heading tape the width of
the seat from arm to arm, plus 300 mm (12 in)

tack or tape roll long enough to go round the
sides and across the top of the chair back (see
figure 56)

cushion of Dacron-covered foam (see project 1,
figures 31 & 32) or feathers to fit the chair
seat

# Figures 1–19  The arms

Reupholstering this type of chair begins with the arms, because once the seat is in place, the bottom rails to which you anchor the arm padding and cover are virtually inaccessible.

The diagram on the right shows the names of each section. Repeat all the following instructions for the second arm.

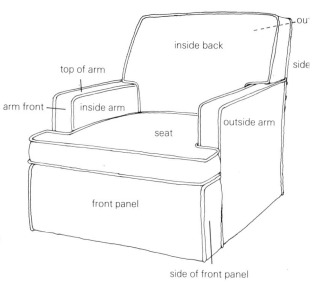

top of arm — inside back — ou

arm front — inside arm — side

outside arm

seat

front panel

side of front panel

### Figure 1  Attaching the webbing and hessian

Attach several strips of webbing to the arm frame on the inside, about three fixed vertically and two horizontally. Detailed instructions for attaching webbing are given in project 1, figures 3–8.

Cut a piece of 340 g (12 oz) hessian about 25 mm (1 in) larger all round than the arm frame. Temporarily tack it over the inside of the frame (**1**). Make sure the hessian is smooth and taut, then drive the tacks home. Now turn up a 13 mm ($\frac{1}{2}$ in) hem all round and tack it down, placing the tacks between those already in position under the hem.

**Figure 1**

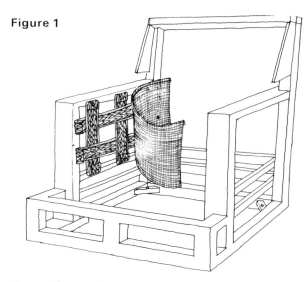

### Figures 2–8  Putting on the padding

In order to soften the front edge of each arm, roll up a little linter felt or Courtelle lengthways in a piece of webbing the same length as the arm is wide. Tack this, rolled edge forward, slightly over the front of the arm frame (**2** and **3**).

**Figure 2**

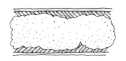

**Figure 3**

**Figure 4**

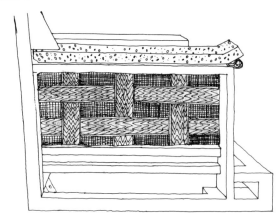

Cut a piece of 40 mm (1$\frac{1}{2}$ in) thick D7 polyether foam the same width as the top of the arm and 25 mm (1 in) longer. (Use a very sharp trimming or kitchen knife, or one with a serrated blade, or ask the foam retailer to cut it for you.) Glue this piece to the top of the arm by applying a layer of contact adhesive, then pressing the foam in place firmly, sliding it under the side pieces attached to the back frame, as shown (**4**). Fold the end of the foam down over the rolled edge at the front of the arm so that the top edge of the foam is butted against the front of the arm frame (**5**). Tack or staple in place, to form a smooth, curved edge.

**Figure 5**

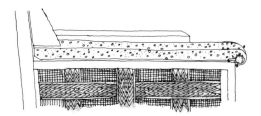

With a springing needle and twine, make bridle ties on the hessian on the inside of the arm in the pattern shown (figure 6). For full instructions, see project 1, figures 12–14. Take a handful of horsehair, tease it out with your fingers and insert it under and around the ties (**6**), blending the handfuls together and adding more until you have a firm, smooth, even layer of hair about 25 mm (1 in) thick. The horsehair should cover only the hollow area in the centre of the inside arm and not the frame itself.

Cut a piece of skin wadding about 25 mm (1 in) larger all round than the inside arm frame plus enough to go over the foam along the top of the arm. Staple or tack it to the frame all round (**7**), then trim it to the frame as closely as possible, fitting it round the back frame as shown in figure 7.

Cut a piece of 60 g (2 oz) Courtelle large enough to cover the inside arm and attach it to the outside frame as shown in figure 8. Staple or tack it in position in the usual way, cutting and/ or folding at the corners and trimming where necessary (**8**).

**Figure 6**

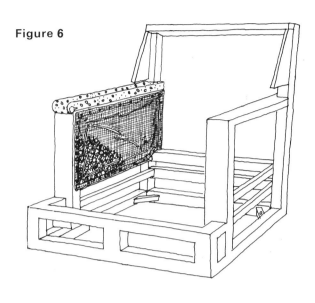

### Figures 9–17  Putting on the arm covers

Measure and cut a piece of your covering fabric 25 mm (1 in) wider than the width across the top and front of the arm, and about 150 mm (6 in) longer, centring the pattern if necessary. Now measure and cut a piece of covering fabric 75 mm (3 in) longer and wider than the outside of the arm frame, and another for the inside, taking these inside measurements from the top of the arm to the bottom of the topmost side rail, where you attached the hessian (see figure 9). Lay the appropriate piece of fabric in position along the top of the arm and down the front. Cut a small nick into both sides of this piece, at the point where the top of the arm becomes the front (**9**).

**Figure 7**

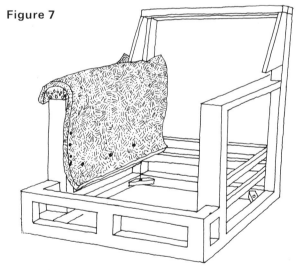

Figure 8

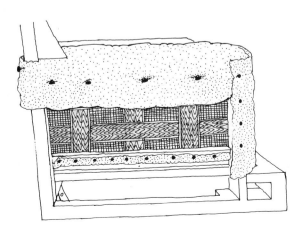

Figure 9

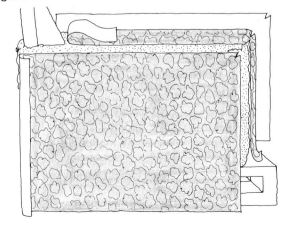

Cut diagonal strips of fabric, join them together and wrap them round a length of piping cord. The amount you need depends on the measurements of the seams to be piped. Pin and baste the fabric as close to the cord as possible, then machine-stitch along the edge of the cord, starting 50 mm (2 in) from the end.

Right sides together, pin a strip of piping to each side of the central arm strip, then sew the inside and outside pieces to this strip, folding the strip at the nicks so that they fall at the front corners of the side pieces (**10**).

Turn the arm cover right side out and place it in position, anchoring it with one temporary tack at the back of the top arm strip. Pull it taut towards the front and temporarily tack it to the bottom of the front arm panel at each side (**11**).

Pull the inner arm fabric towards the back and anchor it at the back with another temporary tack. Repeat for the outside arm.

Make a cut just inside and parallel to the piping, from the top of the back towards the front until you reach the frontmost edge of the back rail, as shown in figure 12. Remove the inside temporary tack (**12**).

At the other side of the back rail, make a second parallel cut in the fabric, again as far as the front edge of the back rail. Pull the fabric firmly to the back round the rail and temporarily tack it (**13**).

**Figure 10**

**Figure 11**

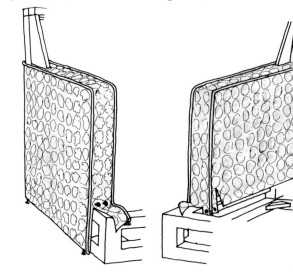

**Figure 12**          **Figure 13**

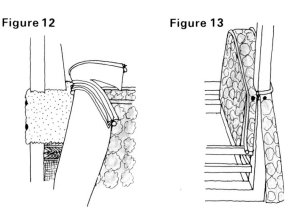

At the bottom of the front of the arm, make a cut inside and parallel to the piping up to the point where the front arm forms a right angle with the top of the front panel. Remove the temporary tack from here. Pull the fabric firmly down at the front of the outside arm cover and temporarily tack it under the bottom rail (**14**).

Make another cut inside the piping at the other side of the front of the arm, remove the other temporary tack, pull the fabric down and anchor with another temporary tack to the inside of the arm at the bottom (see figure 15).

**Figure 14**          **Figure 15**

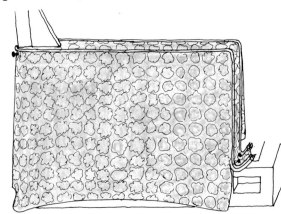

From the bottom inside front of the arm, make a diagonal cut up to the bottom inside corner of the side rail. Anchor with a temporary tack as shown (**15**). Remove the temporary tack at the outside back and pull the inside fabric under the rail and through to the outside (**16**).

Lift up the outside arm cover and fasten it out of the way. Temporarily tack down the inside arm cover you have pulled through to the outside face of the rail (**17**).

Remove the temporary tack holding the inside arm cover to the back of the arm rail. Smooth the cover down and towards the back until it feels smooth and taut, and put another temporary tack inside the back rail to hold it in place. Trim and tack the fabric neatly round the lower back rail. There is no more to be done to the arm covers until the chair has reached a further stage.

**Figure 16**

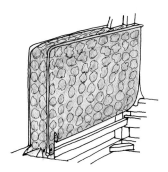

**Figure 17**

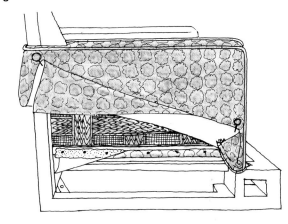

## Figures 18-54 The seat

These instructions refer to a seat with a cushion which rests on top of the springs and padding.

### Figure 18 Attaching the webbing

Tack strips of webbing to the underside of the frame as described in project 1, figures 3–8. The strips should be no more than their own width apart and attached in a woven pattern (**18**).

**Figure 18**

### Figures 19 & 20 Attaching and lashing the main seat springs

For an average-size chair, you will need twelve 250 mm (9 in) gauge 9 springs spaced in three rows of four across the seat, with a gap between the front edge and the first row of springs as shown in figure 18. Lay them on the webbing, making sure that all the knots in the tops of the springs are facing away from the frame to prevent them wearing through the hessian which will be stretched over them. Attach each spring to the webbing in three places in the same way as explained in project 3, figures 2–5 (and shown in figure 18). Begin with the middle row, then do the front row, then the back row.

To lash the springs to the frame, first drive in temporary tacks along the bottom back rail, aligning each with the centre of each row of springs. Cut four pieces of laid cord twice as long as the frame is deep. Leaving a loose end of at least 30 cm (12 in), knot each length of cord around one of the tacks, then drive it home.

Now lash the springs to the frame in much the same way as described in project 3, figures 6–12; only the position of the knots varies slightly. The first knot is made at the waist of the first spring in each row. The second is made at the top of the same spring, in a straight line toward the front. The second spring is lashed twice at the top only, continuing the straight line, and the front spring is lashed first at the top, then at the waist. Drive in a row of similarly positioned tacks along the bottom front rail, then anchor the pieces of cord to them in the same way (**19**).

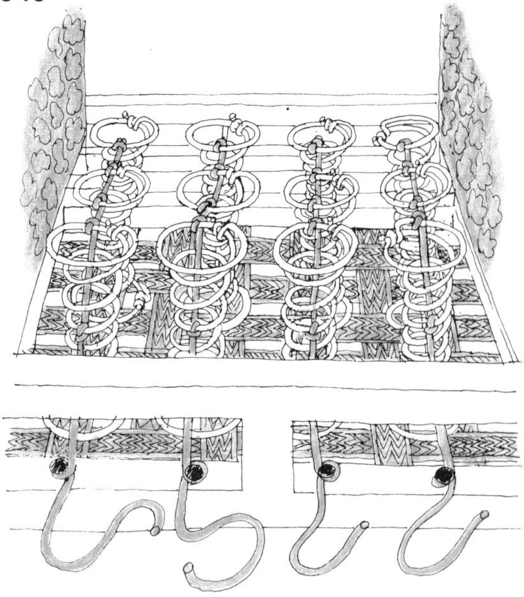

Now use the lengths of cord left over at both ends to knot round the top of the springs at the front and back respectively, near the frame. Pull on this cord so the back springs lean very slightly towards the back rail and the front ones towards the front (**20**). Repeat this lashing from side to side so that the side rows of springs lean toward the nearest rails and the four corner springs lean slightly toward their corners.

### Figures 21–25 The front rail springs

You will need some 130 mm (5 in) gauge 10 springs to go on the top of the front rail. Making sure the knots are in the correct position as shown in figure 21, space these springs evenly along the rail, against the front edge, and anchor each one with two or three galvanized staples round the bottom coil (see figure 21). If you are using an electric staple gun, two staples on each spring will hold them.

Cut a strip of webbing about 104 mm (4 in) longer than the front rail and lay it on the rail over the bottom coils of the springs. Tack or staple it in position round the inside and outside of each spring and at the two ends of the rail (**21**).

To lash these springs, cut a piece of laid cord one and a half times the length of the front rail. Drive a temporary tack into the top of the rail at one end, knot the cord around it tightly and drive the tack home. Drive in one temporary tack between each spring but towards the front edge of the rail, and one at the other end of the rail. Make a knot around the waist of the first spring, then pull the cord so the spring leans forward. Knot the cord around the next temporary tack and drive it home. Continue in this way until all the springs have been lashed and are leaning toward the front (**22**). It is very important that the springs remain level with one another, so when you have lashed each one, push it back to an upright position and check that it is the same height as its neighbours. Knot the cord around the last tack, drive it home, then trim the cord.

**Figure 19**

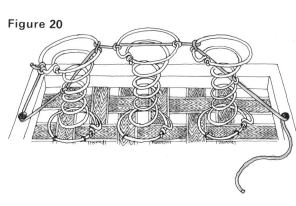

**Figure 20**

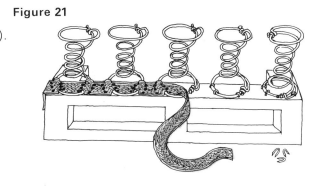

**Figure 21**

**Figure 22**

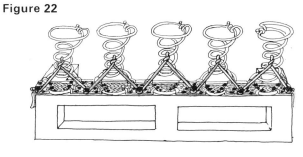

**Figure 23**

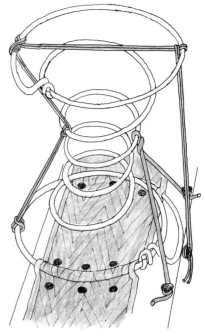

Cut a piece of twine about 1.25 m (4 ft) long and double it. You will need as many of these double lengths as there are front springs (five for this chair). Put a temporary tack into the front of the rail at the centre of each spring. At each spring, loop the twine round the bottom of the spring at the back, then round the waist of the spring as shown in figure 23. Take the twine to the top coil and loop round the back and front of the spring. This process involves three kinds of loops so study the diagram carefully. Making sure your spring is standing straight up and level with its neighbours, pull the twine down to the front of the rail, loop it around the temporary tack, and drive the tack home (**23**). Lash all the springs in this way and trim the twine.

Cut a single piece of twine twice the length of the front rail. Drive a temporary tack into one end of the front rail as shown in figure 24. Lash the first spring at the waist and top, then at the existing lashing, then at the other side. Continue along the row, lashing at the tops of the springs and at the cord in the middle of each, and anchoring at the other side in the usual way (**24**).

**Figure 24**

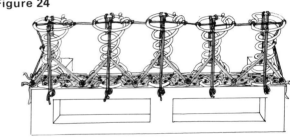

Take the piece of cane (or metal) which you removed from the top of the springs when you stripped off the old upholstery. Put it back in position and tape it temporarily to the springs, as shown in figure 25. To lash the cane, cut eleven pieces of twine each about 1.25 m (4 ft) long. Double one of these lengths and lash the cane to one spring with a loop like a blanket stitch, but made without a needle. Continue making these on the same spring until your twine is used up and there is a 26 mm (1 in) area of lashing.

**Figure 25**

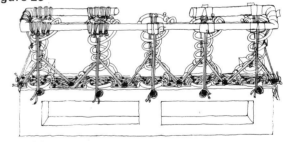

*detail of the blanket-stitch lashing shown in figure 25*

Knot the twine to finish. Lash all the springs to the cane in this way, then lash again at each end of the cane rail, at the back of the end springs and at the ends of the cane, as shown (**25**).

**Figure 26**

## Figures 26–34 Attaching the hessian

Measure and cut a piece of hessian large enough to go from the back of the seat, over the springs (and down between the main springs and the front springs) to under the bottom front rail, and from under one side rail, over the springs and under the opposite side rail, allowing for a 25 mm (1 in) hem all around. Turn under a hem and temporarily tack the hessian along the top of the bottom back rail (**26**); tacks can be 75–100 mm (3–4 in) apart.

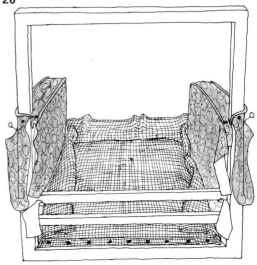

# Upholstery Project 5

Pull the hessian forward and tuck it down to make a gully between the main sprung section and the front row of springs. To anchor this in position, cut a small hole in the hessian at each inside front corner of the bottom front rail (at the bottom of the gully), and put in a temporary tack at each side of the bottom rail at the nearest point. Now cut a piece of laid cord slightly longer than the front rail and knot it around one temporary tack. Drive the tack home, pass the cord through the first hole, across the tucked-in section of the hessian as in the cross-section (**27**), through the other hole, knot it round the other temporary tack, and drive the tack home.

Cut into the hessian at the front corners and tuck the excess down the sides between the springs and the side rails.

Fold back the hessian at the front over the seat as shown in the cross-section (**28**). Cut a second piece of laid cord double the length of the front rail and thread it on to a springing needle. Put in temporary tacks across the top of the bottom front rail, about 100 mm (4 in) apart (see figure 29). Knot one end of the cord round one of the tacks and drive it home. With your needle, stitch the hessian, catching the strip of laid cord previously attached, anchoring each stitch to one of the tacks just inserted (**29**) and driving it home. Finish off with an anchoring tack.

Fold the hessian back over the front springs so that it hangs over the front rail and between the front springs and the front of the arms (**30**). Pull the hessian down gently to the centre of the bottom front rail and put in a temporary tack. Add more temporary tacks all along this front rail about 75 mm (3 in) apart, making sure that the hessian is smooth and straight. If necessary, trim the hessian at the front to about 50 mm (2 in) from the tacks.

Pull the hessian down over the sides of the bottom front rail, folding it neatly over the corners, and anchor with temporary tacks, two at the bottom and one halfway up (**31**). Trim the hessian close to these tacks.

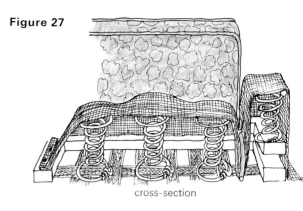

**Figure 27**

cross-section

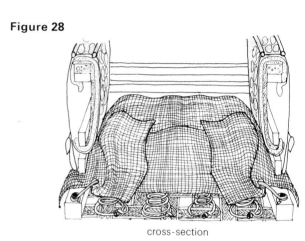

**Figure 28**

cross-section

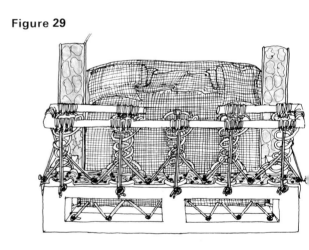

**Figure 29**

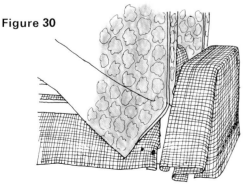

**Figure 30**

**Figure 31**

Thread your springing needle with twine and use a large blanket stitch to sew down the front edges as far as the upper rail, making them neat as shown in figure 32. Still with a springing needle and twine, anchor the hessian to the cane and front springs with a continuous line of blanket stitches round the cane (**32** and **33**).

**Figure 32**

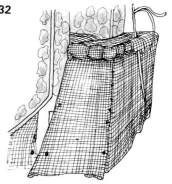

Pull the hessian down between the main seat springs and the side rails. Anchor with a line of temporary tacks, cutting and folding the hessian at the back corners for neatness. With a springing needle and twine, stitch the main seat springs to the hessian as described in project 3, figure 18. Now stitch the front springs to the hessian in the same way, in the pattern shown (figure 34). To stop the edge springs separating from the main ones when the chair is sat on, cut a piece of laid cord about 1.25 m (4 ft) long, thread it on to a springing needle and sew each front main spring to its nearest edge spring, pulling them together (**34**). Finish with a simple knot.

**Figure 33**

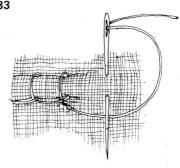

**Figure 34**

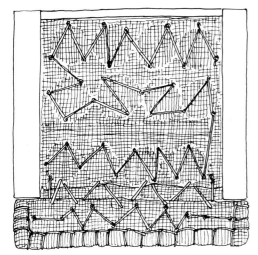

### Figures 35-39  Putting on the padding

Take handfuls of ginger fibre and stuff them down between the edge springs and the main springs until the fibre feels firm and fits nicely under the stitches you have just made (**35**).

Remove the temporary tacks along the bottom back rail of the chair, pull the hessian taut and drive in permanent tacks more closely spaced; say 25 mm (1 in) apart. Do the same along the side rails and trim the hessian (figure 36). Tack around the back corners neatly. Remove the temporary tacks along the bottom front rail, pull the hessian taut, and add more tacks. Remove the temporary tacks from the folded hessian at the sides of the front rail, pull it taut and tack it down to the upper rails as shown (**36**). Trim.

**Figure 35**

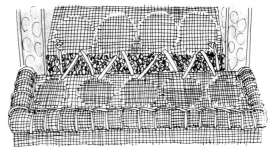

**Figure 36**

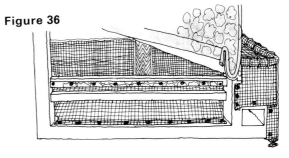

With large, sharp scissors, cut a piece of 25 mm (1 in) thick rubberized hair wide enough to go over the springs and reach the bottom rails on each side, and long enough to reach from the top of the bottom back rail to about 75 mm (3 in) beyond the front edge of the chair. Place it in position and make straight cuts into the corners so that you can tuck the side and back edges into place on their respective rails (**37**). The hair should not be tucked directly on top of the hessian, but over the rail above the bottom one. If there are any hollow places between the main springs and the front edge ones, lift up the rubberized hair and tuck in a little more fibre.

Fold under the front edge of the hair so it is flush with the front edge of the springs, and anchor it temporarily with upholstery skewers (or sharp kitchen ones) (**38**). Trim the corners so they fold under neatly then fold under the side edges, anchoring with skewers. Tuck the excess hair down between the edge springs and the front of the arms. Cut a piece of laid cord one and a half times the length of the front rail, then drive in a temporary tack on the bottom side rail as shown in figure 38. Anchor the cord to the tack, pull it taut so that it goes under the arm and across the seat to the other arm, then anchor it at the other side in the same way (see figure 38).

Cut a piece of twine about 3 m (10 ft) long and thread a double bayonet needle. Sew a row of top stitches around the front edge of the seat as shown (**39**), through the hessian (below the cane) and the rubberized hair. Instructions for this stitch are in project 2, figures 25–28. Remove the skewers as you go.

In order to build up the sides of the main sprung area so they are tight against the arms, stuff some ginger fibre up between the rubberized hair and the hessian. You should not now be able to get your hand down the side of the seat. Do the same at the back so that the hair is right against the rail.

Anchor the rubberized hair to the top of the bottom side rails with temporary tacks which need be only about 150 mm (6 in) apart.

To anchor the hair to the hessian and springs, thread a double bayonet needle with twine, push the needle into the hair about 100 mm (4 in) from one corner, pull it almost all the way out at the bottom, re-angle it slightly and push it out at the top, catching the hessian and springs inside. Make three stitches like this along each side until you are back where you started, then move into the centre and make a stitch there (see figure 39 for pattern of stitches).

**Figure 37**

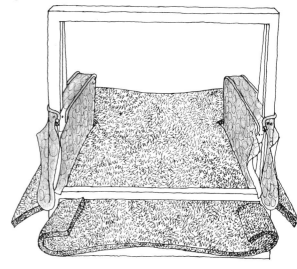

**Figure 38**

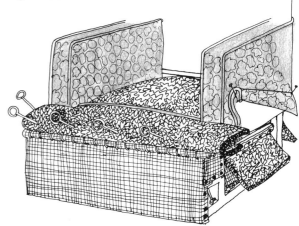

**Figure 39**

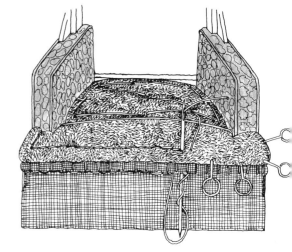

## Figures 40-54 Putting on the seat cover

Cut a piece of covering fabric to cover the seat from below the front bottom rail to the first rail from the bottom at the back, and from one bottom side rail to the other. Lay this fabric in place and temporarily tack it to both ends of the bottom front rail. Trim the fabric to about 13 mm ($\frac{1}{2}$ in) from the tacks along the bottom, and also up the side and top edges of the seat front until you reach the inside of the arms. Make a small nick at each side to indicate where the front edge of the seat comes (see figure 40). Now make two cuts at the inside front corners (**40**) and tuck the fabric in neatly round the corners of the arms and down to anchor it temporarily.

Cut out two pieces of fabric about 300 mm (12 in) wider than the sides of the front edge panel and about 150 mm (6 in) deeper (**41**).

Attach a length of piping to both sides of the front panel section up to where it comes in front of the arms (**42**). Sew the side panels to the front of the main seat section (**43**), then along the top, forming a box shape and leaving the excess width at the back of this panel to tuck in.

Put the covering fabric in place on the seat and mark a line across the underside of the material with chalk about 175 mm (7 in) in from the front edge, from the front of one arm to the front of the other. Sew a length of 40 mm ($1\frac{1}{2}$ in) curtain heading tape to the underside of the fabric along this line, leaving about 150 mm (6 in) free at both ends (**44**).

**Figure 40**

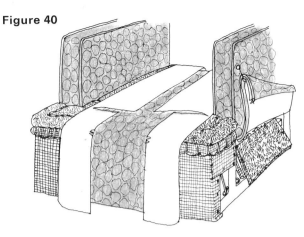

**Figure 41**

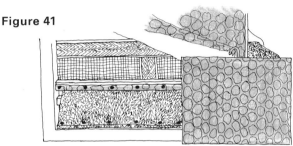

**Figure 42**

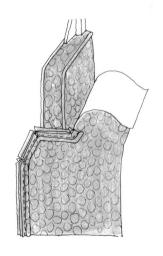

**Figure 43**

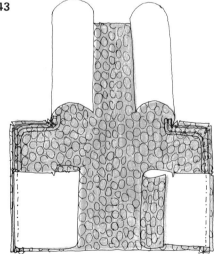

**Figure 44**

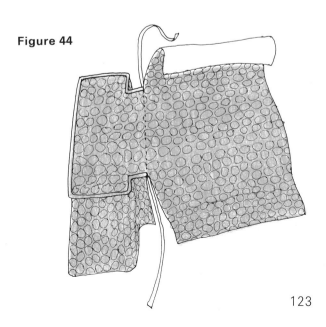

Put the cover back on the seat neatly and pull it into place. Take the ends of the tape, push them down over the hair and pull them through under the arms to the outside. Pull on these tapes gently so the cover fits smoothly over the top of the seat, then anchor the ends of the tape to the bottom rail with tacks in the usual way. Anchor the cover to the seat along the tape line with long pins and fold the seat cover back from the front so the edge of the tape is exposed (see figure 45).

Thread a double bayonet needle with a piece of twine two and a half times as long as the width of the seat at the front, and knot one end. Now sew the seat cover to the seat itself by means of long running stitches along the tape: beginning at one side of the seat, put your needle down into the tape, through the seat, until the point comes out underneath. Then angle the needle towards the centre of the chair and push it out 40 mm (1½ in) from the point where you went in. Continue making these stitches along the tape, pull them taut, and knot to finish (**45**).

**Figure 45**

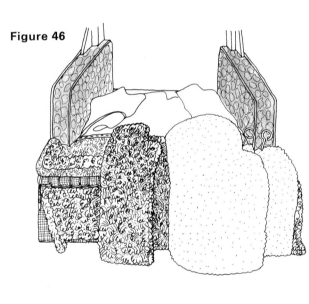

Tear off small pieces of linter felt and place them on top of the rubberized hair along the front edge, to fill in the hollow formed by the top stitches, as shown in figure 46. Now cut a piece of linter felt large enough to cover this front panel and go just over the front edge. Cut another piece of linter felt wide enough to cover the front edge panel from side to side and long enough to reach from the tape line, over the edge, to the bottom of the chair (see figure 46). Press this in place; it is not necessary to fasten it down.

**Figure 46**

Cut a piece of Courtelle about 150 mm (6 in) larger all round than the second piece of linter felt. Lay it over the felt and anchor it in place along the tape line with skewers, as shown (**46**). Pull the Courtelle down at the front and tack or staple it along the bottom front edge of the chair. Trim as closely as possible.

At the sides of the front edge panel, pad the gaps with pieces of linter felt, then lay over one large piece as you did at the top (**47**). Pull the Courtelle down from the top, beyond the felt slightly, then cut it diagonally, trim and fold over from the front (**48**). Tack the Courtelle into place and trim (**49**).

**Figure 47**

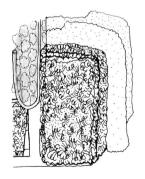

**Figure 48**

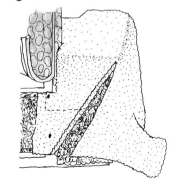

**Figure 49**

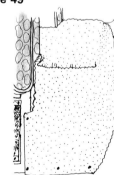

Pull the covering fabric into position over the Courtelle and check for fit.

Lift up one inside corner, near the front of the arms, make a diagonal cut into it from the raw edge, and extend it bit by bit so you can pull the front sides of the cover neatly down between the front edge panel and the front of the arm. Repeat on the other side (**50**).

Pull the finished cover down into place at the front and temporarily tack it under the centre of the front rail. Put in more temporary tacks along this rail (see figure 51).

Fold the rear half of the seat cover to the front at the tape line (see figure 51). Cut a piece of linter felt large enough to cover the top of the seat from tape to back, and be tucked in slightly all around. Lay this on the seat, then cut a piece of Courtelle the same size and lay it on the top (**51**).

Fold the seat cover back over these layers and tuck it down at the sides and back so you can pull it through the rails from the outside, cutting and folding at the corners where necessary. Tack this fabric down with a few temporary tacks along the bottom rail at the sides and back (**52**).

Check that the front of the chair is now the same height on both sides. If one side is slightly higher, adjust it by removing the temporary tacks under the side panel pieces, pulling the cover down firmly to compress the filling, and re-tacking it.

Make a slightly angled cut into the fabric from below, from the back edge of the side front panel to the point where the two rails meet (**53**). It is better to make your cut slightly too short and extend it with tiny cuts around the area until you can push the cover down neatly between the front section and the arm. The blunt end of a regulator needle will help you with this tricky process.

The bottom section of fabric can be simply pulled toward the back and stapled or tacked. Release the fabric covering the outside arm so its piping falls down over the side panels you have just been working on. Slip-stitch the two covering sections together (**54**), or use a thin line of suitable adhesive.

If you are satisfied with the front section of your chair, drive home the tacks underneath the bottom rail.

**Figure 50**

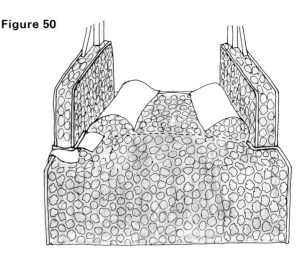

**Figure 51**

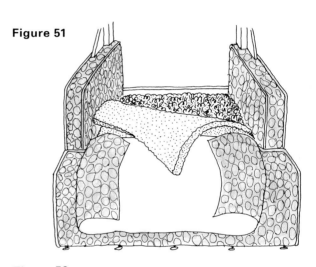

**Figure 52**

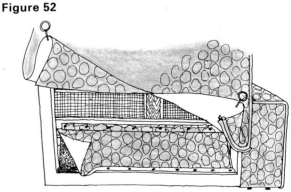

**Figure 53**          **Figure 54**

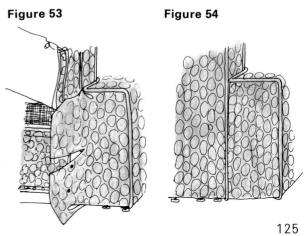

125

## Figures 55–72  The back

### Figure 55  Attaching the webbing

Attach three rows of webbing horizontally and three vertically to the back of the frame, arranged in a woven pattern as usual. Leave the tacks as temporary ones, however, since you may have to remove them later to fix the back and seat fabric. These strips of webbing should be at right angles to each other and in straight rows, even if the back frame is wider at the top. Tack the vertical rows of webbing to the top face of the top rail.

### Figures 55 & 56  Attaching and lashing the springs

You will need six springs of one size and three of a slightly smaller size. The larger ones should be placed in two rows of three at the top and centre of the back and the smaller springs in a single row at the bottom, since more pressure will be exerted at the top. The larger of these sizes should project slightly beyond the frame of your chair; the smaller should be about level with it. For this chair, we used six 156 mm (6 in) gauge 12 springs and three 130 mm (5 in) gauge 10 ones. Tip the chair so it is lying flat on its back with the top rail nearest you. Position the springs with all the knots possible at the one o'clock position, as explained for the seat springing.

With a springing needle and twine, attach these springs to the webbing as for the seat (**55**).

Cut a 2 m (6 ft 6 in) length of twine and double it; treat this as if it were one piece of twine. Put in three temporary tacks across the top and bottom rails, aligning with the centre of each spring. Starting with the central spring farthest away from you, loop the twine first around the waist of the spring, then pull the twine to the tack, bending the spring slightly toward the bottom rail. Loop the twine around the tack and drive it home. Now loop the twine around the top of the spring at the back, go straight across to the front and loop, then make two loops at the back and front of the middle spring, and two at the top of the spring nearest to you, back and front again. Now pull the spring sharply forward, more than you did at the bottom, loop the twine around the tack and drive it home. Repeat this for the rows of springs on each side of this one as shown in figure 56, and then for the top two horizontal rows, putting in only two tacks on each side rail. The top two rows should be lashed from the top of the side rails rather than from the waist of the edge springs. It is not necessary to lash the bottom row horizontally.

**Figure 55**

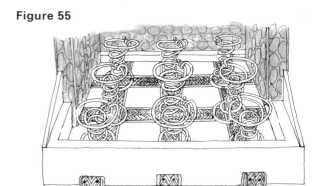

**Figure 56**

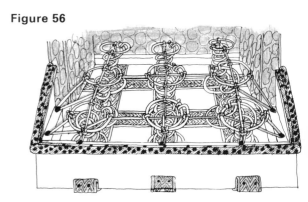

Cut three lengths of tack or tape roll long enough to go across the back and up the two sides of the back rail. Tack or staple this around the inside of the rail, mitring the corners (**56**).

## Figure 57 Attaching the hessian

Cut a piece of hessian 150 mm (6 in) larger all around than the T-shape of the chair back. Tack this to the frame over the springs in the usual way. At the bottom of the back, pull the hessian down behind the seat to reach the rail, and tack. Tuck it in between the sides and the arms where there is no rail, cutting into the corners where necessary, and tack in position along the top and side rails, turning under a small hem. With a springing needle and twine, anchor the springs to the hessian in the usual way (**57**).

## Figures 58-63 Putting on the padding

Again in the usual way, make bridle ties around and across the back in the pattern shown in figure 58. Stuff ginger fibre under and around the bridle ties, blending one handful with the next and adding more until it feels thick and firm (**58**). Tuck some more fibre down the sides by the arms to fill any gaps.

Cut a piece of rubberized hair 50 mm (2 in) larger all around than the shape of the chair back, including the arms (**59**). Place it in position and make straight cuts into the corners at the top of the arms so you can tuck the hair down between the back and the arms. Tack or staple it down around the top, inside the tack roll, and trim (**60**).

Tear off some pieces of linter felt and stuff them round the edge of the back to fill in the hollows where the tack roll meets the rubberized hair. Anchor the rubberized hair through the hessian and springs as you did with the seat, then cover the stitches with more linter felt (**61**).

**Figure 57**

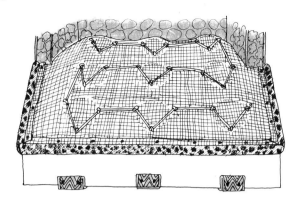

**Figure 58**

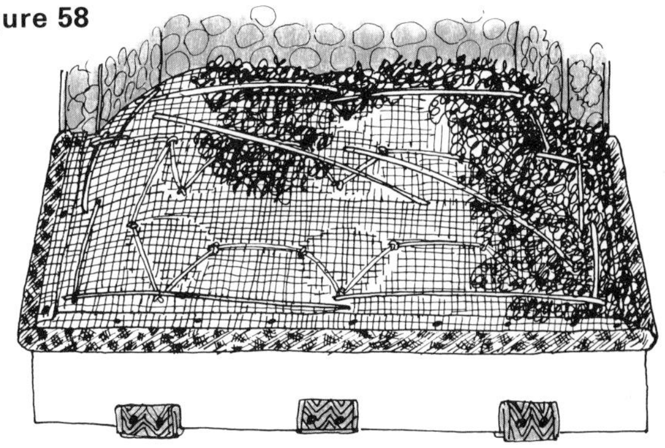

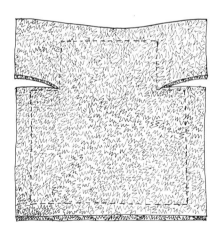

**Figure 59**

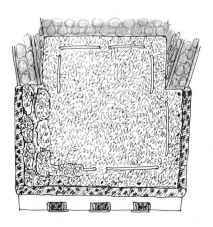

**Figure 60**

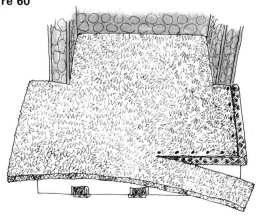

**Figure 61**

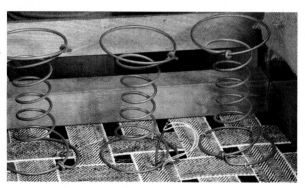

*Attaching springs to webbing with twine.*

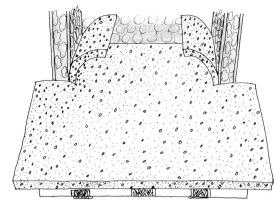

**Figure 62**

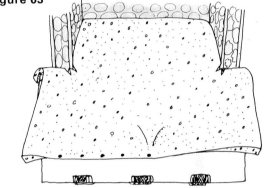

**Figure 63**

Cut a piece of 40 mm (1½ in) Supersoft foam 75 mm (3 in) larger all around than the back and arms. Making cuts and nicks where necessary at the tops of the arms (**62**), tuck this down between the back and sides of the chair, over the rubberized hair. Pull the foam down over the top and sides of the back and anchor it with tacks to the top and side rails (**63**). Trim the foam with a sharp knife.

Cut a piece of Courtelle 150 mm (6 in) larger all around than your T-shape. Tuck it in around the bottom and the arms, tack it to the frame and sides in the usual way and trim.

### Figures 64–70 Putting on the back cover

Cut a piece of covering fabric in a rectangle 100 mm (4 in) larger all round than the back, including the arms. Lay it in position and anchor it with skewers. Make horizontal cuts in from the sides at the top of the arms so the fabric fits around the top of the arms. Leaving a 13 mm (½ in) seam allowance, cut around the arms to make the fabric a T-shape, but try to leave a narrow piece at the bottom corners (as shown in figure 64) to use as a pull. Cut round the top and sides of the chair, again leaving a 13 mm (½ in) seam allowance. Sew piping round the top and sides of this piece, then sew a 150 mm (6 in) wide piece of any fabric or lining to the bottom for tucking in (**64**).

**Figure 64**

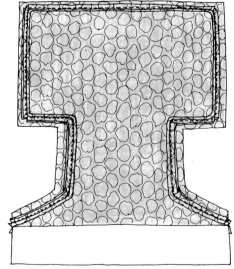

**Figure 65**

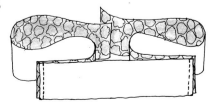

Cut three strips of fabric, each 13 mm ($\frac{1}{2}$ in) larger all around than the top and side borders of the chair back, all the way down to the seat at the sides for tucking in. Sew these together at what will be the top corners (**65**) and then sew this long border strip to the inside back cover along the piping edge. (If you wish, you can divide this border into two strips separated by piping to give the impression of a loose cushion, as shown in the picture on page 113).

Put the cover in place on the chair, anchor it to the back of the frame with temporary tacks, and pull the excess fabric through to the back of the chair at the bottom (**66**).

At each corner, where the back meets the arms, pull the fabric out and make a cut to about 26 mm (1 in) away from the piping so the fabric can be spread out and tucked in neatly.

Pull the fabric down and make more cuts into it as shown so that it can be pulled down through the rails without puckering and tacked there (**67**).

Remove the temporary tacks from the top of the chair. Cut a piece of Courtelle large enough to cover the top rail without going over the edges, and push this into place along the rails, under the cover, paying particular attention to the corners. Temporarily tack the fabric down again, along the back of the top rail, as before (**68**).

**Figure 66**

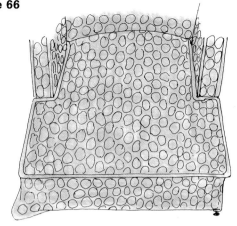

**Figure 67**

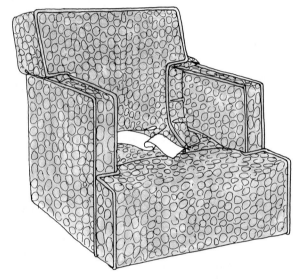

**Figure 68**

Pull the cover over the two sides of the chair back, above the arms, and anchor it to the back of the side rails with temporary tacks (**69**).

Make a cut into the fabric near the piping at the point where the side of the back meets the outside arm as shown. Pull the resulting flap of fabric through between the back and the arm to the back and anchor it with temporary tacks. Fold the remaining piece of fabric under, against the piping and temporarily tack it to the back of the rail (**70**). It may be necessary to undo the temporary tacks holding the back webbing in place in order to reach in and pull this fabric through. Repeat on the other arm.

**Figure 69**          **Figure 70**

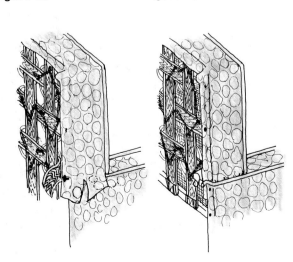

129

Examine the top rail to make sure the cover is absolutely smooth and straight. If necessary, remove the temporary tacks and adjust the cover until you are satisfied with it. Drive the tacks home. Do the same along both sides of the back to the arms, trimming and folding neatly at the top two corners (see figure 71).

### Figures 71–75 Finishing off

Check the temporary tacks holding the seat cover in place at the back, to see if the cover is straight. If it is not, adjust and trim any excess rubberized hair underneath before you tack or staple along the top face of the rail.

Do the same thing at each side, putting in tacks along the top face of the bottom rail. Trim and fold the fabric neatly at the corners.

You will have a lot of excess padding and fabric coming through to the back of the chair. Trim and tack it down where possible to make the back of your chair neat. Retack your webbing with permanent tacks.

Pull the outside arm covers down at each side so the fabric is straight, taut and smooth, making sure the piping along the arms falls in the right place. Temporarily tack it under the bottom side rails. Now pull this fabric toward the back of the chair, again so it is smooth, taut and straight, and temporarily tack it at the back faces of the vertical back rails. If you are satisfied with the look of the cover, drive the tacks home and trim the fabric (**71**).

Cut a piece of covering fabric 13 mm ($\frac{1}{2}$ in) larger all around than the back of the chair. Make a length of piping long enough to go along the top of it and down both sides, to the bottom of the chair. Place this fabric in position, fold under the top edge and pin it in place along the top of the chair, with the piping strip between this fabric and that which has already been attached, as shown (**72**). Slip-stitch in place along the top. Fold the cover out of the way over the front of the chair and tack the piping into place down the sides of the chair (**73**).

Cut a piece of hessian slightly larger than the back of the chair. Turn under a small hem and tack it permanently across the outside face of the top rail. Pull this hessian down so it is taut and firm over the back and tack it along the outside face of the bottom rail, then tack the sides, again making a hem. Trim all around (see figure 74).

**Figure 71**

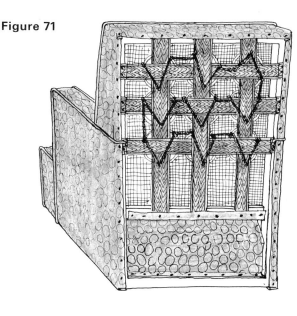

**Figure 72**

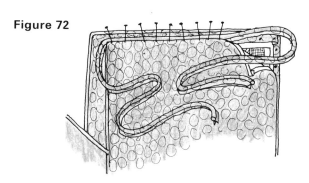

**Figure 73**

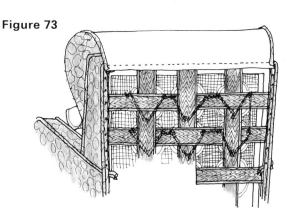

Cut a piece of Courtelle the same size as the back of your chair but long enough to fold under at the top and anchor it in position (**74**). Fold the covering fabric back into position, pull it straight and taut and temporarily tack it in place underneath the bottom rail. Trimming and folding neatly at the corners, turn the fabric under at the edges and slip-stitch it through the piping to the outside arm fabric with a slipping needle (**75**).

Turn the chair upside down, drive the tacks home underneath the back rail and trim the fabric. Cut a piece of black linen or hessian slightly larger than the base of the frame, turn under a small hem and tack it into place to cover your work.

## Making the cushion cover

If the existing cushion is reusable, make a new cover for it by taking the old cover apart carefully and using it as a pattern to cut your covering fabric.

If the cushion itself is too damaged to use, you will have to provide a new one, which should be made either of feathers or of best-quality rubber foam wrapped with Dacron. Cut a template the same size and shape as the chair seat.

If you are having a feather cushion made, mark on the template that this is the size you want the finished stuffed cushion to be and the pad will be made slightly larger so that it will look plump and firm inside the cover.

If you are using foam, have a specialized dealer cut it for you and explain to him that you want your pad to be the same size as the template so the cover will fit tightly.

When your pad arrives, use the same template to cut two pieces of fabric for the top and bottom of your cover, leaving a 13 mm ($\frac{1}{2}$ in) seam allowance all round. To make the border, measure the perimeter of the template, add 25 mm (1 in) for two seam allowances, and cut a strip of fabric this length and the height of the seat cushion (plus seam allowances). Sew a strip of piping to each long edge of the border, then sew the top and bottom sections to the border, right sides together and stitching over the piping stitches (see figure 10), leaving a gap along one back edge to insert the cushion pad. Finish by oversewing this open edge (or insert a zip).

**Figure 74**

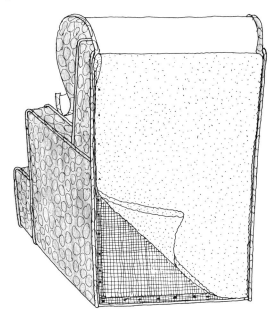

**Figure 75**

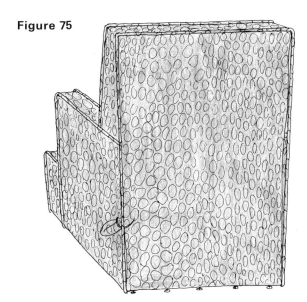

# Upholstery Project 6: Buttoned Wing-chair

## Introduction

There are many similarities between this project and the previous one so, before you begin, turn back and read the instructions for the square armchair. This armchair, however, differs from the other one, not only in the shape of the arms and back but also because it has no cushion on the seat, which must be built up with thicker padding. As with all the projects, you should begin this one by carefully stripping off the old upholstery and keeping it so that you can refer to it as you work. This process is particularly vital with buttoned furniture, since you will need the old back cover to give you the positions of the buttons on the new one. (Working out this positioning from scratch is not a job for the amateur; it is fairly tricky and really requires the skill of a master upholsterer.)

Because this chair is generally rounded, with few flat surfaces, the cover is applied in a different way from that in project 5 in that it is moulded round the curves and tacked directly on to the frame, rather than assembled in sections and then fitted over the padding. Because of this, a new technique called back-tacking is introduced which makes it possible to attach the final cover to awkward places so that no tacks are visible.

## Tools

scissors
pencil or tailor's chalk
tape-measure
hammer
webbing stretcher
springing needle
regulator needle
double bayonet needle 450 mm (18 in) long
paper (for template)
pins, skewers
small slipping needle

## Materials

black and white (first-quality) webbing: see project 2, figure 3 for measurements and add 500 mm (20 in)

20 mm ($\frac{5}{8}$ in) improved tacks

13 mm ($\frac{1}{2}$ in) fine tacks

340 g (12 oz) hessian — 12 pieces slightly larger than the arms (see figures 2–6), the seat, the wings, the back (front and back) and front panel

twine (upholsterer's twine is always sold by the reel)

ginger fibre for padding the arms, the wing rails, and round the seat springs — use the old stuffing to estimate quantities

horsehair — gauge approximately how much you need from the old stuffing

sheet (skin) wadding to cover the padded arms, wings, seat and back

60 g (2 oz) Courtelle — enough to cover the arms, back (front and back) and side sections, and front panel (optional)

piping cord — enough to go round the fronts of the scroll arms and along the front of the seat.

scrim — two pieces large enough to go over the wing rails (see figure 18), and two pieces about 150 mm (6 in) larger all round than the chair seat and chair back

covering fabric — enough to go over all surfaces of the padded chair and attach to the frame

springs — we used nine 350 mm (14 in) gauge 9 and four 175 mm (7 in) gauge 10 springs for the seat, and nine 125 mm (5 in) gauge 12 springs for the back

galvanized staples

laid cord

cane for the seat front: you will probably be able to use the piece you removed with the old upholstery

linter felt — a piece slightly larger than the top of the seat

slipping thread

back-tacking strip or strip of card, long enough to go along the outer back and wings, along the top rails

## Figures 1-15 The arms

See the diagram of the bare frame (**1**) for the names of different rails.

### Figure 2 Attaching the webbing and hessian

Attach three strips of webbing vertically between the top arm rail and the one immediately below it, on the inside, as shown (see figure 2). Instructions for attaching webbing are given in project 1, figures 3–8. It may be necessary to angle the strip nearest the back so it is parallel with the back rail. Cut a piece of 340 g (12 oz) hessian slightly larger than the area contained within these rails. Turning over a small hem and starting in the middle of each side, tack or staple it along the inside of the top, bottom and front rails of this section, pulling it taut as you go. At the back, leave an opening of about 25–40 mm (1–1½ in) between the hessian and the back rail as shown in figure 2. Later on you will need to tuck in and anchor various layers here.

### Figures 2-6 Attaching the first layer of padding

Beginning at one inner corner, make bridle ties with twine in a criss-cross pattern across this area as shown (see figure 2). Instructions for making bridle ties are given in project 1, figures 12–14. Now cut a piece of twine slightly longer than the top arm rail and anchor it by driving in a temporary tack at the back of the arm rail, knotting one end of the twine, looping it around the tack and driving the tack home. Pull the twine to the front of the rail and anchor it there in the same way (**2**).

Cut a piece of hessian about 150 mm (6 in) wider than the length of the arm and about two and a half times longer than the distance between the top rail and the one under it. Temporarily tack this down along the outside of the first arm rail from the top, leaving the hessian hanging down below the tacks (see figure 3). Take handfuls of ginger fibre and stuff them around the twine at the top of the arm (**3**), and around the bridle ties on the inner arm, blending one section into the next. Keep adding fibre until you have a firm, thick layer which extends to the back rail along the top and the inside of the arm. Push the hessian through to the inside of the chair, under the rail to which it is attached and pull it firmly over the top of the arm (**4**),

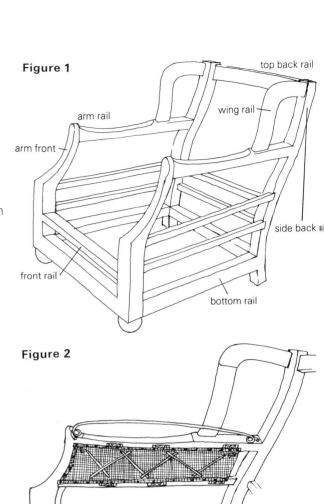

Figure 1

top back rail
wing rail
arm rail
arm front
side back r
front rail
bottom rail

Figure 2

Figure 3

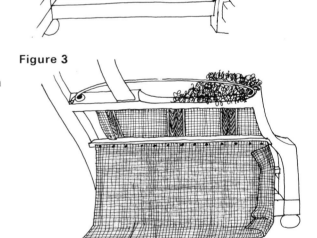

Figure 4

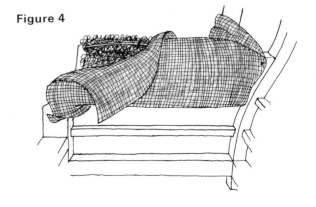

adjusting the fibre underneath as you go, and adding more if necessary. Pull the hessian firmly again and temporarily tack it to the outside of the top rail, first at the centre, then in a row along the arm as shown in figure 5, adjusting the fibre along the rail and teasing it into shape with the point of a regulator needle. Do not tack the hessian to the back rail, but leave a space there To neaten the hessian round the back of the arm, cut into it and fold it around the front wing rail (**5**). Take out the temporary tacks to readjust the filling and hessian if necessary. Repeat these steps for the other arm.

At the front of each arm, stuff more fibre under the hessian to make a smooth, plump roll over the edge of the frame. Pull the hessian down from the top and across from both sides and anchor it with temporary tacks, always smoothing the surface, arranging or adding to the filling and teasing it forward as you go. Now remove these temporary tacks and turn the front edges of the hessian under around the scroll shape now formed, adjusting the fibre and trimming and folding where necessary. Now temporarily tack it into place at the inside front edge and around the top (**6**). To get the shape and finish right you may have to go over your work several times, taking out the tacks, adding to and arranging the fibre with a regulator, and pulling and folding the hessian.

Remove the temporary tacks from along the outside of the top arm rail. Tuck under this edge, pull the hessian straight and taut, replace the temporary tacks, check your work and drive the tacks home. Remove the temporary tacks holding the bottom edge of the hessian in place, pull it tight, and retack.

With twine and a double bayonet needle, make giant running stitches right through the hessian and the fibre across the inside of the arms (see figure 8) to hold these layers together.

### Figures 7 & 8 Making blind and top stitches

Now make a row of blind stitches around the front of each arm in the position shown in figure 7. Detailed instructions for this stitch can be found in project 2, figures 18–24. While making these stitches, use your needle to pull the fibre towards the front to form a firm edge.

Following the same line, make a row of top stitches around the front of each arm (**7**), pulling the twine tight and teasing the fibre forward frequently, as before. See project 2, figures 25–28 for instructions on how to make

**Figure 5**

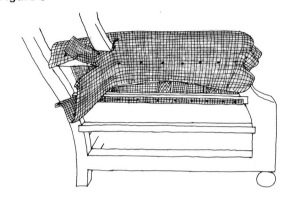

**Figure 6**

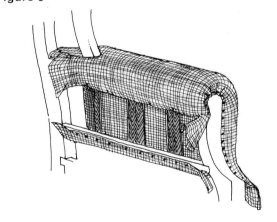

**Figure 7**

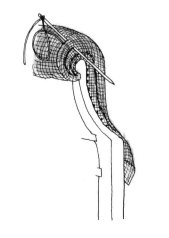

top stitches. This stitching will make a firmly anchored and clearly visible edge roll. The rows of blind stitches and top stitches should meet at the bottom of the padded section (see figure 8).

In order to make the padding along the outer arms firmer, make a row of top stitches along their top edge slightly larger than those at the front, to form a thick edge roll (**8**).

**Figure 8**

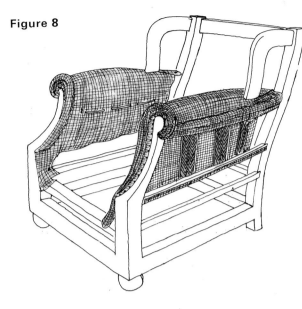

### Figures 9 & 10  Adding the final padding

Turn the chair on its side. Take small pieces of horsehair and lay them in the gaps left by the stitching round the front of the arm, along the top, along the inside and underneath the arm (**9**). Lay a piece of sheet (skin) wadding over the work you have just done and tack it in place along the outside of the first rail from the top, where you first attached the hessian. Pull it smoothly under this rail, up over the padding and round to the outside again, anchoring it to the underside of the top arm rail (see figure 10). At the front, pull the wadding down over the edge and tack it round the front arm rail, pleating and cutting where necessary (**10**). Trim. Tack a small piece of wadding of the shape shown in figure 10 to the front of the arm.

At the back, cut, fold and trim the wadding so that it fits round the frame, then anchor it in exactly the same places as you did the hessian (see figures 5 and 6). Although not strictly necessary, you can cover this with a layer of Courtelle, attached in exactly the same way as the wadding, for an especially smooth finish.

**Figure 9**

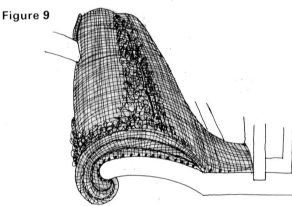

**Figure 10**

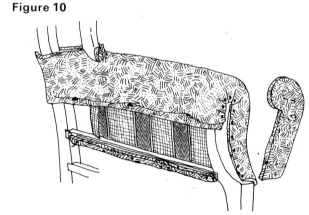

### Figures 11–15  Putting on the cover

Make a template of the front of the arm to the floor by tacking a piece of paper to the front section and drawing a line round the scroll shape from the back of the paper. Cut this shape out and use it as a pattern to cut a piece of covering fabric, leaving a 13 mm ($\frac{1}{2}$ in) seam allowance all round. Cut another piece of covering fabric about 50 mm (2 in) wider than the widest part of the inside arm and long enough to cover all the padded area over the arm. Anchoring it in place over the arm with skewers, cut the fabric round the front of the arm (**11**), again leaving a 13 mm ($\frac{1}{2}$ in) seam allowance. Press into position the piece of fabric you cut for the front and make a nick in both pieces at the top of the arm (**12**).

Make a length of piping (see project 5, figures 10 and 42–3) long enough to sew round the right side of the front fabric from under the curve, up

**Figure 11**

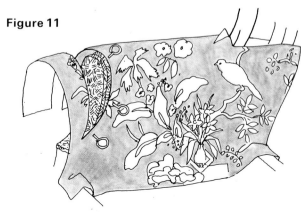

**Figure 12**

round the top, then down to where the chair's concave curve becomes the flat front, as shown in figure 13, leaving enough at each end to go down to the floor. At the curve of the fabric make small cuts into the seam allowance so the cover will fit neatly (**13**). Now sew the main piece of fabric to the front fabric, matching nicks.

Put the cover in place over the arm and temporarily tack it to the outside of the top arm rail, at the front facing and at the back rail, near the wing (**14**). Keep adjusting and retacking until the cover fits perfectly. At the rails, cut carefully into the fabric as shown in figure 15 so you can tack it round the wing and back rails at the top, and the back rail further down. Cut and tack similarly at the inside front so you can pull the bottom of the cover to the outside (**15**).

**Figure 13**     **Figure 14**          **Figure 15**

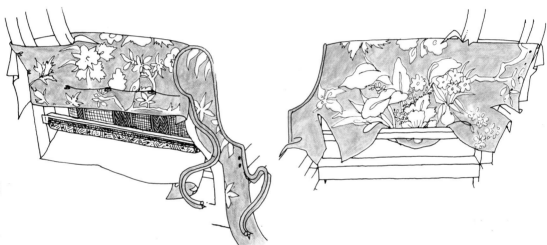

## Figures 16–25  The wings

### Figures 16 & 17  Attaching the webbing and hessian

In order to make the webbing especially strong, and also to save space, fold it in half lengthways and attach a single strip vertically to the inside of each wing frame at the back.

Cut a piece of hessian one and a half times larger than the wing area. Temporarily tack it to the wing, first along the inside front of the wing rail, pulling it between the webbing and the back rail, to the outside, cutting into the edges where necessary. Now temporarily tack it to the inside top of the rail (**16**). Now, at the outside of the wing, temporarily tack the remaining long edge along the inside face of the back rail (see figure 17). At the bottom of the wing, pull the hessian to the outside, cutting where necessary, and temporarily tack it to the top arm rail (**17**).

**Figure 16**          **Figure 17**

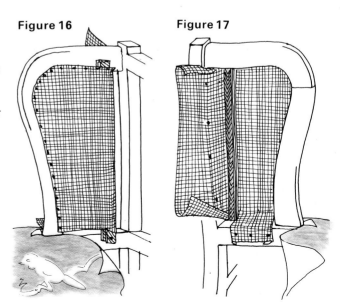

### Figures 18 & 19  Padding the wing rails

Cut a piece of scrim about 200 mm (8 in) longer than the whole wing rail and about 275 mm (11 in) wider. Turning under a small hem, temporarily tack this around the inner edge of the inside of the wing (**18**), so that the scrim hangs over the outside of the wing. You will have to make small pleats in the scrim around the curve.

Cut a piece of twine the same length as the scrim, for bridle ties. Put three temporary tacks inside the wing rail (as shown in figure 19), one at the top back, one at the top front and one at the bottom near the arm. Knot one end of your twine around this last tack, drive it home, then, leaving your twine loose, loop it around the second tack and drive it home. Loop it round the third tack and drive it home in the same way. Take large handfuls of ginger fibre and push them under and around the loops you have just made, blending the handfuls together (**19**).

Pull the scrim over the fibre and round to the other side of the rail. Keep adding fibre and working it in until you have a smooth, firm roll about 65 mm ($2\frac{1}{2}$ in) thick under the scrim, using your regulator needle to work the fibre into place. Turn under the scrim and temporarily tack it down at the top of the outside edge of the rail (see step 20). Keep checking the fibre as you tack, arranging it and adding more if necessary since this is how you form the basic shape of your wing. When you are satisfied that your roll is smooth, even and firm, drive these tacks home. Insert your regulator needle and ease the fibre towards the outside of the wing.

### Figures 20 & 21  Making top stitches

Thread your double bayonet needle with twine and sew a row of top stitches around the outside edge of the rail as shown (**20**), starting from the bottom of the wing and constantly working the fibre toward the edge. Stop sewing a few centimetres from the end, but do not remove your needle and twine. Finish off this top end by neatening the fibre, adding more if necessary, trimming and folding the end of the scrim neatly and tacking it down (**21**). Continue

**Figure 18**

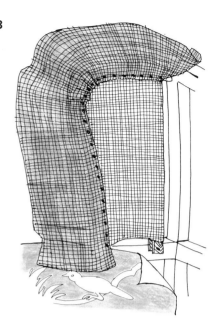

**Figure 19**

**Figure 20**

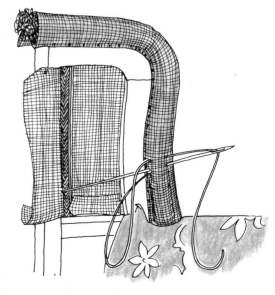

**Figure 21**

op stitching to the end of the wing and across
he back of the wing rail. Drive home all the
emporary tacks along the inside of the wing.

Figure 22

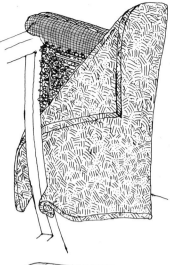

## Figure 22 Padding the inside wing

Thread your springing needle with twine and
make bridle ties across the inside of the wing.
Tuck handfuls of horsehair under and around
these ties in the usual way until the surface is
smooth, thick and even. Add hair also along the
edge roll and into the grooves made by the top
stitching.

Cut a piece of skin wadding large enough to
cover the inside of the wing and round to the
outside of the roll (**22**). Tack it to the outside of
the rail just beyond the scrim. Remove the
temporary tacks holding the hessian to the back
rail and push the wadding through in front of the
back rail, as with the hessian. You will have to
make cuts in the wadding so it will fold neatly
around the rails (see figure 22). Cover this with a
layer of Courtelle attached in the same way.

**Figure 23**

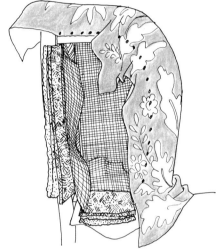

## Figures 23–25 Putting on the cover

Measure the wing area covered by the hessian
and padding and cut a piece of covering fabric
about 250 mm (10 in) larger all around. Lay the
fabric in place and temporarily tack it along the
outside of the wing rail, easing it into gathers at
the curves (**23**). Tuck the back edge of the
cover through between the webbing and the
back rail and fold under the lower edge above
the arm (**24**). Temporarily tack it behind the
back rail at the top, then pull the fabric firmly
back from the side and temporarily tack it to the
back rail (**25**). Where the wing meets the arm,
you will have to make cuts in the fabric (see
figure 24) so it will tuck neatly under the wing.
Use your regulator needle to ease this fabric into
place.

**Figure 24**

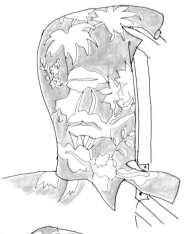

When this part is taut and smooth, check the
fabric around the outside of the wing rail,
readjust if necessary by removing the tacks,
then replace the tacks and drive them home.
Make small cuts in the fabric where the top rail
meets the back rail (see figure 24) so that the
fabric can be pulled taut, folded and tacked
neatly around it, and completely tucked
between the webbing and the back rail. Leave
the wings now until you have done the seat and
back.

**Figure 25**

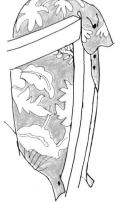

## Figures 26-40 The seat

### Figures 26 & 27 Attaching the webbing and springs

Some old chairs without seat cushions have very large springs in them — up to 350 mm (14 in). If this is the case, and your old springs are in good condition, you should use them again, since it is not always possible to buy such large ones. If you have to use shorter ones than this, attach the webbing to the top of the bottom rails instead of underneath them.

Now lay your springs in place on the webbing (in this case, in three rows of three with a slightly larger space left just behind the front rail). Make sure the knot in the top of each spring is positioned so that it will not rub against the hessian which will go over the springs. Anchor the springs to the webbing in the usual way.

Because of their size, these springs must be lashed at two levels. At the lower level lash the springs in both directions, anchoring the laid cord to the bottom rails and looping the cord around the waist of each spring at both sides. The springs should lean slightly toward the nearest rail, and the knots made exactly as described for the square armchair, project 5, figures 19 & 20. The second lashing should be through each spring in the usual way (**26**).

For the front rail springs we used four 175 mm (7 in) gauge 10 springs; you may need slightly smaller or larger ones but they should be slightly higher than the lashed seat springs when in position. Space these springs evenly across the front rail, and have them protruding slightly beyond the front edge of the rail. Anchor them to the rail (**27**) and lash them as described in project 5, figures 21–24.

Now cut a piece of cane as described in the introduction to project 5, or use the old one if it is still in good condition and attach it to the springs as described in project 5, figure 25.

### Figure 28 Attaching the hessian

Following the instructions given in project 5, figures 26–34, you should now attach the hessian to the seat, using laid cord to anchor it between the main sprung section and the front edge springs. Note that, in this chair, the hessian is tacked to the outside of the back rail above the bottom one (i.e. the rail into which the top set of lashings are anchored) rather than the bottom rail as on the square armchair.

**Figure 26**

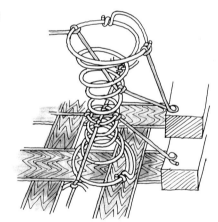

**Figure 27**

Pull the hessian down to the centre of the bottom front rail and put in temporary tacks about 75 mm (3 in) apart, making sure the hessian is smooth and straight (see figure 28). If necessary, trim the hessian here to about 50 mm (2 in) from the tacks. Pull the hessian through to the side rails, cutting and folding at the corners where necessary, and attach it with a row of temporary tacks to the top of the rail above the bottom one.

Using a springing needle and twine, attach the hessian to the cane and front springs with blanket stitches along the cane as shown in figure 28, then stitch all the seat springs to the hessian as described in project 3, figure 18, in the pattern shown in figure 28. Now thread a springing needle with a piece of laid cord 1·25 m (4 ft) long and sew each front spring to the nearest edge spring, pulling them together.

### Figures 28–32 Putting on the padding

Stuff some ginger fibre down between the edge springs and the main springs until the fibre feels firm under the stitches you have just made (**28**). Remove the temporary tacks from the back rail of the seat, pull the hessian taut and drive in permanent tacks more closely spaced (say 13 mm (1 in) apart). Do the same along the side rails and trim the hessian. Tack around the back corners neatly. Remove the tacks from the bottom front rail, pull the hessian taut and retack permanently, adding more tacks as you go. Remove the tacks from the folded hessian at the sides of the front rail, pull it taut and tack it down. Make bridle ties over the seat and two more in a straight line across the front springs. Stuff handfuls of horsehair around these ties until you have a layer of hair 50 mm (2 in) thick (**29**).

Cut a piece of scrim about 150 mm (6 in) larger all round than the chair seat. Temporarily tack it to the same back rail as you did the hessian, pull it over the hair, tuck it in between the hair and the caned edge and anchor it with skewers. Pull the scrim down the sides of the chair, cutting and folding it around the front of the arms (see figure 30) and the back rails where necessary. Temporarily tack it to the top of the side rails above the bottom ones.

Thread a double bayonet needle with twine, push it into the seat about 100 mm (4 in) from one corner, pull it almost all the way out at the bottom, reangle it slightly and pull it out at the top, catching the padding and hessian together inside. Make two stitches like this along each side, then two in the centre (**30**).

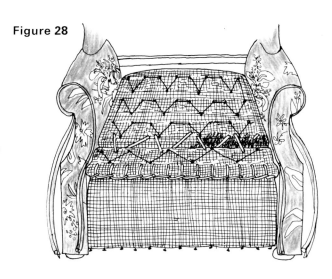

Figure 28

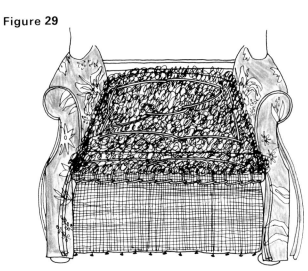

Figure 29

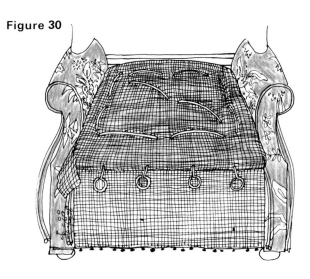

Figure 30

141

Run a row of top stitches along the front edge of the seat, putting your needle into the edge right against the top surface of the cane and working as much hair forward as possible (**31**). Pull your stitches tight to give a firm edge roll about 50 mm (2 in) thick. Now drive home the temporary tacks holding the scrim to the side and back rails. Trim where necessary. With small pieces of horsehair, fill in the grooves in the top of the seat left by the top and anchoring stitches.

Cut a piece of skin wadding very slightly larger than the top of the seat, lay it in place and tuck it in; it does not need to be fastened down. Now do the same thing with a piece of linter felt, tearing and trimming it at the front edge to exactly the same size as the seat.

Cut a piece of Courtelle about 150 mm (6 in) larger all round than the top of the seat, place it in position and tuck it down at the sides and back, trimming and folding where necessary. It should tuck in so tightly that no anchoring is necessary. At the front, pull the Courtelle over the front of the chair and leave it (**32**).

### Figures 33–40  Putting on the seat cover

Cut a piece of your covering fabric wide enough to go across the seat from rail to rail (the side rails where you tacked your hessian and scrim), and long enough to go from the tacking rail at the back to about 75 mm (3 in) below the top rail at the front.

Place the covering fabric in position, pull it through to the outside back and sides and temporarily tack it to the rails where the other layers have been anchored. Anchor it firmly in place with skewers along the front (**33**).

Now remove the temporary tacks from along one side of the seat, pull the front corner of fabric free and make a diagonal cut in it (**34**) so it will fit round the arm at the front. Push the fabric behind the cut back through to the outside. Repeat on the other side. Now remove the skewers at each side of the front edge and make a neat fold at both front corners, cutting into the fabric where necessary.

With a large springing needle and twine, and beginning at one end of the front section, sew down the fold you have made and stitch along the front edge, using running stitches and joining the covering fabric to the hessian on top of the cane. At the other end, sew down the corner fold in your final stitch as you did at the other corner (**35**).

Figure 31

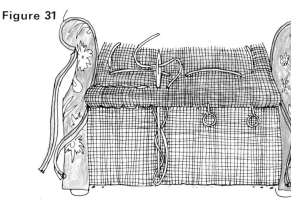

Figure 32

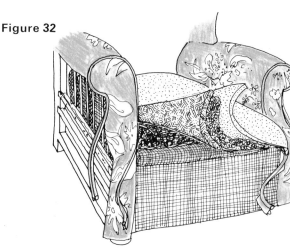

Figure 33

Figure 34

Measure and cut a piece of covering fabric the same width as the front panel, plus the arms, and long enough to go from your front edge stitching line to under the bottom rail. (Try to match the pattern, if there is one, to that on the seat.) Attach a strip of piping to the top edge of this piece and temporarily pin it in position on the front along the piped edge, anchoring it with skewers at the two front corners (**36**). Lift up this border and trim the seat fabric underneath it below the stitches, if necessary.

The front panel must now be padded. This padding really should be a layer of horsehair (fixed with bridle ties and covered with wadding and a layer of 115 g (4 oz) Courtelle (**37**)), but if you do not want to be bothered with this, simply tack a single layer of 230 g (8 oz) or a double layer of 115 g (4 oz) Courtelle over it.

Pull the covering fabric back down over the front panel and temporarily tack it along the bottom rail. Fold one end of the front panel back and make a diagonal cut in it as shown in figure 38, and another cut just below the piping (**38**) and pull the top two sections (piping and fabric) between the front of the seat and the arm. Pull the remainder of the fabric straight across the bottom of the arm under the front facing and temporarily tack it there (**39**). Repeat on the other side. If there are any hollows under this front panel, reach up and fill them in with linter felt or Courtelle. When you are satisfied with the look of this section, drive home the temporary tacks along the sides and bottom edges, adding more to make a really strong anchor.

Now release the temporary tacks holding the seat cover to the back rail, pull it taut and attach it with permanent tacks, stopping about 130 mm (5 in) short of the side rails. Pull the seat cover down through the side rails (**40**) and tack it permanently, again stopping 130 mm (5 in) short of the back rails.

**Figure 35**

**Figure 36**

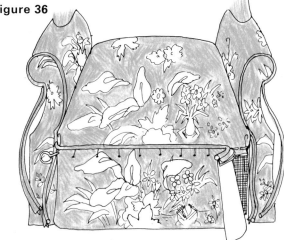

**Figure 37**

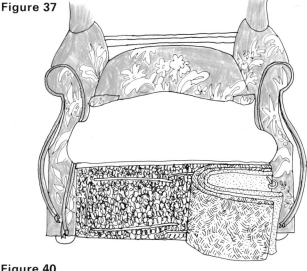

**Figure 38**

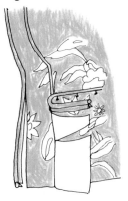

**Figure 39**

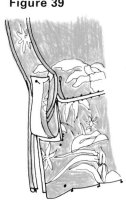

**Figure 40**

At the two back corners of the seat, pull the covering fabric back through to the inside, carefully make diagonal cuts in from the corners so that the fabric can be folded round the back rails, pull the fabric to the outside again, round the back rails, then fold neatly and tack it to the rails permanently.

Slip-stitch the front panel to the seat cover along the piping and remove the pins and skewers holding it in place.

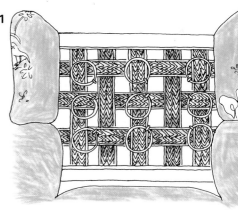

Figure 41

## Figures 41–63 The back

### Figures 41–43 Attaching the webbing and springs

Attach five parallel strips of webbing in the usual way from the top rail to the seat, starting with the strip in the middle. Now attach three rows horizontally. Your chair may require more or less webbing than this one; as a general rule, the strips should be approximately their own width apart (**41**). Leave out the turnings at the end of each strip, to avoid bulk under the final cover.

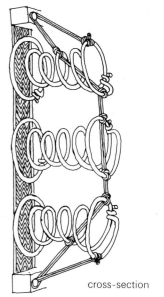

Figure 42

cross-section

We have used nine 125 mm (5 in) gauge 12 springs; if the back is very much larger or smaller, the number you need may be different, but nine is the most usual for this type of chair. Put the springs in place on the webbing with the knots in the positions shown, and attach them in the usual way.

With doubled twine, lash the springs down the three rows vertically (**42**) and across the top two rows horizontally, as shown in figure 43. The arms of the chair will probably prevent you lashing the bottom horizontal row. If there is not enough room for the tacks to go in the usual position on top of the rails, put them into the sides as shown for the horizontal webbing (**43**). Note the angles at which the springs are lashed.

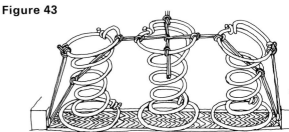

Figure 43

cross-section

### Figure 44 Attaching the hessian

Measure and cut a piece of hessian large enough to cover the back, over the springs (allowing for a hem), and attach it with permanent tacks or staples to the front face of the top and bottom rails. Remove temporary tacks where necessary, push the hessian down by the wings through to both sides (see figure 44) and temporarily tack it to the front face of the side rails, cutting and folding at the corners where necessary. With a springing needle and twine, attach the hessian to the springs in the usual way (**44**).

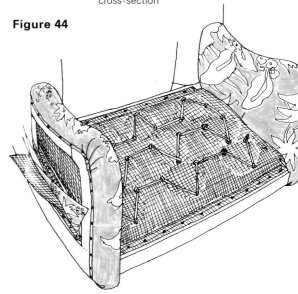

Figure 44

## Figures 45-50 Putting on the padding

Now make bridle ties across the back, roughly following the random pattern laid out in the diagram (see figure 46).

Although it is usual to add stuffing now, then scrim, it is a good idea to anchor the scrim at the bottom of the back at this stage, since this is more difficult to do with the stuffing in place. Cut a piece of scrim about 150 mm (6 in) larger all round than the area of the back and tack it to the back face of the rail just above the seat, as shown in the cross-section (**45**). Fold it out of the way over the seat.

Now stuff handfuls of horsehair around the bridle ties in the usual way, until the distance from the padding on the back to the front edge of the seat measures 575 mm (23 in) when the scrim is pulled up over the back and fastened. (This gives the seat the right depth for comfort.) Using tacks and twine, make two bridle ties across the top rail of the back, loose enough to allow for a very thick layer of hair. Add horsehair around these ties (**46**) to make a firm, thick, soft layer along the top rail, blending into the hair over the back. When you are satisfied with the padding, pull the scrim over the hair and temporarily tack it in place along the outer face of the top rail near the bottom edge (**47**). Tuck the scrim a little way down the sides, by the wings.

With a double bayonet needle and twine, make large stitches across the back through all the layers, anchoring them together as you did with the seat (see figure 30), but in a zig-zag pattern. Take out the temporary tacks holding the scrim in place at the back, add more hair to the roll at the top if necessary, pull the scrim back over it firmly and temporarily tack again, this time along the outer edge of the top face of the top rail. Use your regulator needle to tease the hair into the roll and make it even and smooth. Work along the row of tacks from the middle out, releasing each one, adding more hair if necessary, turning the scrim neatly under and retacking permanently (**48**). At the corners, fold the scrim neatly, adding more hair if necessary, then tack it down. To reinforce this rolled edge, sew a row of top stitches along it in the usual way (**49** and **50**). Use your regulator often to pull the hair into the roll.

Tuck the scrim all the way down the sides, by the wings, cutting and folding it around the arm rails and back rails. Pull any loose hessian at the back to the nearest rail, tack it down and trim. Remove the tacks holding the scrim in place

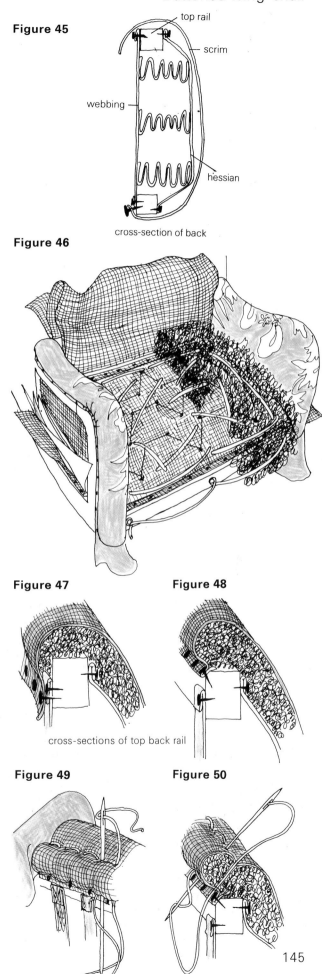

**Figure 45**

top rail

scrim

webbing

hessian

cross-section of back

**Figure 46**

**Figure 47**

**Figure 48**

cross-sections of top back rail

**Figure 49**

**Figure 50**

cross-sections of top stitching

145

along the bottom, pull it taut and retack permanently. Pull the scrim through the wings, turn, and tack it along the same face as the hessian is tacked, cutting and folding where necessary.

### Figures 51–63  Buttoning the back

Take the old back padding (or just the cover) which you have reserved and use it as a guide to mark the position of the buttons accurately on the scrim with a piece of chalk. Cut small holes in the scrim at each of these places with the point of a large pair of scissors.

**Figure 51**

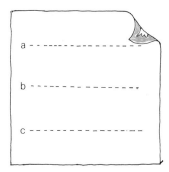

The buttons on our chair are 175 mm (7 in) apart. When marking their position on your covering fabric, you must allow for the amount of indentation made by the buttons and for the amount of give in your fabric. The maximum you should allow is 40 mm (1½ in) on either side of each button, and we have allowed this maximum because the padding will be quite thick and the fabric has a lot of give. (The minimum you should allow is 20 mm (¾ in).)

Measure the distance from the outer face of the top back rail, over the inside of the back, to the outer face of the rail above the bottom one, and from the outer face of one side rail, inside the wing, to the other side rail. Cut a piece of covering fabric 350 mm (14 in) longer and wider than this and lay it out flat, wrong side up, for marking.

**Figure 52**

Check the old cover to find the distance from the top of the fabric to the first row of buttons, and draw a horizontal line across the fabric this distance from the top (see figure 51). In our case, this is also 350 mm (14 in).

**Figure 53**

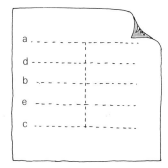

To arrive at the next marking, take the distance between the buttons (180 mm), add it to twice the appropriate allowance (2 x 40 mm = 80 mm) and draw a parallel line this distance (in this case 260 mm (10 in)) below the first one, and another the same distance again below this (**51**). These represent your main working lines which fall at alternate lines of buttoning. Now draw two more lines equally spaced between these as shown (**52**).

**Figure 54**

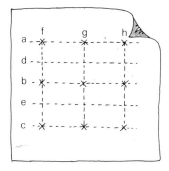

Mark the centre of the fabric crossways on the first three lines you drew (a, b and c) (**53**). Measure your working distance (distance between the buttons plus 2 x allowance (260 mm (10 in) in our case)) and mark this distance on either side of your centre points (**54**). Join these points diagonally as shown in figure 55 to give you the final positions of the

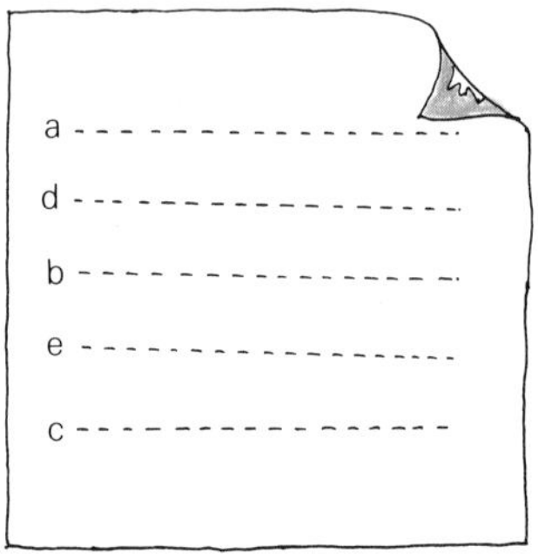

146

buttons on the fabric. Mark these positions with pins (**55**) and tailor's tacks.

Cut a piece of 40 mm (1½ in) Supersoft foam slightly wider than the chair back and long enough to tuck behind the seat and go over the top to the outside face of the top rail. Place the foam in position and stick skewers in where the button-holes will go; do this by feeling under the foam for the holes you made in the scrim earlier. Make pencil or chalk marks where these holes should be (see figure 56), then remove the foam and cut the holes about the same size as your buttons (**56**). Tuck the foam back in place on the chair, press it over the top rail and tack it along the outside face. Measure and cut a piece of Courtelle about 150 mm (6 in) larger all round than the back of your chair and lay it in position. Feel through the Courtelle for the position of the holes and make holes in the Courtelle with your fingers.

Lay the back cover in place so that the tailor's tacks coincide with the holes. Beginning with the hole in the middle, attach the buttons in their positions, removing the tacks as you go. To do this, thread a 300 mm (12 in) double bayonet needle (or a straight buttoning needle) with twine and thread the button as shown in the diagram (**57**). Push the needle through the fabric, fold the fabric back, remove the tailor's tacks and push the needle through the hole and out at the back, making sure you go through a piece of webbing to make the button really secure. Anchor the twine round a tack driven into the nearest rail at the back, driven in lightly so the button can be adjusted later if necessary.

**Figure 55**

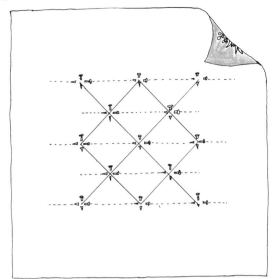

**Figure 56**

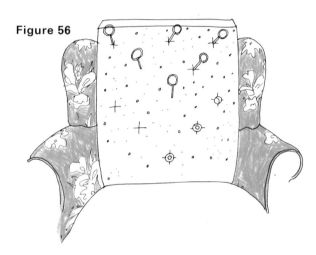

**Figure 57**

Anchor all the buttons in this way, pleating the fabric neatly between them on the inside and pinning the pleats in place as they are made (see figure 60). Do the top ones last.

When you have done all the buttoning, make sure all the buttons are at the same depth. If they are not, take out the temporary tacks holding the twine of any shallow ones, pull them tighter and retack. When they are all satisfactory, undo each tack and knot the two pieces of twine together on the webbing, tucking a small piece of hessian between the knot and the webbing to prevent the knot from

*The Courtelle in position on the chair back.*

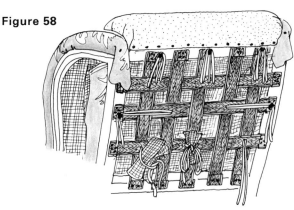

**Figure 58**

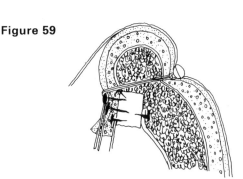

**Figure 59**

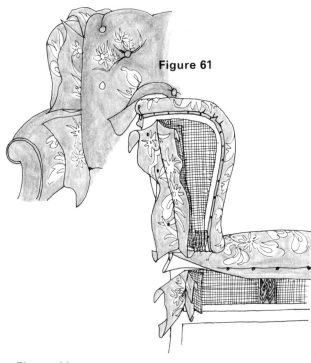

**Figure 60**

**Figure 61**

slipping through (**58**). Since the top three buttons on this chair come above the top rail, their twine goes through the foam, above the top rail, and will be anchored with tacks to the outside face of the top rail (**59**).

Pull the cover through to the outside at the bottom of the back. Now pull the cover over the top, arranging the pleats from the buttons neatly, and temporarily tack it to the outside face of the top back rail. Tuck the sides down slightly.

Make a cut into the fabric at the wing as shown, so it can be tucked through to the back above the arm rail (see figure 60). Now make a cut near the top, under the top wing rail, as shown (**60**), pull the fabric through between the wing and the back, and temporarily tack this piece to the side face of the side rail (figure 61). Pull the rest of the fabric through above the seat (**61**).

Make extra pleats from the outer top buttons to the nearest points on the wings and pin them in place. Cut, fold and trim the excess fabric at the top of the wing, tuck it in, and temporarily tack it to the outside face of the back rail, using your regulator for the tucking (**62**).

When you are satisfied with the fit of the back cover, add more tacks along the outer face of the top rail and drive all the tacks home, folding the fabric over neatly at the corners (**63**).

**Figure 62**

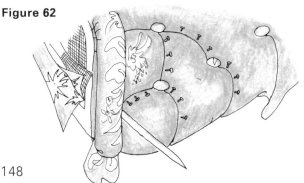

**Figure 63**

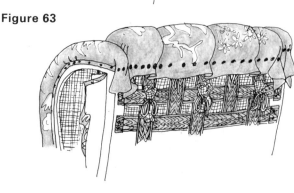

Pull the bottom of the back cover through to the outside face of the back rail above the bottom one, tack it in position and trim if necessary.

## Figures 64-75 Finishing off

First, neaten the tops of the arms by checking any temporary tacks still in place, adjusting where necessary and tacking permanently.

### Figures 64-67 Finishing the wings

At the wings, remove the temporary tacks holding the back cover in place, pull the fabric taut and tack it permanently to the front face of the back rail. (All fastening down must be done to the front face of the rails to avoid bulk when the outer cover is on.) Trim if necessary (**64**). At the bottom of the wing, pull through the wing covering fabric and the hessian flap which has remained loose and attach them permanently to the arm rail. Tack down and trim any remaining ends of hessian or fabric still left (**65**).

Cut a piece of hessian large enough to cover the outside of the wing and tack it in position permanently.

In order to attach the rest of the outside cover invisibly, it is necessary to use a method known as back-tacking. First, cut a rectangle of covering fabric about one and a half times larger than the area formed by the outside of the wing. Now cut a piece of back-tacking strip (or a narrow strip of card) long enough to go across the top of the wing. Place the fabric you have just cut in position on the outside of the wing and turn under a hem of about 25 mm (1 in) across the top. Keeping the hem in the same position (flat against the top wing rail), lift up the fabric from the bottom and tack this hem to the top of the rail just below the fold line. Put the back-tacking strip along this fold line and tack it in place to the rail. Now fold the fabric down over it, leaving a neat top edge. Pull the cover down to the bottom of the wing and anchor it with a temporary tack. Continue turning the fabric under and pressing it into place with your fingers around the curve — you will have to remove the tack, lift up the fabric and make a series of small cuts into the hem in order to do this neatly. Lift up the fabric again and attach a piece of Courtelle over the hessian (**66**). Pull the fabric back down, pin it in place round the curve, and fold and pin it down and round the back of the arm. Pull the fabric smoothly over the outside of

**Figure 64**

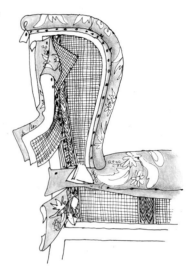

**Figure 65**

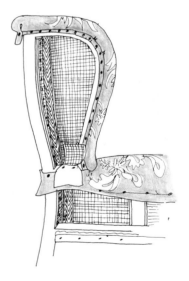

**Figure 66**

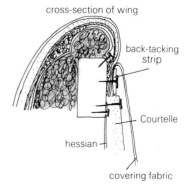

cross-section of wing

back-tacking strip

Courtelle

hessian

covering fabric

the wing and tack it permanently along the back face of the back rail (see figure 67).

Make a cut from the bottom outside corner up to the arm rail so you can pull the fabric down under the arm rail and anchor it permanently there. Slip-stitch all round the inside of the curve of the wing, down to the bottom of the roll at the top of the arm (**67**).

### Figures 68–71  Finishing the arms

To finish off the arms, pull the piped front arm cover into place between the front panel and the arm, pin it there and slip-stitch the opening, taking in the piping. Pull the fabric tightly over the arm rail and permanently tack it to the outside face, taking in the piping which should be falling loose from the curve at the top of the arm. Fold and trim the fabric neatly at the bottom of the chair and tack it in place permanently (**68**).

For the outer arms, cut one piece of hessian and one of covering fabric about 50 mm (2 in) larger all round than the uncovered section. Now cut a strip of back-tacking the length of the arm rail. Place the fabric in position, turn under a hem at the top, fold back the fabric and tack it along the fold line, as you did at the top of the wing. Do exactly the same thing with the hessian, then, with a row of closely spaced tacks, permanently anchor your strip of back-tacking on top of these two layers to the underside of the top arm rail (**69**).

Pull the hessian down smoothly and tack it permanently to the surrounding rails, turning over a small hem, trimming and folding it at the corners where necessary (see figure 70).

Cut a piece of Courtelle about 25 mm (1 in) longer and the same width as the outer arm section. Turn over a 25 mm (1 in) hem at the top to cover the back-tacking strip. Tack it in position up the sides and along the bottom. If you have a staple gun, you may be able to put in a few staples along the top. There is no place here to put tacks, but the Courtelle should stay in place anyway (**70**). Trim the Courtelle to the shape of the outside arm section.

Pull the covering fabric down firmly and temporarily tack it under the bottom rail (see figure 71). Now pull it towards the back and temporarily tack it to the back face of the back rail. Pull the fabric towards the front and fasten it with a temporary tack underneath the front rail. Pull the rest of the fabric forward so that it is taut and pin it in position temporarily, with the

**Figure 67**

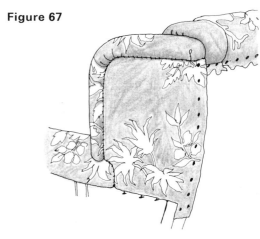

**Figure 68**

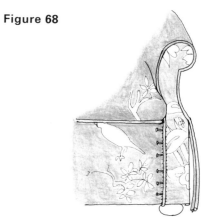

**Figure 69**

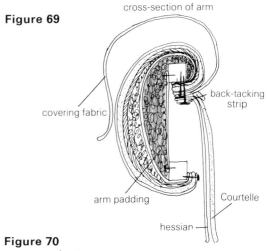

cross-section of arm

covering fabric

back-tacking strip

arm padding

Courtelle

hessian

**Figure 70**

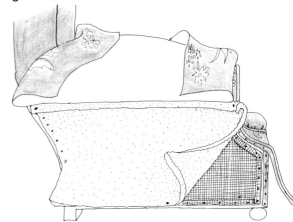

raw edges out (see figure 71). Trim any excess fabric, cut into the curves, then remove each pin, beginning from the top. Turn under a hem and repin.

When you are satisfied with the look of the outside arm, drive the tacks home at the bottom and the back, adding more as you go so your fixing will be secure. Slip-stitch the front edge of this panel in place where you have pinned it (**71**).

**Figure 71**

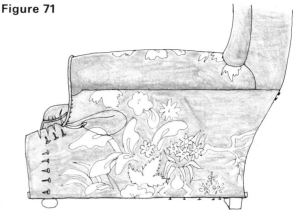

### Figures 72–75 Finishing off the back and the base

Attach the final cover to the back with the hessian and the tacking strip in the same way as you did with the outside arm panels, but this time attach the layers to the outside face of the rail. To fit round the curve formed by the padding, cut into the strip as shown in the diagram (**72**). The sharper the curve, the smaller and more acute these cuts should be.

Tack the hessian down all around, turning over a small hem, then add a layer of Courtelle, turning over a small hem at the top as before and tacking all around – this time you will be able to anchor it along the top as well (**73**).

**Figure 72**

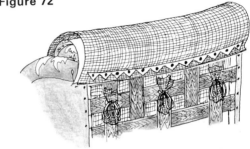

**Figure 74**

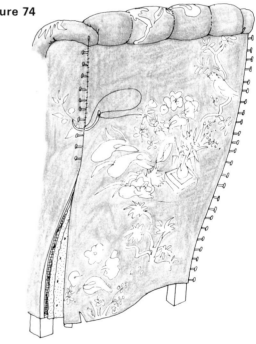

**Figure 73**

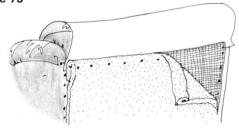

Pull the covering fabric down over the Courtelle, pull it taut at the sides, pin, trim, then turn under hems and re-pin as before. Slip-stitch this back panel to the sides (**74**).

Turn the chair upside-down and, beginning in the middle of each rail, tack down the covering fabric permanently to the four bottom rails, adding extra tacks for strength. Cut and fold the fabric neatly around the legs and trim any excess.

Measure and cut a piece of black upholsterer's linen or hessian slightly larger than the bottom of your chair. Turning under a small hem, tack this in position, cutting and folding it round the legs where necessary (**75**).

**Figure 75**

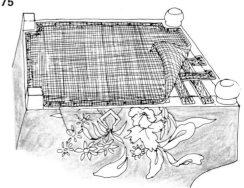

# Upholstery Project 7: Chesterfield

## Introduction

Before you begin this project, read the introduction to project 5 for a general outline of the steps. The techniques are also very similar to some of those for project 6.

## Tools

scissors
pencil
tape-measure
hammer
webbing stretcher
springing needle
skewers
double bayonet needle
pins
slipping needle
tailor's chalk
paper (for template of arm fronts)
rasp
regulator needle

## Materials

black and white first-quality webbing: see
    project 1, figure 3 for measurements and add
    500 mm (20 in)
20 mm ($\frac{5}{8}$ in) tacks
10 mm ($\frac{3}{8}$ in) and 13 mm ($\frac{1}{2}$ in) fine tacks
springs: we used twenty-four 225 mm (9 in)
    gauge 8 ones for the seat, thirteen 150 mm
    (6 in) gauge 10 upright and twelve 175 mm
    (7 in) leaning springs for the top of the arms
    and back, and twelve 150 mm (6 in) gauge 12
    ones for the inner arms and back
twine
laid cord
galvanized staples
hessian — enough to cover the sprung areas of
    the arms, back and seat (see figures 11 and
    31–33)

ginger fibre for padding the back and round the seat springs — use the old stuffing to estimate quantities

scrim — enough to cover the padded arms, back and seat (see figures 19 and 31)

covering fabric — enough to go over all surfaces of the padded sofa and attach to the frame (see figures 21–23 and 31–35)

curtain heading tape (see figure 23)

linter felt — small pieces to fill in hollows and large pieces to cover the whole sprung section of arms and back, and the seat

sheet (skin) wadding — enough to cover the sprung arms and back, the seat and the front panel

60 g (2 oz) Courtelle — enough to cover the sprung arms and back, the seat, the front panel, and facings

horsehair for the seat and front panel — use the old stuffing to gauge approximately how much you need

piping cord — enough to extend along the front border of the seat plus 300 mm (12 in), and round the facings

6 mm ($\frac{1}{4}$ in) thick plywood, for the front facings

contact adhesive

30 mm ($1\frac{1}{4}$ in) panel pins

back-tacking strip or strip of card, long enough to go along the outer back and wings, along the top rails

### Figures 1 & 2  Attaching the seat springs

Although it is the usual practice to do the arms of a piece of upholstered furniture first, in this case you should attach the webbing and seat springs first, before going on to the arms and back. This is because, if the thick padding were put on the arms and back first, it would prevent you reaching the bottom rails on to which the seat springs are lashed.

See figure 1 for the parts of the frame referred to throughout this project. Having stripped the frame bare (**1**), attach webbing to the bottom rail across the seat area, as described in project 1, figures 3–8, remembering to place the strips their own width apart. If there are strips of wood across the frame, position the webbing over them and place the springs on the webbing as shown (**2**); otherwise, position them in the usual way, at the junctions of the webbing. Leave room at the sides and back for the arm and back padding. Stitch the springs to the webbing and lash them together firmly, as described in project 3, steps 2–12.

**Figure 1**

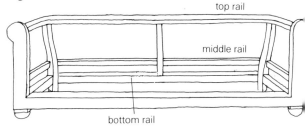

top rail

middle rail

bottom rail

## Figures 3–30  Upholstering the arms and back

The skills involved in springing the arms and making the roll along the top of the arms and back are introduced here.

**Figure 2**

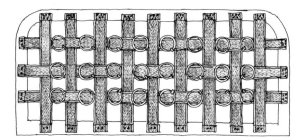

### Figures 3 & 4  The top rail springing

Springs must first be positioned along the top rail in order to support the padding which will go along the top of the arms and back. These springs are attached in a similar way to those on the front edge of a sprung armchair, but with alternate springs leaning in towards the centre of the sofa at a 45° angle, to provide support for the inside top edge.

First place the upright springs in position: start by putting one at the front of each arm and one at each corner. Now add more upright ones, leaving room for an angled spring between each one. There will not be enough room at the corners for an angled spring to bend inwards on both sides, so put an upright spring at each end of the back rail (so that there are two uprights next to each other at the back corners). If the base of the springs is wider than the back rail, they should protrude towards the centre of the sofa rather than to the outside. Now anchor each spring to the rail all round with at least three galvanized staples (see figure 4).

Place one angled spring between each upright one and tack it to the rail with galvanized staples in the same way. If you are not using the old springs (which will already be the right shape), you should bend each one at the waist to the correct angle before placing it on the rail. After putting each one on the rail, hammer the bottom coil over the inside of the rail (**3**). Place a length of webbing along the top rail and tack it down round the base of the springs (**4**), as described for the front rail springs in project 5, figures 21–24.

## Figure 5  Webbing the back and arms

Attach a piece of webbing horizontally halfway between the top and the middle rail, both across the back of the chesterfield and across each arm. Now attach strips of webbing vertically, one directly under each angled spring, anchoring the webbing round the middle rail and pulling it up over the bottom coil of each angled spring. Anchor these rows of vertical webbing to the outside face of the top rail (**5**).

## Figure 6  Attaching the back and arm springs

Using the method described in project 3, figures 2–5, anchor springs to the webbing you have just attached, one at each point where the vertical strips cross the horizontal ones (**6**). (We used three for each arm and six across the back.)

## Figures 7 & 8  Lashing the upright top rail springs

Again referring to the instructions for front rail springs (project 5, figures 21–24), first lash only the upright springs to the rail, running the cord outside the angled springs between tacks as shown in figure 7.

Cut another length of laid cord (with a piece of furniture this large it would be awkward to work with a piece of cord long enough to do the job in one go, so the precise length is not important) and anchor it round a tack at the top of one arm at the front in the usual way, knotting the short end to the top of the front spring as shown (figure 7). Loop the cord round the waist of the first upright spring at the nearest point. Then, using simple knots, knot it to the top coil at the furthest point and continue knotting it to opposite sides of the top coil of each upright spring. At the corners, knot the twine round the top coil at the nearest point, then loop it round

**Figure 3**

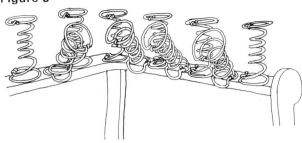

**Figure 4**

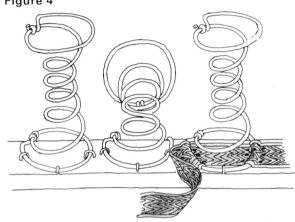

**Figure 5**

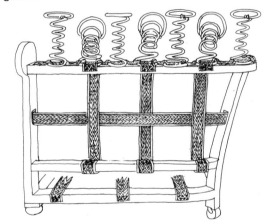

**Figure 6**

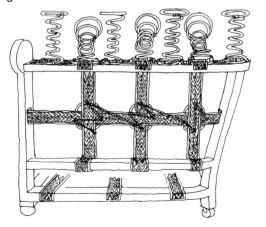

the waist. Take it down to the rail, anchor it with a tack, then loop it round the waist of the next upright (**7**). Continue along the back and second arm in exactly the same way.

Now, with a piece of cord, tie each corner spring to the first back spring as shown (**8**), as they have not yet been lashed together at the top.

### Figure 9  Lashing the angled top rail springs

To lash each angled spring at the top rail to the back and arm springs directly below it, cut a length of twine about 2 m (78 in) long and double it. Drive a temporary tack into the inner face of the middle rail directly below these springs, as shown in figure 9. Loop your doubled twine round the waist of the lowest spring, twist it round the temporary tack and drive it home, then knot it round the top coil of the same spring, first on one side, then on the other as shown in figure 9. Take the twine up to the angled spring above, knot it round the top coil at the nearest point, then opposite. Pull the twine taut and anchor it to the outside edge of the top face of the top rail (**9**).

### Figure 10  Lashing the back and arm springs

The springs on the inside back and arms should now be lashed horizontally. Cut a single piece of twine one and a half times the length of the back and arms. Anchor the end of it with a tack to the inner face of one of the arm fronts in line with these springs. Leave enough twine loose so that you can knot it to the top coil of the nearest spring when you have finished the lashing. Loop the twine at the waist of the first spring, then knot it to the top coil at the furthest point, then to the top of the next spring at the nearest point. Now loop it round the lashing which runs vertically, then knot it to the top coil on the opposite side (**10**). Continue in this way along the back and arms and finish by anchoring the twine to the other arm front, leaving enough twine to tie back to the top coil firmly. Tie the other end you left at the beginning to the top of the first spring, as shown in figure 10.
Now lash the angled springs along the top rail to each other in the same way (see figure 10).

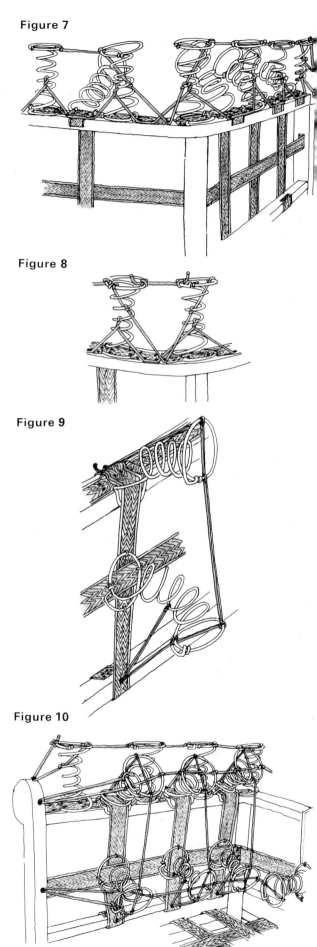

Figure 7

Figure 8

Figure 9

Figure 10

## Figures 11-16  Attaching hessian to the arms and back

Figure 11

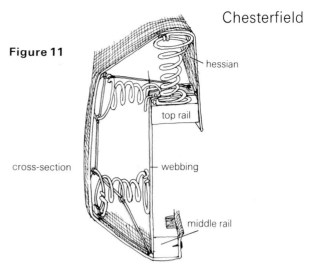

cross-section

hessian

top rail

webbing

middle rail

Cut two pieces of hessian slightly wider than the arms of the chesterfield and long enough to go from the outer face of the middle rail, under the rail, up over the inside arm to the outer face of the top rail. Turning over a hem, temporarily tack the hessian at one arm to the outer face of the middle rail. Pull it under this rail, up over the springs – see the cross-section (**11**) – and temporarily tack it to the outer face of the top rail. Pull the hessian forward firmly and temporarily tack it to the inner face of the front arm (figure 12). Cut and fold the hessian round the middle rail where necessary. At the inner corners, cut into the hessian at top and bottom where the two pieces of horizontal lashing fall (**12**), so that it can be tucked through to the back rail.

Cut a piece of hessian to cover the back in the same way, and lay it in position. Attach it to the rails in the same way as before (figure 11), except that you will have to cut it at the bottom of the central vertical rail at the back, to attach it to the middle rail. At the inner corners place the hessian over the side pieces and make two cuts as shown (**13**). Pull the three resulting sections

**Figure 12**

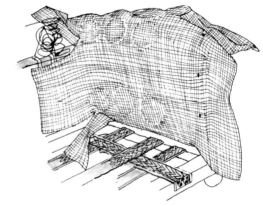

**Figure 13**

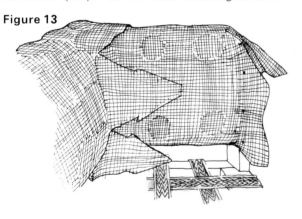

**Figure 14**

**Figure 15**

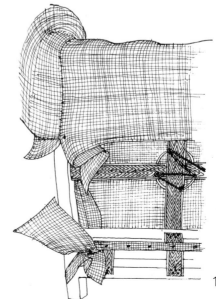

through to the back of the sofa, one above the top rail, one between the top and middle rail, and one below the middle rail. Tack them down out of the way, trimming any excess hessian at the corners but leaving enough to fold the back and arm sections neatly together along the inner corner, over the top and down the back. Anchor this fold with skewers as shown in figure 14, and, starting from the inside bottom, stitch along this fold (**14**), up the inner corner, over the top and down the outside to the level of the top rail (**15**).

Trim the hessian to just above the temporary tacks along the middle rail, then remove the tacks, pull the hessian taut, turn over a small hem and replace the tacks, driving them home. Add more between the existing ones so that the hessian is attached firmly all round the sofa to the outer face of the middle rail.

Now trim the hessian to just beyond the front of the arm and the side of the top rail, turn over a small hem and tack it firmly in place with permanent tacks all round the arm, so that the front face is fully exposed (**16**).

Using a springing needle and twine, anchor the springs to the hessian as described in project 3, figure 18.

**Figure 16**

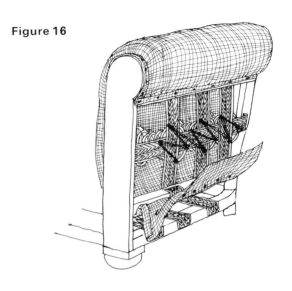

### Figures 17 & 18  The first layer of padding

To provide an anchor for the padding, cover the hessian with bridle ties in the pattern shown (**17**).

Take handfuls of ginger fibre and tuck them under and around the bridle ties you have just made (**18**) until the entire area of hessian is covered and each section of fibre is blended well into the next. At this stage, the fibre should be about 100 mm (4 in) thick and feel very firm and solid. There is no special technique for dealing with the corners; just continue stuffing the fibre around the ties without a break, following the line of the chesterfield.

**Figure 17**

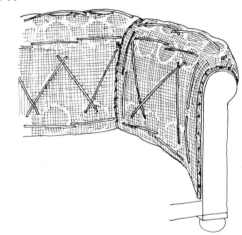

### Figures 19 & 20  Attaching the scrim

Cut three pieces of scrim (one for each arm and one for the back) 100 mm (4 in) larger all round than the area (rail to rail, over the padding) to be covered. Anchor them in position with temporary tacks in exactly the same way as you anchored the hessian (see figure 11). Adjust the scrim to fit neatly, removing the temporary tacks where necessary and cutting into the scrim exactly as you did with the hessian, pulling it into position until it is smooth and taut over the fibre. If there are any lumps or hollows, add more fibre or redistribute the existing fibre with the point of a regulator.

To reinforce the edges of the padded area, you must make a row of blind stitches, then a row of top stitches, round the front face of the arms (see figures 19 and 20). Full instructions for these stitches are given in project 2, figures 18–28. Now anchor the padding to the hessian along the inside back and arms with large running stitches, as shown in project 6, figure 8.

**Figure 18**

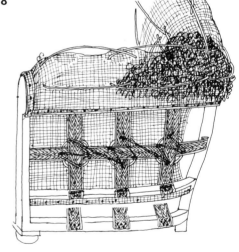

Fold the scrim at the corners and stitch (**19**) as you did with the hessian (see figure 15).

To reinforce the roll formed by the top of the arms and back, make a row of blind stitches all along the roll in the position shown (**20**).

Remove the temporary tacks holding the scrim in place and adjust if necessary. Replace the tacks and drive them home, adding more where necessary to make a firm edge.

## Figures 21–23 Making up the cover

To make the arm covers, measure and cut two pieces of covering fabric 150 mm (6 in) longer than the scrim which covers the same area. To find the necessary width, measure along the outside arm from the front to the outside back corner of the roll, at the back rail, and add 75 mm (3 in).

For the back cover, measure the length in the same way as for the arms (i.e. scrim plus 150 mm) and the width from the seam on the scrim at one back corner to the other, plus 150 mm (6 in). If the fabric is not wide enough to cover this area, have one large panel in the middle and two smaller ones at each side, matching the pattern, if any.

Fold the back piece of fabric in half and make a small nick in the middle of the top edge. Lay the back piece in position, right side up, centring the seams and matching the nick to the central rail. Temporarily tack it in place to this central rail.

To establish the point where the seams should fall, attach a piece of twine with a tack driven into each vertical back rail just below the middle horizontal one. Bring the twine up to the inside, over the padding to the back, and anchor it to the back rail just below the scrim (**21**).

Lay the back piece of fabric over the twine at each corner and trim any excess to about 40 mm (1½ in) beyond the twine, but trim it only as far as the top of the seat, since you will need this excess fabric to tuck down the sides and back. With skewers, anchor this back piece in position along the line of twine. Now lay the arm pieces in position and temporarily tack them to the bottom face of the top rail. Anchor them with skewers to the padding at the front of the arm, as shown in figure 22, then trim the excess fabric at the corners to about 40 mm (1½ in) beyond the twine, down to the top of the seat.

At the inner corners pin the arm and back pieces together to make a neat fit, with seam allowances

**Figure 19**

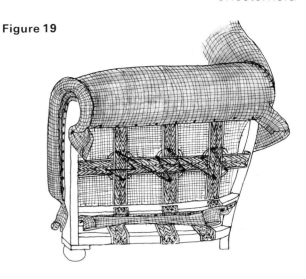

**Figure 20**

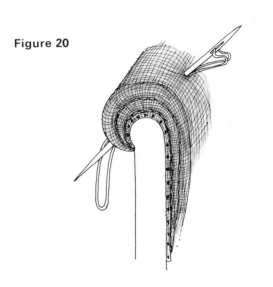

**Figure 21**

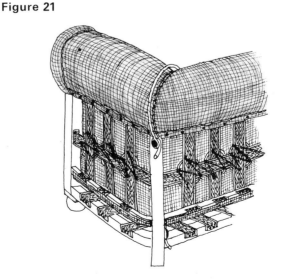

facing out. Trim the seam allowances to 13 mm ($\frac{1}{2}$ in), again to the top of the seat, and make small nicks in the seam allowances every 100 mm (4 in) so that you can match the fabric when you take it off and put it right sides together for sewing (**22**). Carefully remove the cover, turn the pieces right sides together and re-pin, matching nicks. Now stitch the seams, catching in each one a length of curtain heading tape extending about 250 mm (10 in) beyond each end of the seam (**23**). This will help you pull the cover neatly into position at the corners.

**Figure 22**

### Figures 24–26 The final padding

Tear off small pieces of linter felt and lay them in the grooves formed by the top stitching at the front of the arms and in the hollows made by the anchoring stitches on the back and sides (see figure 24). Now tear off enough linter felt in large sheets to cover the inner arms and back, and go right over the curve to the top rail, but not over the front edge of the arm (**24**). When you join pieces, butt them together; do not overlap them. There is no need to fasten the linter felt down.

**Figure 23**

Cut three pieces of skin wadding, one to go over each arm and one to go over the back. Lay them in position and anchor the arm pieces to the side face of the top rail with a few tacks, and tuck it down behind the seat. At the front of the arms, pull it over the front and gather it where necessary round the curve, attaching it with a few tacks (see figure 25). Overlap the pieces of wadding to join them and cut into them where necessary at the inner corners. Cover the wadding with a layer of Courtelle attached in exactly the same way (**25**). The cross-section (**26**) shows where all the layers are attached.

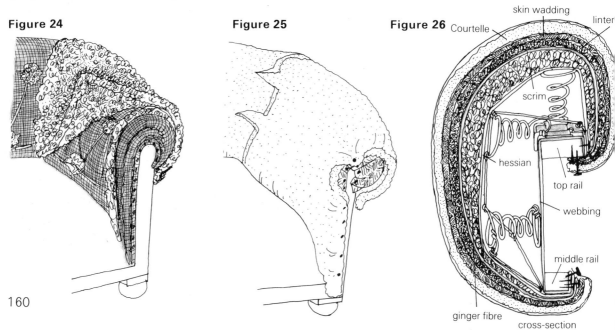

**Figure 24**

**Figure 25**

**Figure 26**

skin wadding

linter

Courtelle

scrim

hessian

top rail

webbing

middle rail

ginger fibre

cross-section

## Figures 27–30  Attaching the cover

Put the made-up cover in place on the chesterfield. Pull it down taut at the outer corners with the tapes and put a temporary tack through each top tape into the outside face of the back rail to keep it there. Pull the cover into position at the front of the arms and anchor it with a temporary tack to the outer and front faces of the front rail. Push the bottom tape down into the inside corners, pull it through to the outside corner of the arms and temporarily tack it to the outer face of the back rail (**27**).

Pull the cover over the top of the sofa to the back and, starting at the centre, drive a row of temporary tacks into the bottom face of the top rail all round, making neat and symmetrical pleats at both back corners (**28**). Smooth the cover round the inside back and arms and tuck it down behind the seat. At the centre of the back, cut in from the bottom so that the cover can be pulled round the upright rail (figure 29).

Pull the fabric through to the outside back, pull it taut and fasten it with temporary tacks to the outside face of the middle back rail (**29**).

At the front of each arm, pull the fabric firmly towards the centre, making even, neat pleats in the same direction (use your regulator to help) and temporarily tack them in place. These tacks should be placed about 6 mm ($\frac{1}{4}$ in) from the edge of the padding so that they go directly into the wood. When you are working on the second arm, measure from the floor to the first inside pleat to make sure that it is on the same level as the one on the first arm. When you are satisfied that the pleats are even and straight, drive the tacks home and add more to make a close row all the way round them (**30**). Trim the fabric.

At the bottom front of the inside arm, make two cuts up from the bottom of the fabric as shown in figure 30 so you can pull the fabric down round the front rail to the outside. It is a good idea to begin by making a short cut, then lengthen it bit by bit. Cut, fold and neaten.

## Figures 31–35  Upholstering the seat, front panel and facings

### The seat

To attach the padding and covering to the seat follow the instructions for project 6, figures 26–40. The only difference here is that if one width of fabric will not cover the chesterfield seat, you will have to add two small panels at each side as you did with the back.

Figure 27

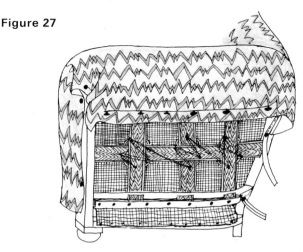

Figure 28

Figure 29

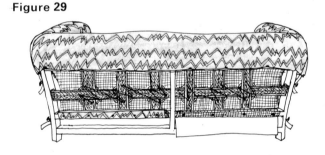

Figure 30

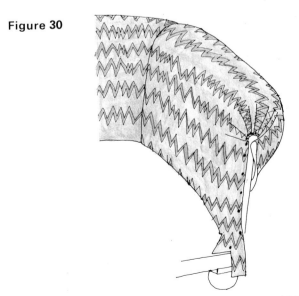

### Figures 31–33  The front panel

Cut a piece of covering fabric large enough to go from under the front edge roll of the seat to the bottom of the front rail, plus 50 mm (2 in), and right across the front of the chesterfield. If your fabric is not wide enough, you will have to sew a narrow piece on either side of a central piece as you did with the back and the seat. Attach a length of piping along the top edge of this panel, extending about 150 mm (6 in) on either side. (See project 5, figure 10.)

**Figure 31**

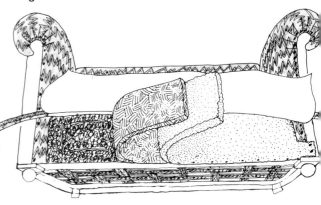

Lay the fabric panel in place across the front of the chesterfield and anchor it with skewers (matching any seam lines with those on the seat). Fold the fabric back over the seat. Using your springing needle and twine, make bridle ties across the hessian (attached to the front panel when you padded the seat), and stuff them with a fairly thin layer of horsehair in the usual way (figure 31). Cover this with a piece of skin wadding large enough to lay over the top, tuck down at each side between the seat and the arms, and fasten over the bottom rail. Anchor this at the top with skewers, tuck it down the sides and tack it to the front of the bottom rail. Now add a layer of 60 g (2 oz) Courtelle, cut to the same size. Anchor it under the same skewers that go through the wadding, tuck it down the sides and tack it along the bottom (**31**).

**Figure 32**

Remove the skewers. This top line of the padding remains unattached. Fold the covering fabric for the border down into place and anchor the piped edge under the front roll with large pins or skewers stuck straight in. Pull the border down gently and temporarily tack it to the bottom face of the bottom front rail.

Cut in from each side of the border just below the piping to about 75 mm (3 in) before you get to the seat. Push this piping down between the seat and the arm and pull it to the outside (as shown in figure 32) by reaching up underneath the middle rail at the outside arm.

**Figure 33**

Cut into the front panel from the side to a point near the top of the bottom rail (**32**). Fold the fabric under to make a continuous curve coming down from the top corner of the seat. You may need to push a little stuffing in here to make a smooth curve. When you are satisfied that the front border is smooth and straight, slip-stitch it to the seat along the piping, using the blunt end of your regulator to push the fabric between the arm and the front border (**33**), then tack it permanently below the bottom rail. At the bottom corners, trim and fold the fabric at the inside leg (see figure 34).

## Figures 34 & 35  Making the front facings

Cut a paper template to the scroll shape formed by the front faces of the arms, about 13 mm ($\frac{1}{2}$ in) beyond the row of tacks and extending to the bottom of the front of the arm, flush with the outside edge, as shown (**34**). Tack it lightly to two pieces of 6 mm ($\frac{1}{4}$ in) plywood in turn, trace round them carefully and cut out the shapes with a jigsaw or hacksaw. These two pieces of plywood become the facings.

Chamfer the front edges of the facings all round with a rasp, so there will be no noticeable edge when it is covered with fabric. Cut a piece of Courtelle the same size as each facing and glue it to the front. Place each facing, padded side down, on a piece of covering fabric, wrong side up. Cut the fabric about 50 mm (2 in) beyond the facing, wrap it round the facing except at the straight inner edge and fasten it with staples: you will have to make a cut underneath the curve so that the fabric will stretch smoothly (see figure 35). When the fabric is stapled down, trim it close to the staples, leaving the loose flap.

Make up some piping long enough to go all round the facings. Unpick the piping about 25 mm (1 in) at one end and cut off the end of the cord inside. Fold the fabric down over the top of the cord and then in half lengthways to neaten. Lay this along the straight side of the facing, at the back (**35**) and fasten it down with 10 mm ($\frac{3}{8}$ in) fine tacks or staples. Take the piping round the facing, cutting into the curves.

**Figure 34**

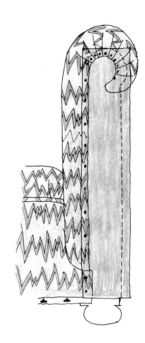

**Figure 35**

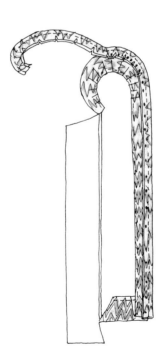

## Attaching the facings to the arms

Place the facing in position on the arm, lift up the loose flap and attach the facing under the fabric with 13 mm ($\frac{1}{2}$ in) fine tacks placed as far in as you can reach from the edge. The heads of the tacks will be hidden under the fabric. Now anchor the facing to the inside front of the arm by driving 30 mm ($1\frac{1}{4}$ in) panel pins through the fabric into the wood. It is very important that these pins remain straight so they can be concealed. When you have driven them in, use the point of a pin to ease the fabric free of the head of the pin, so that it is no longer visible.

Pull the loose flap of fabric round to the outside arm and tack it in place along its length. Pull the loose piping down and fasten it in place along the outside edge where you tacked the fabric. Trim and neaten the piping.

The outer arm and back covers are back-tacked and slip-stitched, and the project finished off, in exactly the same way as project 6.

# The Care, Repair and Recovering of Upholstery

## Upholstery fabrics

The time and care you put into your upholstery work will be wasted if you choose a covering fabric which is not strong enough for furniture. Many pretty materials are really only suitable for curtaining, and even those which can be made into loose covers are often too thin or loosely woven for tight upholstery, so be sure to check with your supplier before you buy.

There is a huge range of fibres to choose from and each has its own peculiarities; fibre content must, by law, be marked on all fabric, so you should have no difficulty in finding one to meet your needs.

## Natural fabrics

These fabrics are made from fibres that come either from plants, like cotton and linen, or from animals, like wool and silk. They have many

*Make sure that any pure cotton you choose for upholstery is strong and tightly woven.*

*Top: for a crisp look use linen as a covering fabric and add contrast piping. Above, left: wool is expensive but wears well and resists burning. Above, right: linen union in a traditional print is appropriate for a chesterfield.*

advantages but are in some cases becoming scarcer and more expensive, and you will find that many suitable materials are now made from a combination of natural and artificial fibres.

**Wool** Used extensively for upholstery, wool has many advantages as a furnishing fabric. Because it lacks the static electricity of many artificial fibres, it attracts less dirt. It is very tough and has a natural resilience which helps it to keep its appearance even after several years of hard wear.

This fabric is used widely for contract jobs such as hotels and airports, not only because it is soft and warm to sit on, but also because it has a natural and very efficient flame resistance: a lighted cigarette dropped on to wool will

smoulder and die, rather than flare up as it would with many synthetics. Wool absorbs moisture easily and therefore takes dyes readily, so it can be made in an enormous range of colours and patterns.

Almost all furnishing wool sold by the metre will have been treated with a moth-proofing solution; but make sure that this is so. All materials which show the Woolmark (pure new wool) or Woolblend mark (at least 70 per cent pure new wool) will have had this treatment; these are trade marks of the International Wool Secretariat.

Wool should be dry-cleaned and any spots treated with a slightly dampened cloth, since over-wet wool tends to become lumpy and matted.

**Cotton** An easy material to care for, pure cotton has to be extremely thick, strong and closely woven to be suitable for tight covering. Stiff, glazed cotton, called chintz, used to be popular for upholstery, but it has become very expensive in recent years. The glaze will eventually come off if you clean it with water and you may have difficulty finding a company willing to reglaze the fabric.

**Linen** A vegetable product like cotton, linen is rather more expensive and somewhat coarser; it also loses it strength more quickly than cotton when wet, and creases if not specially treated. Not all linen is suitable for upholstery.

**Linen Union** This material has a cotton warp and a linen weft. (Warp threads run along the length of a fabric, while weft threads run across its length.) When two different fibres are woven together in this way, the fabric is described as a 'mix' (as opposed to a 'blend', where each thread is comprised of two or more different fibres). Linen union is a very common and highly suitable fabric for upholstery and comes in a huge range of traditional and modern prints and plain colours.

**Silk** Too weak to be used as a tight covering on its own, silk is often mixed with tougher fibres such as linen and cotton for upholstery fabrics.

**Velvet** Although widely used in the last century as an upholstery fabric, real velvet (as opposed to its synthetic imitators) is not really suitable for people who give their furniture a great deal of hard wear, since under these conditions the pile is quite likely to be rubbed off. Velvet also has a tendency to show 'shading' — patches of apparently lighter or darker fabric caused by a change of the direction in which the pile runs.

### Artificial fabrics

Science has brought us many new, chemically produced materials which relieve the huge demand for natural fabrics and often help to give these fabrics properties which they would not have on their own. Artificial fibres can be divided into two main groups, regenerated and synthetic.

**Regenerated fibres** These have their origin in nature, although not in the fibrous form needed for textile production. The best-known of these is viscose (also called rayon or viscose rayon) which comes from the cellulose material in wood. The trade name Durafil often describes viscose when it is used in upholstery fabric. All regenerated fabrics should be sponged carefully since they lose strength when wet.

**Synthetic fibres** Chemically produced, these substances originate from raw materials such as oil and coal.

*Nylon* One of the first synthetics produced, nylon is lightweight and very strong; it is also resistant to staining because it does not absorb moisture readily, but looks and feels unpleasant.
*Acrylic* Known as Courtelle, Acrilan, Orlon or Dralon (a fibre which is often woven into a fabric resembling velvet), acrylic is strong, stain-resistant and easy to look after. Often blended with wool, this material does not matt easily and retains its shape well.
*Modacrylic* Like acrylics, these fibres — sometimes known as Teklan or Dynel — are similar to wool in appearance and texture and often blended with wool.

## The care of upholstery

### Preventing wear and tear

All fabrics suffer to a greater or lesser extent from exposure to sunlight, either because it weakens the fibres or fades the colours, or both. There is no material which can withstand being in bright sunlight (especially when it is magnified by glass) all day over a long period of time, so try to position furniture out of the direct rays of the sun. Dirt also damages fibres, so clean all fabrics regularly, either with a proprietary cleaner or with a brush or vacuum cleaner as described below.

Try to keep children and animals from abusing your furniture, since they can shorten its life by many years. Bouncing will ruin springs; buckles and buttons may catch the cloth (as will animal claws); and rubber or plastic soles on shoes will quickly wear through it. Extra back and arm covers are very useful on chairs and sofas since they protect the most vulnerable areas from heavy wear. Restrict the use of aerosols such as polishes, air fresheners and insect sprays as much as possible, as these too can damage fibres.

### Cleaning upholstery

Try to make a habit of vacuuming your upholstery regularly, since if you spring-clean it only once a year the dirt will become embedded in the fabric, making it very difficult to remove as well as damaging the fibres. Most suction cleaners have a special attachment for cleaning upholstery and for removing dust and dirt from awkward places in the backs and sides of chairs.

If possible, you should remove any spillage immediately after it happens. Treatment will depend on the type of fabric, so before you begin always check the manufacturer's instructions to make sure the cleaner you have in mind is suitable. You should test for such things as shrinkage and colour-fastness by experimenting with the cleaner in an inconspicuous place on the upholstery. To avoid over-dampening the fabric and the padding beneath, it is best to use a dry-cleaner to get rid of spots and stains. This type of cleaner only wets the surface and dries very quickly to a powder; when you brush off the powder, it should take the stain with it. At least one make of this type is suitable for cleaning both upholstery and carpets. Dirty marks can often be removed from fabric if you rub them with a piece of white bread.

Very badly soiled areas can be cleaned by using a special upholstery shampoo. Again, to avoid over-dampening the fabric, you can use a dry shampoo with an applicator. The shampoo foam is forced through a sponge head in a controlled flow which eventually dries to a powder and is then removed with an upholstery attachment on a vacuum cleaner. To make sure the shampoo will not harm the fabric, test it on a small, hidden area first.

Alternatively, if you are going to spring-clean your carpets by hiring a hot-water soil-extraction machine, you can clean your upholstery at the same time. Ask for a special upholstery tool attachment when you are hiring one of these machines, which are available by the day or half-day from specialist hire shops and some carpet retailers. These machines are fairly heavy to manoeuvre, but this should not be a problem when you are cleaning upholstery, since you will probably be able to reach several chairs from one position. A shampoo is mixed with hot water, 'vacuumed' over the upholstery with one sweep and sucked back with the grime and dirt in the next sweep, which takes out most of the moisture. It is best to treat very dirty areas with a spot remover to loosen the stain before using the machine. The upholstery will dry out fairly quickly in a warm room.

## Repairing upholstery

A tiny tear or hole can eventually lead to a major recovering job, so it is a good idea to give your furniture a quick examination from time to time in order to catch any small accidents before they get out of control.

### Tears

Burst or frayed seams and tears near piping can be repaired by slip-stitching which, if done with care, will conceal the damage. Neaten any frayed edges by trimming, but do not cut into the fabric. If necessary, turn under a tiny piece along the torn edges to neaten them. Use large darning needles fixed down firmly into the padding along the torn edges, to hold them together while slip-stitching the tear (see figure 1).

You will need matching strong thread and an upholsterer's half-circle needle. Knot one end of the thread and insert the needle into one side of the tear a little way in from the end, hiding the knot on the underside of the upholstery. Bring the two edges together by using very tiny stitches on either side, pulling the thread through very firmly each time and keeping the stitches parallel (**1**). Remove the darning needles as you go and finish by fastening off the thread, working the thread end into the seam.

**Figure 1**

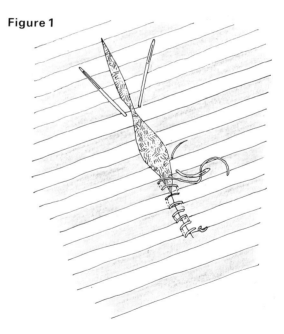

### Patches

A hole can be successfully repaired by taking replacement fabric from elsewhere (the underside of the chair or sofa, for example) to use as a patch. If this is not possible and you feel it is worth the effort, try locating a piece of matching fabric from the manufacturer. Carefully cut away all the damaged fabric, tidying up the edges as you cut. The replacement patch should be slightly larger than the hole size and match any pattern on the fabric. If there is a pile make sure it runs in the same direction.

# Renewing buttoning

Push the patch down into position on the padding, underneath the hole edges (**2**). Coat the edges of the patch and the undersides of the fabric edges round the hole with a fabric adhesive, taking care not to let the adhesive touch anywhere else. Hold the two pieces apart for the few seconds it takes for the adhesive to become tacky, press the two surfaces together and leave them to dry. This type of patch will satisfactorily disguise small damaged areas. For anything larger you will need to fit a replacement cover for that particular section.

**Figure 2**

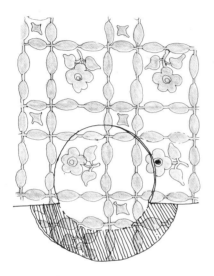

## Leather and vinyl

Covers made from leather and vinyl cannot be slip-stitched, but if the material is soft, either by nature or through wear, you can repair holes and tears with a special repair kit available from most hardware stores. This kit enables you to match not only the colour but also the grain, which is particularly important if you want an inconspicuous repair.

Clean the surface with white spirit to remove grease and dirt and insert a small piece of bonding sheet (provided with the kit) through the tear to form the base for the repair paste. Mix the paste to the exact colour and use a knife or spatula to spread it on to the area. To match the grain, use one of the patterns provided with the kit; alternatively, if the grain pattern is an unusual one, you can use the rubber compound (also supplied) to make a mould of an area identical to that which is damaged, to provide a pattern. Place the grain pattern or rubber mould face down over the paste, put a piece of card on top and press down on it for two minutes with a warm iron to imprint the pattern on the paste.

## Renewing and recovering a buttoned back

If you have an old chair or sofa needing some attention but which is basically in good condition, you can usually improve its appearance by renewing the buttoning, so that it looks deeper and plumper, without actually repadding the whole back. This, along with the addition of an attractive cover, will give it a new lease of life. Upholstery buttoning, however, requires some experience and should be attempted only after you have mastered some of the simpler upholstery projects (1–4).

### Tools and materials

mallet
ripping chisel
tape-measure
double bayonet needle
regulator needle
slipping needle
linter felt (see figure 1)
covering fabric (see figure 2)
buttons (see project 6, figures 51–55)
twine
slipping thread
pieces of hessian – one for each button (see
    figure 3)
13 mm ($\frac{1}{2}$ in) fine tacks

*The sofa before and after rebuttoning.*

168

## Figures 1 & 2 Preparing the covering fabric

With a mallet and chisel, carefully remove the old cover, then stretch the calico underneath taut, making a smooth surface to work on. Poke your fingers into each hole, making them as deep as possible, since the deeper the holes are the better the pleats will be between them.

Cover the back with two layers of linter felt long enough to reach from the front of one arm to the front of the other, and to tuck down between the back and the seat. The first layer should reach just to the outside edge of the top roll, and the second layer should be larger than this so that it can be tacked to the back face of the top back rail (**1**). Poke through the holes with your fingers after you have added each layer.

**Figure 1**

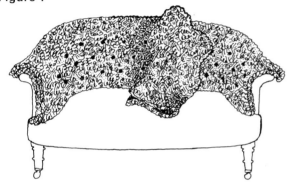

To determine how many widths of covering fabric you need, measure from the outside front edge of one arm at the widest part, in and out of each button, until you come to a measurement near to that of the fabric width — usually 122 cm (48 in). Now go back to the previous button diagonally and measure from here until you reach the width of your fabric again. Repeat until you get to the outer edge of the other arm. Now count up the total number of widths needed.

**Figure 2**

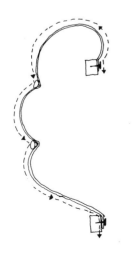

To find the length of each piece of covering fabric, measure from the bottom of the top back rail, over the back, into each hole, then down through between the back and the seat to the top of the back face of the lower back rail (**2**).

Mark out the first piece of fabric for buttoning as described in project 6, figures 51–55. Lay it in position at one arm, making sure you have enough material to pleat round the front face of the arm and to tack to the outer face of the bottom rail.

## Figures 3–8 Attaching the first fabric width

Begin with the first button of the bottom row at the front of the arm. Push the fabric down into the bottom of the hole with your finger, making sure you do not take up any of the fabric which will go over the front of the arm or down between the arm and the seat.

Cut a piece of twine about three times as long as your button-holes are deep. (Our stuffing is 150 mm (6 in) thick, so each thread was cut 450 mm (18 in) long.) You will need this length of twine for each button. Thread a button on to it, then double the twine, hold the two ends together and thread them through a 150 mm (18 in) double bayonet needle.

Now insert the needle into its hole (**3**) and attach the button as explained in project 6, figures 57–58. Finish off the button completely, tying the twine on the webbing with a piece of hessian in the knot as shown in figure 6.

**Figure 3**

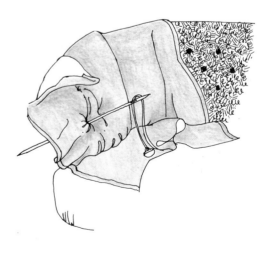

Repeat for all the buttons along the bottom row on this first piece of fabric except for the last button, leaving enough loose fabric to reach from

# Renewing buttoning

the bottom of one hole, down into the bottom of the adjoining hole (**4**).

**Figure 4**

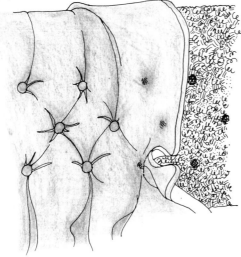

Attach the middle row of buttons, then the top row, in the same way.

Using the flat blade of a regulator, arrange the vertical pleats from the bottom row of buttons to the seat, pushing the fabric between the seat and the back and cutting into the fabric carefully at the inside corner so that it can be pushed down at both sides of the back rail (**5**). From the outside, pull both pieces of fabric through and, with your regulator, arrange the bottom row of vertical pleats again. Insert temporary tacks into the rail at the base of each pleat (**6**). When all the pleats have been done, check to make sure they are as even as possible, then drive the tacks home.

**Figure 5**

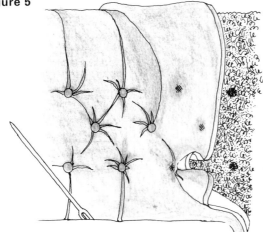

At the front of the arm, cut into the fabric at the inside towards the back of the front arm rail. Pull the fabric down behind the front arm rail. Trim. Pull the front edge of the fabric over the front of

**Figure 6**

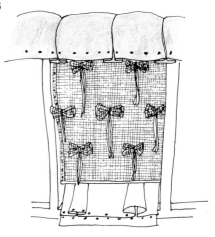

the arm, towards the outside (**7**), so that its edge is parallel to the vertical edge of the front rail, and anchor it at the lowest point with a temporary tack, making sure the horizontal grain of the fabric is parallel with the seat.

**Figure 7**

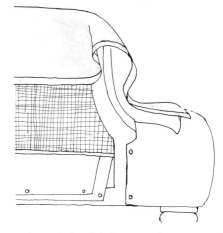

Pull the top edge of the fabric over the curve of the arm towards the outside, making the fabric as smooth and tight as possible. Temporarily tack it to the outer face of the front arm rail. Pull the rest of the front edge of fabric to the front of the chair in the same way and temporarily tack it here. It will probably be necessary to do a lot of pulling, rearranging and retacking for a

**Figure 8**

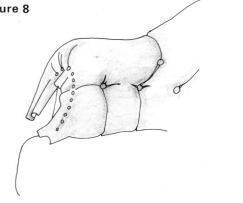

satisfactory result and no buttoning over a curved, traditionally padded surface will ever be perfect.

When you have done the best you can, drive home the temporary tacks along the outside rails.

Release the temporary tacks at the front of the arm, cut off any excess fabric, arrange the fullness into even pleats and tack these permanently to the front of the arm (**8**).

### Figures 9–11 Finishing the arm front panel

Cut a rectangle of fabric large enough to cover the arm front generously. Lay it over the inside of the arm, right sides together (see figure 9), with one edge of it over the inside of the arm front. Tack down a strip of back tacking (or stiff card) over this fabric edge from the bottom of the front of the arm up as far as you can go without going round the outside of the curve (**9**).

**Figure 9**

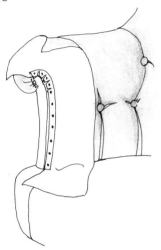

Pull the fabric over towards the outside arm and insert a piece of Courtelle (or linter felt) slightly wider than this piece of fabric to make a lightly padded curve (**10**). Fold the fabric under to make a neat edge at the bottom. Turn under a

**Figure 10**

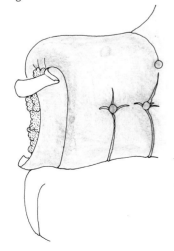

small hem at the top and, with a slipping needle, slip-stitch the fabric around the curve with tiny stitches (**11**).

**Figure 11**

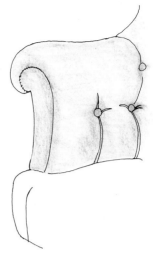

### Figures 12–14 The second fabric width

At the other, buttoned end of your fabric width, cut a V-shape as shown, leaving at least 25 mm (1 in) beyond each last button-hole.

Line up the top edge of your next fabric width (marked as before) with the existing fabric. Lay the new width on the first width, overlapping the next holes to be buttoned by at least 25 mm (1 in). Cut a V-shape parallel to the V-shape in the first width.

Thread a button on to the needle and, beginning with the central button-hole, insert the point of your needle through the two layers of fabric at the point of the V-shape (**12**). (Hold the first width of fabric in place with your fingers so it will be caught in the point of the needle.)

**Figure 12**

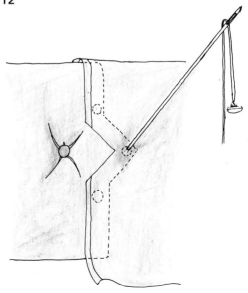

## Making a skirt

Attach the button in the usual way. Before you finish the join, you should attach a few more buttons so the fabric is secure; to do this, first attach the next button in the middle row, then the one in the top row, above and between the two you have just attached, then the equivalent one in the bottom row (**13**).

**Figure 13**

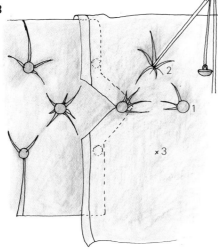

Now go back to where the widths are being joined, at the top row of buttons. Again anchoring the first width with your finger, pull the new width into position with your other hand so it fits tightly over the stuffing and into the hole. When you are holding the two layers securely together, put your needle through them and attach the button as before. The pleat formed should face down.

Attach the nearest button to the join in the bottom row in the same way. Ideally, all the pleats going between the buttons should face down toward the seat, but this one will face up (**14**). This is not very important with most fabrics and it should not show, but if it does, and you are worried about it, make a tiny cut very carefully just above the lowest button,

**Figure 14**

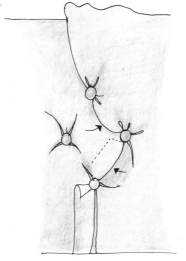

so that you can lift the first width up and put it down over the second one. This is a very tricky process and can easily cause the fabric to tear, so do not take it on unless you really must.

Continue buttoning and joining widths as described until you reach the other arm. Finish this in exactly the same way as you did the first. Now tack down along the back, arranging the pleats as you did at the bottom (see figure 5). Finish off according to the appropriate instructions in the earlier projects.

## Making a tailored skirt

A tailored skirt with box pleats at the corners is simple to make and attach round the bottom of an upholstered chair or sofa.

### Tools and materials

pins
string
tape-measure
scissors
covering fabric to match the rest of the chair, as wide as the height the skirt will be and 1110 mm (44 in) longer than the perimeter of the chair, plus bias strips for piping
lining fabric the same length and 13 mm ($\frac{1}{2}$ in) narrower than the covering fabric
piping cord the length of the perimeter of the seat plus 50 mm (2 in)
slipping needle and thread

*A tailored skirt with corner pleats gives an attractive finish to any chair or sofa.*

## Figures 1–5 Making up

With a pin, mark on one corner of the chair the point where you want the top of the skirt to be. Measure its distance from the floor on the other three corners. Join up these four pins with a length of string running all round the chair. This will give you a guide for attaching the finished skirt, and an indication of the width of fabric needed. (Since there will be a 13 mm ($\frac{1}{2}$ in) seam allowance, the finished skirt will clear the floor by this amount.)

Cut out four strips of fabric as wide as the height of the skirt, each one the length of one of the four sides of the chair, plus 90 mm ($3\frac{1}{2}$ in).

Now cut four extra pieces of fabric to the same width, but 190 mm ($7\frac{1}{2}$ in) long; these will form the insides of the pleats. With right sides together and allowing 13 mm ($\frac{1}{2}$ in) for seams, stitch all the pieces end to end in a continuous band, each long one in the sequence in which it will fall round the chair.

Make up a circle of lining fabric to the same length but 13 mm ($\frac{1}{2}$ in) narrower – it does not matter where the joins fall. Sew this to the right side of your fabric strip, edge to edge, again leaving a 13 mm ($\frac{1}{2}$ in) seam allowance. Turn the skirt right side out and press it so that the two free raw edges meet. This will ensure that the lining is well concealed behind the skirt.

Pin the skirt temporarily into place on the chair with the lining side out, raw edges at the top and the centre of each short piece falling at each corner. Attach it so that it fits tightly round the chair except for a large loop of fabric at each corner. Pin the loops in position at the top at each corner (**1**).

**Figure 1**

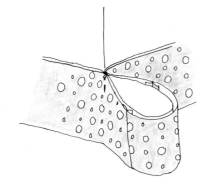

Take the skirt off the chair and sew each loop down at the point where you pinned it to 50 mm (2 in) from the top edge (**2**). Now press and pin the loop flat so that there are equal amounts of fabric at each side of the vertical seam, forming a pleat (**3**).

**Figure 2**

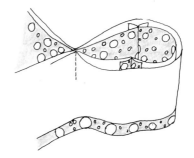

**Figure 3**

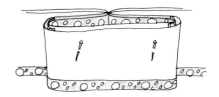

Pin a length of piping to the top of the skirt, right sides and all raw edges together. (Instructions for making piping are given in project 5, figure 10.) Sew the piping to the skirt, stitching straight across the pleats at the corners (**4**). Neaten the ends and press so that the seam allowances are tucked down behind the piping.

**Figure 4**

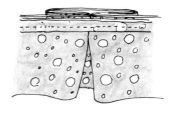

Ease the finished skirt (**5**) back into position on the chair from below, pin and slip-stitch it to the cover.

**Figure 5**

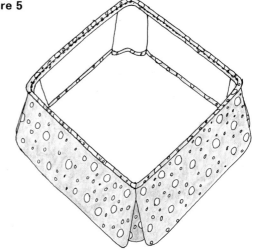

# Glossary

**Applied Moulding** Decorative moulding which is glued onto surfaces such as drawer fronts, doors and cabinet fronts.

**Batten or caul** An end piece of narrow waste wood, which can be up to about 30 inches (75 centimetres) in length, used for clamping.

**Bevelled** Sloping edge cut in timber. The sloping edge of a chisel, for example, is bevelled.

**Blind Stitching** A series of stitches around the edge of the piece to pull the stuffing to the edge.

**Blister** A small section of veneer which has lifted because of lost adhesion.

**Bracket Foot** A short foot that forms an extension of the plinth member on a chest of drawers. It can be plain or rectangular, and may be carved or shaped in a number of ways.

**Bradawl** Like a gimlet, the bradawl is a tool which makes holes for starting screws. Bradawls have either square or tapered points.

**Bridle Ties** Long loose stiches sewn on the fabric under which the stuffing is positioned and partially held in place.

**Carcass** The main structure of a piece of furniture, excluding such parts as drawers, mouldings or feet.

**Cocked Beads or raised bead** Decorative beads which are placed above the main surface of drawers and doors.

**Cross Banding** A slice or band of wood used as inlays or mouldings and consisting of a solid core of cross-grained blocks flanked by two sheets of veneer. Only used with certain types of furniture, such as that made from walnut.

**Dovetail** A joint made by a piece of wood lapped in series which receives the similarly shaped tails made in the wood to be joined.

**Dowel** A small, rounded piece of wood, usually made of birch, used for making or strengthening joints.

**Flush** When two adjacent surfaces are in the same plane, they are said to be flush.

**Glazing Bar or mullion** The framework used as a glazing foundation and moulding core on glass cabinet doors.

**Glue Blocks** A triangular block of wood where the two adjacent faces are at 90° and the pointed ends are squared off. Glue blocks are usually about two inches (five centimetres) long but can be longer for chairs. Used to strengthen jointed rails.

**Knuckle Joint** The revolving wooden joint used for swinging the flap leaves on gate-leg tables.

**Loose Tenon** A tenon inserted into a mortise which has its underside opened by cutting with a saw. Also a separate tenon glued into an open mortise or notch.

**Mitre** A piece of wood which has had its end cut at an angle of 45° is said to be mitred. Used for jointed picture frames.

**Panel Stitching** This holds the centre of a seat firm and attaches the scrim to the hessian through one layer of stuffing.

**Plinth** The base, usually separate, of cupboards, cabinets and desks.

**Plugging** Filling old screw holes with small, shaped wooden plugs.

**Reviving** Cleaning and renewing the polished surface of furniture.

**Rubbed Joint** A glued joint where no clamping is needed. Surfaces are planed flat and rubbed together slowly and gently until surplus glue is expelled and a kind of vacuum adhesiion is felt.

**Rule Joint** A hinged joint used on the leaves of gate-leg tables.

**Stub Tenon** A mortise and short tenon joint where the tenon cannot be seen once it is glued into place.

**Stuck Moulding** A moulding which has been cut from the solid carcass.

**Top Stitching** This forms the hard, firm edge after blind stitching has gathered the stuffing to the edge.

**Turning** A method of carving legs or arms of chairs and tables by means of a revolving lathe.

**Veneer** A thin layer of wood, noted for its grain and colour, used to decorate the showing surfaces of most kinds of furniture.

**Windsor Chair** A comfortable type of English country-made chair, usually executed in oak or beech, generally with arms and an arched back with numerous spindles. They were popular from the eighteenth century in America.

# Further Reading

BLANDFORD, PERCY W. *The Upholsterer's Bible.* Blue Ridge Summit, Pa.; Tab Books, 1978.

JONES, PETER. *Fixing Furniture.* New York: Butterick Publishing, 1978.

JONES, ROBERT. *Repairing Furniture.* Chicago: Time-Life Books, 1980.

HAND, JACKSON. *Wood Finishing.* 2nd ed. New York: Harper and Row, 1976.

HOWES, C. *Practical Upholstery.* New York: Sterling Publishing Co., 1980.

GIBBIA, S. W. *Wood Finishing and Refinishing.* 2d ed. New York: Von Nostrand Reinhold Co., 1971.

MARSHALL, MEL. *How to Repair, Reupholster and Refinish Furniture.* New York: Harper and Row, 1979.

NESOVITCH, PETER. *Reupholstering at Home.* New York: Crown Publishers, Inc., 1979.

SCHARFF, ROBERT. *Practical Wood Finishing Methods.* Pittsburgh, Pa.: Rockwell International Tool Group, 1978.

RODD, JOHN. *Repairing and Restoring Antique Furniture.* New York: Van Nostrand Reinhold Co., 1976.

SERGIO, LISA. *You Can Upholster!* Philadelphia and New York: J. B. Lippincott Co., 1978.

VISHER, M. A. *The Finishing Touch.* Englewood Cliffs, N.J.: Prentice-Hall, Inc., 1979.

# Index

Anchoring twine, 80
Applied moulding, 32, 68
Armchair, square, 112–131, *113*
Artificial fibres, 166

Back-tacking, 80
Batten, 174
Beading, 48, 51, 52
Beads, cocked, 63
Bevel, 174
Bias, 80
Blanket stitch, 80
Blind stitch, 80, 97, 106, 135–136, 158–159, *97*
Bowing, in old furniture, 12
Bracket foot, 30, 62, 174
Bradawl, 174
Bridle ties, 80, 88–89, 98, 105–106, 158
Bruises, removing, 35
Buttoned wing-chair, 132–151, *133*
Buttoning, 146–147, *146, 147*
    renewing and recovering, 168–172
    thread, 82

Cabinet, glass-fronted, 68–77, *69, 70, 71, 77*
Calico, 80, 89–90, *89, 90*
Cane, bamboo, 80
Caning, 46–52, *47*
Carcass (box), 22–25, 23, 78, *22*
    repair, 23–25
Carving, 32, *32*
Caustic soda, 29 *28*
Chairs, 12–13, 26, *13*
    cane, 46–52, *40, 46, 53*
    drop-in seat, 84–91, *85*
    furniture repair, 26, 40–53
    oak, 42–45
    occasional, 108–111, *109*
    sprung dining, 100–107, *101*
Chamfer (bevel), 80, 94
Chest of drawers, 61–67, *60, 67*
    moulded front, 63, *62*
Chesterfield, 152–163, *152*
Chips, repairing, *36*
Chisel, ripping, 82
Cleaning upholstery, 166
Cleaning wood, 28–29
Cocked beads, 63
Cord, piping, 82
Cording, 81
Cornice moulding, 68, *70*
Cotton, 165
Cross banding, 78

Dating furniture, 10–14
Doors, repair, 25, 75, *74*
    staining, *75*
Dovetail joint, 25
Dowels, 44, 56
Drawer runners, 25, *73*
Drawer stops, 63

Drawers, repairing, 25, *65*

Fabrics, 19, 164–166
    calculating amount needed, 19
Facing, 81
Feet, chest of drawers, *65*
Felt, linter, 81
Finding furniture, 10
Finishing, 29–30
Foam, 81
French polish, 12, 30, 39

Gate-leg table, 54–59, *54, 56, 59*
    replacing leaf, *57, 58*
Gimp, 81
Gimp pin, 81
Ginger fibre, 81
Glass-fronted cabinet, 68–77, *69, 77*
Glazing bar, 78
Glue blocks, 78
Grain, 29, 81

Hair, rubberized, 82
Hammer, magnetic, 82
Handles, *31*
    cleaning and replacement, *38*
Hardwoods, 15–17
Hessian (burlap), 81, 88, 94, *88, 89, 94*
Hinges, 56, 75–76, *74*
Horsehair, 88–89, 105, *88, 89, 105*

Inlay, 18
Intarsia, 18

Joint, dovetail, 25, *25*
    mortise and tenon, 24, 41–3, *24*
    stub tenon, 25, *24*

Knobs, 66, *66*
Knot, slip, 82
Knuckle joint, 78

Lashing, 81, 102, 117–119, 126, 140, 144, 155–156
Leather, repairing, 168
Legs, broken, 26
Linen, 166
    union, 166
    upholsterer's, 83
Linter felt, 82
Locks, 66
Loose tenon, 78

Magnetic hammer, 82
Mallet, 82
Marquetry, 18
Mirror, mahogany, *8, 9*
Mitres, 52, 68, 70
Mouldings, 32, 68, 74
    cornice, 68, *70*
    applied, 32, 68
    stuck, 32, 68

Needle, double bayonet, 81

# Index

regulator, 82
slipping, 82
springing, 83
straight, 83

Oak chair, 42–45, *40, 45*
Occasional chair, 108–111, *109*

Padding, 98, 106, *98, 106*
Paint removal, 35, 37, 39, *37, 38*
Panel pin, 82
    stitching, 78
Parquetry, 18
Patches, 167–168
Pine desk, 35–39, *34, 39*
Piping cord, 82
Plinth, repair, 74, *72, 73*
Polishing, 12, 30
Polish removal, 28–29

Rail repair, 26, 63
    replacement, 42, *42, 43, 44, 47*
Rasp, 82
Regulator needle, 82
Repairing upholstery, 167–168
Ripping chisel, 82
Rubbed joint, 57
Rubberized hair, 82
Rule joint, 55
Runners, repair, 25, *73*
Running stitch, 82

Scratches, 35
Screws, *36*
Scrim, 82, 92, 96, 158, *95, 96*
Seat, drop-in, 84–91
    repair, *44*
Selvedge, 82
Seven Step Tradition, 46–47
Sheet wadding, 82
Shelf repair, *71*
Shrinkage, 24
Silk, 166
Skewers, 82
Skin wadding, 82
Skirt, tailored, 172–173
Slip knot, 82
    stitch, 82
Slipping needle, 82
    thread, 82
Softwoods, 15, 17
Splits, repairing, 35, *36, 44*

Springing needle, 82
Springs, 83, 102, 103, *102, 103*
Stain removal, 35
Staining, 29–30, 38–39, *75*
Staples, 83
Steel wool, *75, 76*
Stitch, blind, 80, 97, 106, 135–136, 158–159, *97*
    running, 82, 95
    slip, 82, 131, 151, 163
    top, 83, 98, 106, 110, 122, 135–136, 138, 145, 158
Stool, 92–99, *92, 93*
    covering, 98–99, *98, 99*
Straight grain, 83
    needle, 83
Stripping, 28–29
Stub tenon, 25, *24*
Stuck moulding, 32, 68

Table, gate-leg, 54–59, *54, 56, 59*
    replacing leaf, *57, 58*
Tack (tape) roll, 83
Tacks, 83
Tailor's tacks, 83
Tears in upholstery, 167
Template, 57, 62–63, 83
Temporary tacks, 83
Thread, slipping (buttoning), 82
Tools, 9, 81–83, *20, 21*
Top stitching, 83, 98, 106, 110, 122, 135–136, 138, 145, 158
Trestles, 83
Turning, 174
Twine, 83

Upholsterer's linen, 83
Upholstery, care of, 166–167
    cleaning, 166–167
    removal of old, 86, 94, *86*
    repair, 167–168

Velvet, 166
Veneers, 19, 32, 174, *18, 19, 74*
Vinyl, repairing, 168

Waxing, 30, 39
Webbing, 83, 86–88, 94, *86, 87, 88, 94*
Webbing stretcher, 83
Wing-chair, buttoned, 132–151, *133*
Wood, 14–18, *16, 17*
Woodfiller, 76
Woodworm, *14, 42, 44*
Wool, 165

# Guide to Materials and Suppliers

In the specialized area of furniture restoration, it can be difficult for those outside the trade to obtain traditional materials. The few mail-order suppliers who sell to the retail customer sometimes require minimum orders and prepayment. With persistence, however, you should be able to find the product you want or a suitable alternative from the list of suppliers and manufacturers given here.

## Wood and Fittings

To find the small amounts of wood needed to restore old furniture, scour the second-hand furniture shops or buy seasoned wood from a lumberyard or building-materials supplier. Frequently, modern wood is not of the same quality as that used in the past, when it was often seasoned for more than 50 years before being used.

Veneers to match missing pieces are hard to find in shops, and you will have to spend time looking for the better-quality materials. Antique restorers may be prepared to sell you small amounts. Two suppliers of good-quality veneers to the public are Constantine's, 2050 Eastchester Road, Bronx, NY 10461 (212/542-1600), and the Woodworkers' Store, 21801 Industrial Boulevard, Rogers, MN 55374 (612/428-4101).

Brass reproduction fittings are sometimes available from hardware stores and locksmiths. If you have any difficulty finding what you want, Ritter and Son Hardware, Gualala, CA 95445 (800/358-9120; 800/862-4948 in California) has a large selection.

## Stripping

Paint remover is available under many brand names. You will probably find Raiz-off, Strip-eez, TM-4 or Zar, all quite adequate paint removers, on the shelves of your local hardware store. If you would prefer to order through the mail, the Woodworkers' Store offers several other brands.

Caustic soda, available from well-stocked pharmacies, is the last resort in removing old polish. It should not be used on veneers, as it will soften the glue. Caustic soda darkens the wood. To bring it back to its original color you can use a peroxide bleach. Behlen's Color Dissolvent, available from the Garrett Wade Company, 161 Avenue of the Americas, New York, NY 10013 (800/221-2942), is a good bleach for this purpose. To remove small stains, use an ordinary chlorine bleach, available from any grocery store.

If the stains persist, nitric or oxalic acid can be used, diluted with two parts of water. These substances can be hard to obtain, but they are available from large independent pharmacies. Ask the pharmacist for instructions on safe handling.

Sandpaper is available in several different grades, and with garnet, aluminium oxide, and silicon carbide coatings. Ask the salesperson for advice on the best grade and coating for your particular stripping job, or read about sandpaper before ordering from the Garrett Wade catalog.

Titebond Glue, by Franklin Chemical Industries, is an effective glue for all jobs. It may be purchased directly from most hardware stores or mail-ordered from the Woodworkers' Store.

Scratches and stains on light-colored furniture can be treated by rubbing with sandpaper and applying linseed oil, which is readily available at paint and hardware stores.

## Finishing

Before finishing the pieces, you must smooth the surface of the wood with a paste wood filler or patch stick. There are a number of brands on the market. Behlen's Pore-O-Pac Paste Wood Filler (from Garrett Wade) is a good consistency and can be tinted with Japan Colors. Putty Stik, available at most hardware stores, comes in many shades so that you can match the existing wood. Shellac Tuffy Patch Sticks, which can be ordered from the Woodworkers' Store, look a little like sealing wax and are used to fill cracks and knotholes.

After filling and staining, the wood can be coated with a lacquer or oil-based polish or treated to shellac. You can mix up your own shellac with shellac flakes and solvent, available from Garrett Wade.

A wax covering gives the final protective coating to the wood. Beeswax is traditional, but manufacturers' formulations also give excellent results. Constantine's Natural Finish Wax is a good one to try.

## Upholstery Equipment

Len's Country Barn, Inc., 9929 Rhode Island Avenue, College Park, MD 20740 (301/441-2545) is one of the largest mail-order upholsterers' suppliers in the United States, and also stocks many furniture refinishing supplies. Foam N' Fabrics for Furniture, 319 Washington Street, Brighton, MA 02135 (617/782-3169) will try to match any fabric swatch you send them from their vast warehouse stock. The Woodworkers' Store supplies cane by mail.